CONTEMPORARY ISSUES IN COMPARATIVE EDUCATION

Professor Emeritus Vernon Mallinson

CONTEMPORARY ISSUES IN COMPARATIVE EDUCATION

*A Festschrift in Honour of
Professor Emeritus Vernon Mallinson*

EDITED BY : KEITH WATSON AND RAYMOND WILSON

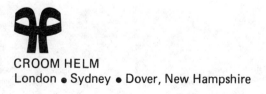

CROOM HELM
London ● Sydney ● Dover, New Hampshire

© 1985 K. Watson and R.Wilson
Croom Helm Ltd, Provident House, Burrell Row,
Beckenham, Kent BR3 1AT

Croom Helm Australia Pty Ltd, First Floor,
139 King Street, Sydney, NSW 2001, Australia

British Library Cataloguing in Publication Data

Contemporary issues in comparative education.
   1. Comparative education
   I. Watson, Keith, *1939-* II. Wilson, Raymond
   III. Mallinson, Vernon
   370.19'5   LA133

   ISBN 0-7099-3607-9

Croom Helm, 51 Washington Street, Dover,
New Hampshire 03820, USA

Library of Congress Cataloging in Publication Data
Main entry under title:

Contemporary issues in comparative education.

   Bibliography: p.
   1. Comparative education – Addresses, essays,
lectures. 2. Mallinson, Vernon. 3. Mallinson,
Vernon – Bibliography. I. Mallinson, Vernon.
II. Watson, Keith. III. Wilson, Raymond, 1925-
LA132.C625   1985   370.19'5   84-21402
ISBN 0-7099-3607-9

W 26331 £15.95. 2.85

Printed and bound in Great Britain
by Billing & Sons Limited, Worcester.

CONTENTS

CONTEMPORARY ISSUES IN COMPARATIVE EDUCATION

INTRODUCTION

Keith Watson and Raymond Wilson

This volume of essays on contemporary issues in comparative education has a twofold purpose. The first is to honour Vernon Mallinson, Emeritus Professor of Comparative Education in the University of Reading and Visiting Professor of Education in the University of Kent at Canterbury. Mallinson´s scholarly and distinguished contribution to the development of comparative studies in education, especialy with his perspective on national character as a major cause of differences in societies and their education systems, has earned him an international reputation, especially in the context of Europe. We feel it is fitting to recognise this contribution on the occasion of his seventy-fifth birthday.

The second purpose is to look at a number of issues in comparative education as well as a number of educational issues from a comparative perspective. Sadly, this latter perspective is all too frequently overlooked in most of the educational debates of the present time. The parochialism with which we view and discuss educational issues is frightening, whether they are implications of contraction and falling rolls, the financing of students in higher education or the reform of examinations, the curriculum, the school system or teacher education. As Edmund King argues in one of the essays in this volume, we are in a situation whereby all education is becoming education for uncertainty(1) and to ignore the wider, international implications of this situation is to court disaster. As societies become more complex and the problems faced by these societies, whether industrialised or newly industrialising, become increasingly common, the need for more comparative and international perspectives grows. Why? Because much can be learnt from the reforms and developments taking place in other societies; because the way problems and crises are being tackled can illuminate the way we might tackle our own national or local problems; and because, in this time of economic recession and financial retrenchment, costly mistakes may be avoided. This has always been part of the stock in trade of comparative educationists since the beginning of the

1

nineteenth century. As Nicholas Hans, amongst others, has argued, "The analytical study of these factors (which help to form a nation) from an historical perspective and the comparison of attempted solutions of resultant problems are the main purpose of comparative education".(2)

There is another reason why comparative studies in education should lay claim to some importance in the present age: it is that they can help us to appreciate, and reflect upon, our own situation from a broader and different standpoint. This was certainly Vernon Mallinson's viewpoint and in his influential <u>Introduction to the Study of Comparative Education</u> he wrote:

> To identify the problems of education thus becomes the most important preliminary task of the research worker in (the comparative study of education). To become familiar with what is being done in some other countries than their own, and why it is done, is a necessary part of the training of all serious students of educational issues of the day. Only in that way will they be properly fitted to study and understand their own systems and to plan intelligently for the future which....is going to be one where we are thrown together into ever closer contact with other peoples and other cultures .(3)

Unfortunately, as a recent survey has shown,(4) far from all students training to be teachers being made aware of developments in other countries, the opposite is the case: fewer students are being introduced to comparative studies in education and fewer teacher trainers have a comparative dimension in their own work. What is important in most schools/departments of education is what is practical and utilitarian in the classroom and what can be measured easily.

The paradox is that this situation has arisen at a time when economically and politically Britain has drawn closer to the European Community and at a time when, as the Brandt Commission has argued, globally we have become ever more "interdependent". As a result of technological change, it is true to say that our world has conspicuously contracted during the course of the twentieth century. In Marshal McLuhan's metaphor, it has become a "global village", and it is imperative that we, as villagers, should understand one another. If we do not, as Alvin Toffler,(5) in one sense, and Olav Palme,(6) in another, have shown, we are heading for disaster. The fact is that neither science nor technology can do anything in themselves to resolve the complex social, cultural and moral problems that are the necessary consequence of the increasingly important part they play in our lives. Our most urgent need is to relate technological advance to the subjective, divergent and what often seem irreconcilable value-systems to which all of us owe allegiance, whether as Russians, Americans, Indians, Chinese or West Europeans. It is precisely here that, in an effort to answer this need, the justification for comparative studies lies. Education systems both shape and reflect the values of the societies in which they are embedded. By studying them comparatively we can at least arrive at a more tolerant and sympathetic understanding of one another, and more often than might be supposed, we can learn from reforms and developments in other systems some useful lessons for the development of our own system.

Throughout his professional career Vernon Mallinson certainly believed this to be the case and in his writings and teaching he inspired countless students to look sympathetically at other education systems and the societies which they reflected and shaped as well as to appraise their own. Perhaps his inspiration and ideas developed during the second world war, when, as a member of the Intelligence Corps, he served behind enemy lines in Belgium. Because of his love for, his service to and his writings about that country at the heart of the post war reconstruction of Europe, Vernon Mallinson was made an Officer of the Order of Leopold II, later of Leopold, both honours of the highest distinction.

Born in Barnsley, in South Yorkshire and a graduate of Leeds University, Vernon Mallinson was always proud of his Yorkshire origins, not least, perhaps, because one of the greatest of all comparative educators, Sir Michael Sadler, was also born in Barnsley and later became Vice Chancellor of Leeds University (1911-23).(7) Whether or not Sadler acted as an inspiration, Mallinson's progression at Reading University (1945-75) from lecturer through to Professor of Education was very much in the tradition and wake of another famous comparative educator, H.C.Barnard (1937-51). Between them they shaped the development of and left their stamp on comparative education studies at Reading, the only university in the U.K. outside London, that was ever able to boast of a chair in comparative education.

As the bibliography of Vernon Mallinson's publications, found at the end of this volume and compiled by Graham Geogeghan, the Education Librarian at Reading, shows, his range of interests has been enormous, and the development of his thinking and his output of materials has likewise been varied. The chapters in this volume reflect these wide interests and at the same time reflect the development of his thinking and writing. They are written, in the main, by experts in the field of comparative education, many with international reputations and all with some close knowledge of, or connexion with, Vernon Mallinson either as colleagues, friends or former students.

The chapters that follow offer a shrewd appraisal of education as it is today in developed and developing countries. Their authors are too realistic to indulge in a facile optimism, and they face the fact that the expansion of education does not guarantee economic growth or necessarily lead to a more equal society. At the same time, they indicate what possibilities do exist within the field of education for the promotion of both the material and cultural welfare of nations. The first few are devoted to themes as they evolved in Vernon Mallinson's writings; the remainder are concerned with the practical outworkings of a comparative analysis in modern times.

It is appropriate that the first chapter is concerned with Michael Sadler and is written by the foremost authority on Sadler's work, Harry Higginson, since Sadler's influence on the development of comparative studies in education and on Vernon Mallinson's thinking, both in perceptions of cultural and other influences on schools and in his view of national character, were considerable. Sadler, as Higginson shows, is remarkably contemporary, even though many of his most important writings were published at the end of the last century and in the first three decades of this. He picks a topic of current interest - how best to educate the masses, especially at secondary level - and shows how the questions on this topic raised first by Sadler, and later by Mallinson, remain unresolved. Higginson also shows that while we can learn from overseas and can borrow ideas, we cannot borrow wholesale because of the different cultural factors prevailing in different societies.

One of the most lasting aspects of Vernon Mallinson's work in comparative education is that of "national character". The term itself, while frequently used by comparative educators throughout the first half of the twentieth century as a means of distinguishing why different education systems are different, has angered critics and puzzled friends alike. This is partly because of the apparent vagueness of the term, partly because it cannot be quantified and used in accurate, statistical measurement, partly because the understanding of national character is subjective rather that objective. William Kay, a former student of Mallinson, seeks to unravel some of the complexity surrounding the topic and to show, from the literature of psychology, that far from being a discredited idea, it has much validity for educational analysis.

For many years it appeared that the cultural, historical approach of Vernon Mallinson, laying emphasis, as it does, on national character, was at loggerheads with the scientific analysis and problem (solving) approach of Brian Holmes. It would appear, however, that the differences are ones of degree rather than essential substance as can be seen from Holmes' chapter, which seeks to reconcile the two approaches. In fact it is one of the clearest statements from Holmes on the how and why of his problem (solving) approach to comparative education, and it is fitting that it should appear in this volume of essays honouring Vernon Mallinson, since the latter, a humanist to the core, was so often puzzled by the empirical demands of scientists in comparative studies.

National character and literature are intertwined since
literature frequently reflects the daily life and attitudes of
"ordinary" people and Mallinson is one of the few scholars to
refer to the need to understand the literature of a country
before, or as a means to, understanding the education systems
and the "philosophy" behind it.(8) Margaret Sutherland examines
this suggestion and explores some of the literature that she
has found most useful in the study of education. This author
knows of only one journal for teachers which regularly
addresses itself to the literature aimed at children. This
chapter, therefore, is a challenging one because it not only
shows the value of looking at literature as a means of
understanding schools and society, but it opens up many new
avenues for thought and study in this direction.

The other major area of comparative studies, and the one
country more than any other that is associated with Vernon
Mallinson, is Belgium. As a result of his wartime experiences
he developed a great affection for a country he has adopted as
his own. Few Englishmen have written so lucidly about Belgium.
It is fitting, therefore, that in this book there should be a
chapter on educational developments in Belgium since the late
´sixties, when Mallinson´s major works on the country first
appeared. John Owen, for many years associated with Reading
through what is now the Buckinghamshire College of Higher
Education, whose PGCE students were validated by Reading staff,
and associated with Belgium through visits and research work,
takes as his theme, Choice and Reform in Belgian Education. He
takes us through the intricacies of modern Belgium and shows
how, with all the reforms of the past decade, there is still a
considerable degree of choice for parents and for pupils alike.
How far should children attend Roman Catholic schools, how far
should they attend "neutral" schools, how far should they
negotiate over the curriculum? The discussion makes interesting
reading in the light of current debates in the U.K. about
uniform, comprehensive education, the freedom of parents to opt
for different types of school, and the recent debate about the
provision of school transport. The discussion is also
interesting in the light of current attempts to provide
technical and vocational education for youngsters at secondary
level, and in negotiations about closures and mergers of
schools. Owen offers us one of the most up to date accounts of
educational reform in the complex nation state of Belgium.

The state is the theme of Kenneth Smart´s chapter on West
Germany. It is important and interesting to examine this
because on it hinges so much of the idea of national character
and the role of the modern nation state. It is also interesting
to take Germany as an example, because, while it is at the
heart of Europe and while in some ways educationally it
resembles the U.K., its historical, religious and political
developments have evolved along very different lines. Smart´s
concern is to look at the concept of "the state". What is it?

Whom does it represent? Who makes the decisions and who is accountable? He gives a very clear exposition of the constitutional, legal and administrative framework of West Germany. There is a particularly interesting discussion on the relationship between local (State/Land) authorities and the central (i.e. federal) government, especially in the light of the present confrontation between central government and local authorities in the U.K. There is also a fascinating discussion about the role and responsibilities of the teacher which anyone advocating that U.K. teachers should become civil servants would be well advised to read.

From the particular to the general, Sixten Markland reviews Vernon Mallinson's thesis of the Western European idea in education. The belief that there is such a thing as a Western European idea, and that there are certain features common to all Western European education systems is one that Mallinson has built on over the years. It is an attractive idea and Western Europe lends itself to comparative analysis admirably, though as Markland points out there is a danger of interpreting Europe too narrowly.

One feature common to all the educational thinking and reforms in Western Europe since the second world war has been the belief that by widening access to the secondary level of education and by equalising educational opportunity more children of the lower socio-economic groups would be able to enter the universities and reach the top jobs in society. Bill Halls' account of the progress towards equality of educational opportunity in Western Europe during the past twenty years is both masterly in its historical and social analysis as well as showing how comparative studies can throw light on a very emotive issue. There has been much criticism in the U.K. that, in spite of comprehensivisation and the widening of opportunities at the tertiary level of education, there has been little progress towards a more equal society. Halls shows from his study of other countries in Western Europe that their success has been even more limited. He gives a pessimistic, but realistic, view in the hope, as he says, that "one of the failures of education may nevertheless stimulate fresh efforts to realise the ideal".

While it is common to respect developments in Europe, even if we do not always understand them or only know a little about them, it is all too common to denigrate education in the U.S.A. as inferior or lacking in academic rigour. Nigel Grant not only explodes some of the commonly held myths about higher education in the U.S.A. but, once again using comparative studies for practical purposes, argues that in the changing economic, social and financial climate we find ourselves in, we have much to learn from the flexibility and creativity of the United States' experience. He cites several very specific ways in which lessons from the American experience could bring benefit to British developments.

It has long been recognised by comparative educationists
that no education system can be studied or understood in
isolation from its social, historical, cultural and political
milieu and two chapters in this volume seek to expand on this
aspect of comparative education in the contemporary world.
Colin Brock is concerned to apply the geographical factor to
educational analysis, while Keith Watson looks at the impact of
demographic, socio-economic and political changes on
educational provision. Brock´s concern is that for too long
geography has been both misunderstood by non-geographers and
that its impact on educational planning and provision has too
easily been ignored. He gives a detailed literature survey and
shows how geographical analysis can be applied to education.
Watson is more at pains to show how those in school systems -
teachers, administrators, curriculum planners, etc. - have had
to respond and react to external changes over which they have
neither influence nor control. He draws examples from both
developed and developing countries.

The last two chapters relate to the practical application
of comparative education studies and to reform. It is often
suggested that comparative education is too theoretical, or is
interesting but lacks practical relevance. Paul Mercier shows
that this image is far from the truth and cites examples, such
as curriculum development, the in-service training of teachers
and the preparation and training of headteachers, where
comparative studies have actually stimulated practical change
and reform.

Reform has always been one of the chief purposes of
comparative studies in education: using ideas, experiments and
developments from other countries in order to enlighten and
encourage developments in one´s own. Edmund King, while not
selecting any specific examples, gives an apologia for
comparative education, showing that in the changing context of
a technological society and in the changing relations between
North and South, education is no longer for certainty. Its
processes and purposes need to be reformed, but such reform as
may be introduced should only come after, or as a result of,
comparative studies.

The contributions to this volume are informative and up to
date, but their analyses are more challenging and provocative
than conclusive. Taken together, they offer a range of insights
into the problems that beset education as it is today, both at
national and at international levels, and it is fair to say
that they offer a lively introduction to the issues that are
now being most urgently discussed by comparative educationists
in five continents.

No one knows better than Vernon Mallinson that if
comparative education is to continue to develop and make a
full contribution to the study of education, it can do so only
by being responsive to important living issues. It is,
therefore, entirely appropriate that this volume of essays

Introduction

should be dedicated to him.

NOTES AND REFERENCES

1.See also King,E.J. (1976): <u>Education for Uncertainty</u>, Inaugural Lecture at King's College, University of London.

2.Hans,N. (1949): <u>Comparative Education</u>, London, Routledge and Kegan Paul, p.10.

3.Mallinson,V. (1975): <u>An Introduction to the Study of Comparative Education</u>, London, Heinemann, pp.10-11. 4th Edn.

4.Watson,K. (1982): Comparative Education in British Teacher Education in Goodings,R., Byram,M. and McPartland,M.: <u>Changing Priorities in Teacher Education</u>, London, Croom Helm.

5.Toffler,A. (1981): <u>The Third Wave</u>, London, Pan Books.

6.Palme,O. (1982): <u>Common Security</u>, London, Pan Books.

7.See Higginson,J.H. (1979): <u>Selections from Michael Sadler: Studies in World Citizenship</u>, Liverpool, Dejall and Meyorre.

8.Mallinson,V. (1968): Literary studies in the service of comparative education. <u>Comparative Education</u>, 4, pp.177-181.

Chapter One

AN ENGLISH EDUCATION FOR ENGLAND

J.H. Higginson

Possibly I should begin this contribution to the
Festschrift with three admissions. First, I treasure with
Vernon Mallinson, as a near contemporary, memories of the same
Alma Mater, and also a European decoration, in his case
Belgian, in mine, French. Second, we have long shared an
admiration for the far-sightedness of an English pioneer in
foreign studies, about whose influence he has written a
comprehensive appreciation.(1) Third, the title of this
contribution is borrowed from that same forward-looking
Englishman who wrote a paper on this theme for the
Contemporary Review in the early days of the first world
war.(2) It is a title that seems to me to sum up much of the
teaching and writing of Vernon Mallinson as I have known it
over the years. To make such a claim implies no reduction in
the breadth of vision, and certainly no insularity, in the
author of The Western European Idea in Education.(3) Rather, it
is to say that Vernon Mallinson´s scholarship affords a superb
illustration of a dictum that he and I both cherish:

> The practical value of studying, in a right spirit
> and with scholarly accuracy, the works of foreign
> systems of education is that it will result in our
> being better fitted to study and understand our
> own .(4)

In this paper, I propose to examine the contents of Michael
Sadler´s essay on An English Education for England, bearing in
mind Mallinson´s fundamental convictions about the influence of
"the cultural heritage" and "national character": and to imply
what relevance arguments put forward in the context of the
first world war may have to the educational situation in the
United Kingdom today.
Sadler´s essay is carefully constructed. Initially, there
is an obvious reaction to the surrounding context of the war
between Germany and Britain, and this provokes a philosophic
clarification of the values to be associated with "the cultural

9

heritage". Sadler then attempts to look ahead and identify what the educational priorities should be when the time for reconstruction comes. The projection of thought of this son of a Radical from the West Riding of Yorkshire, schooled at Winchester and Rugby, and fired by sitting at the feet of Ruskin in Oxford, is distinctly interesting. His preoccupation is with the "education of the masses" - indeed the whole essay elaborates the quotation with which he concluded his 167 pages of analysis in 1901 of <u>The Unrest in Secondary Education in Germany and Elsewhere</u>, where he writes:-

> The problem for statesmen of this age is how to educate the masses .(5)

First, in Sadler's view, should be reform in what at his time of writing was still thought of as Elementary Education. Inevitably, this would lead to a reconsideration of Secondary Education. Next should come Further Education of young school-leavers, a part-time education in continuation classes for young wage-earners. As a background to these advances, comes the question of enough teachers, adequately prepared. Notably, from one who at the time was Vice-Chancelor of a Redbrick University, (Leeds), there is no attention to University education, and not even a tacit recognition of a principle dear to Sadler, as he expounded to an American audience many years later:

> Education must produce an élite. The élite must emerge from the whole range of human society. How then can these two functions of education - the furtherance of a common interest and the fostering of an élite - be effectively combined? (6)

Before scrutinizing each of the strands of Sadler's proposed strategy, it is worth noting how the convictions of the former Director of the <u>Office of Special Inquiries and Reports</u> had been shaped. By the time of writing this paper he had made extensive studies of education both in Germany and in the U.S.A., as well as elsewhere. Though there may well be practical lessons to be learnt from these studies of other systems, Sadler is cautious about cultural borrowings. He warns against trying to apply, with too little discimination, American or Continental ideas to English educational practice. In one lucid paragraph he makes explicit the views he has formed, after half a century of research, about English education, as a result of his foreign studies. Thus he writes:-

> From the experience of the United States and from the experience of Central Europe....we can obviously learn a good deal in matters of educational thought, just as we can learn a good deal from American and

> German experience in methods of industrial and
> commercial organization....Great Britain is one of
> the bridges between East and West and is open in some
> degree to new ideas (and to their educational
> applications) coming from the Continent of Europe and
> from America. But, in spite of this, the English view
> of education is distinct from the view now prevailing
> in America and in Germany. It is not merely a <u>via
> media</u> between two extremes, a middle way between
> State control of ideas on the one hand, and the
> untrammelled unfolding of the individual personality
> on the other. It is a distinct doctrine, or rather a
> practice in which a doctrine is latent .(7)

Vernon Mallinson´s discussion of pragmatism, in his survey of
basic schooling in England and Wales, can be read as an
illumination of this dictum about English education - "a
practice in which a doctrine is latent".(8)

A substantial portion of Sadler´s essay is devoted to
discussing the philosophic basis of English education - the
relation of education to the individual and the relation of the
State to education, a twofold process. He launches this
discussion with some comments on Montesquieu´s judgement that
we English would do well to cling to our liberties because if
we lost them, "we might fall into worse entanglements of
repression than almost any other European nation". Sadler and
Mallinson are at one in their distillation about English
education.(9) Sadler crystallises his comments on Montesquieu
by saying:-

> We in England have been called upon to see a new and
> deeper significance in the idea of political liberty
> and a fuller and more costly meaning in freedom of
> teaching. These are perhaps the chief lessons of the
> War .(10)

When it comes to translating ideals into practice, of
transforming values into structures, Sadler voices his
awareness of the complexity of the problems. He writes:-

> Many of us, whose work has lain mostly in other
> stages of education, are conscious of having felt
> instinctively, from the very beginning of our study
> of educational questions, the capital importance of
> the elementary school problem, but have been dismayed
> by the bigness of it; or dimly aware that the
> elementary school question is interwoven with much
> larger questions of industrial organisation and of
> social tradition, and therefore not to be dealt with
> by methods of educational administration alone.. (11)

An English Education for England

So "the elementary school problem" has deep roots in the economic structure of English society as it has survived from the Industrial Revolution. Crucial to reform at this level of schooling must be the reduction in size of classes. Sadler makes his point graphically:-

> If we do no more than walk through a typical town school for young children we see rooms crowded with pupils, serried rows of faces before the teacher's desk. And sometimes we find that children of the age at which powers of questioning, of self-expression and affectionate trust are the most subtly different and the most sensitive in their tendrils, are packed together in greatest numbers under a single teacher's care .(12)

In this practice, Sadler discerns the perpetuation of an earlier phase of thought on social problems, and he points out that the large class in the elementary school has a long history. It began when charitable people thought of poor men's children "in the lump" - an anticipation of the "lumpen proletariat". Teach the children to read, to write, "to skip about quickly in arithmetic", and this was thought to be enough for their social status. The professional apprenticeship for young people wishing to become teachers, as it was provided in the Normal Schools, was a natural ally of the mass process. An over-simplified psychology reassured observers who would otherwise have been critical. Having weighed the pros and cons of this nineteenth century initiative in educating the masses, Sadler observes:-

> But the English people, like others, gradually discovered that elementary education is a more complex matter than they had at first believed: that it is intimately connected at every point with social, economic, and spiritual issues which at first sight seem remote or separable from it.... (13)

One of the great weaknesses of prevailing practice in school education is its sedentary nature - "our traditional methods of instruction are too sedentary". He exemplifies how schools, under the impact of war, have had to adapt themselves to out of school activities and how the change in educational methods has stimulated the minds of both teachers and pupils. It seems that under the stress of war the English may have stumbled on an educational discovery. Sadler's account reads almost like an anticipation of that influential book by the former soldier, Caldwell Cook, who produced his challenging volume The Playway at the end of the first world war.(14) The crux of Sadler's reforms in elementary education comes when he foresees a much needed link with secondary education. If the

existing mental barrier could be removed, then there would be
some hope of achieving a policy for education that would help
in giving unity to national education.

Prior to the first world war Sadler had made many studies
of the development of secondary education in Germany. He
recognizes:-

> We know what great things Germany had done in
> secondary education, first for boys, and more
> recently for girls: also how profound an effect this
> achievement had had upon German industry and
> municipal life .(15)

However, he suggests that we in England feel that the German
pattern, though it might have pointers from which to learn, was
not automatically applicable in the texture of English society.
He sees our teaching profession as a devoted but badly paid
body of men and women. Nevertheless, he cannot see them willing
to become civil servants like their German counterparts -
"brigaded as servants of the Crown". Sadler often speculated on
the possibility of English teachers becoming civil servants,
but invariably he rejected the notion. What he calls somewhat
vaguely "the English instinct, half-stupid and unimaginative as
it seemed", kept us from a blind admiration of German secondary
education.

One aspect of this second level of education which did
attract Sadler (and about which he had written a paper for the
Bryce Commission as early as 1895) was the underlying concept
of Allgemeine Bildung, that conception of a groundwork of
general education largely examined by those who taught those
candidates they had prepared for the Abitur. He was drawn to
the conviction that such a basis of general culture was a firm
intellectual foundation for intelligent intercourse and co-
operation in a modern State. He was aware that for a century,
the Prussian and other German States had made it a fundamental
part of their policy to maintain higher schools in which boys
destined for public service, for the learned professions and
for the more responsible positions in commerce and industry,
should acquire the elements of general culture by means of a
demanding course of discipline and study extending over at
least six years. In an analysis elsewhere, Sadler was to make
the point that these schools, though not expensive, were "the
appanage of the middle and upper classes" and they left
unbridged a gulf "between the world of the elementary school
and the world of the higher school".(16)

Linked to Sadler´s consideration of reform in the
elementary school, is his interest in continuation classes, and
he says crisply:-

> Impart freshness of interest to the first, and you
> provide more active minds for the latter .(17)

He has, however, a strong reservation. After paying tribute to
scores of people who have made "dogged intellectual application
after their day's wage-work was done", he pleads for a new look
at the whole situation of part-time education. Evening classes
as they were at that time constituted, failed to meet the
wasteful leakage in our educational system between the years of
13 and 17. Not more than one out of every three pupils leaving
the elementary schools received, "in point of general or
technical education, any further systematic care" - a situation
noted in a typical Sadlerian metaphor:-

> We have, as it were, laid down in our elementary
> school system an enormously costly system of water
> supply. But we still allow badly leaking pipes just
> behind our taps .(18)

Sadler looked forward to when the Government would be prepared
to create a great system of continuation classes, but he did
not think this would be the concern solely of the Board of
Education. Other departments such as the Board of Agriculture
should be involved. His conclusion was that:-

> the setting up of a network of continuation classes
> in accordance with national needs is the most
> considerable task which will have been attempted in
> English education since that imposed by Mr. Forster's
> Elementary Education Act in 1870 .(19)

Significantly, when Sadler comes to consider the education
of the young wage-earner, he devotes substantial attention to
the pioneer work of Dr. Georg Kerschensteiner. As long ago as
1907, he had written with enthusiasm of the continuation school
work in Munich. He makes an assessment of Kerschensteiner's
work very similar to that made by Vernon Mallinson who, quoting
Kerschensteiner, writes:-

> The most valuable thing that we can hand down to our
> pupils is not knowledge, but a sound method of
> acquiring knowledge and the habit of acting on their
> own initiative .(20)

Sadler points out that from his personal observations in
Munich, he discovered that the industrial circumstances and
German traditions (to which the continuation schools were
skilfully adapted) were unlike those of an English city. He
detected a close link between elementary education in the
German States and further education, because of the local
conviction that only out of a vigorous system of elementary
education could the effective training in continuation classes
be expected to spring.
One consequence of this realisation was that English

administrators were led to examine more carefully the work of
the German elementary school. From such an examination it was
concluded that these schools presented a formidable rival to
the English, but that they were no model for uncritical
imitation, whether with reference to the training of suitable
teachers, or in methods of discipline, or administrative
control. Dr. Kerschensteiner's original contribution to this
phase of education - so Sadler suggests - was:-

> to utilize a neglected by-product in the mental
> energy of young people during the years of
> adolescence .(21)

On the other hand, research showed English students that the
German system of continuation classes had its roots far in the
past, and that the contemporary development was in part the
revival of the medieval guild, in a modern context but under
the firm aegis of the State. If a system of continuation
classes could be developed after the war, in England, Sadler
hoped they would be based upon obligatory attendance - he could
not foresee that one of the shortcomings of the Fisher Act of
1918 would be its permissiveness in relation to the development
of day continuation schools.

Nowadays it echoes upon our ears a little oddly when
Sadler, turning his attention to teachers, notes that "England
is threatened by a famine of teachers". And this is not solely
the results of conscription. He contends that low rates of
salary are part of the problem, but even more off-putting are
the actual conditions of work in so many schools. He makes his
point with a vivid analogy:-

> The conditions of work in the public elementary
> schools are increasingly distasteful to women and men
> who have experienced the happier atmosphere of our
> secondary schools. Having, so to speak, become
> accustomed to the comforts of the carriages of the
> Midland Railway, they dislike the squalor which I
> remember as a boy on the now admirable South-
> Western .(22)

He wishes to see the reduction in size of classes to 30 pupils.
He commends the work of "the more active-minded Training
Colleges for Teachers". He would like to see experienced
workers drawn from the English industries teaching beginners.
In this sphere we do not fare as well as the Scandinavians, the
Germans, or the Americans. Another reform required is of
liberal advances to be made in the current salary scales and
superannuation allowances. For Sadler the task of teaching in a
school is many-sided - it is "not a mere dexterity but an art
and even a pastorate".(23)

For the Redbrick Vice-Chancellor, who had been led into his

convictions about the importance of secondary education as a
result of his early career in Adult Education, the problem of
how to educate the masses remained a major issue. So it remains
after a multiplicity of post-war Reports, and two major
attempts in the Education Acts of 1918 and 1944 to extend and
reform the education of the rank and file in the State schools,
and to devise workable schemes of part-time education for young
wage-earners. Meanwhile, we have lost the framework of a basic
general education in a welter of topics, projects, areas of
experience and unsuccessful efforts to create new leaving
examinations. Lady Methven, writing in the report of the
Social Affairs Unit in 1982 notes:-

> Too many young people arrive on the labour market
> unqualified and unprepared for work. Our education
> system is failing us and must be challenged and
> changed. Not just by government and educationists,
> but by trade and industry.... (24)

At the end of a searching chapter in his volume A New History
of England, L.C.B. Seaman concludes his survey of post-war
educational development in England with the judgement:-

> While it was right that education at all levels
> should instil values other than those of material
> gain and should develop pupils´ mental and creative
> talents as much as possible, the gulf between the
> way the English were schooled and the kind of life
> most of them lived after full-time education had
> ended added to the tensions of the late twentieth
> century. ....An education philosophy that treated
> working life as an unfortunate adult postscript to
> the joys and opportunities of childhood or as a mere
> tiresome interruption of leisure and pleasure, was
> perhaps something of a luxury for an industrial and
> trading nation wrestling with the competition of
> powerful economic rivals .(25)

Vernon Mallinson has succinctly reviewed this situation in his
discussion of technical and recurrent education, and drawn
enlightening comparisons with practices in Scandinavia,
Belgium, Holland, France, West Germany, Italy and
Switzerland.(26)

To what extent have Michael Sadler and Vernon Mallinson
common ground in a concept of national character? One of the
fascinating outcomes of a close study of Sadler´s work is to
find how he articulates the Englishness of English education,
not only in what is acceptable but also in what is rejected.
Vernon Mallinson is well aware that his critics question the
validity of the notion of national character, which is a
leitmotiv running through his various books. He recognises

An English Education for England

their scepticism and in an Appendix to the Introduction to the Study of Comparative Education he comments:-

> Critics of the concept of national character seem to be baffled that they cannot ´scientifically´ penetrate the mystery of custom. They argue that national character is a generalization and like all generalizations must suffer from imprecision and vagueness .(27)

He argues that the student of Comparative Education, in seeking to identify national character must be primarily:-

> a cultural historian, noting the way of life of a people, and seeking knowledge of their aspirations through their philosophical attitude, their modes of thought, their religions and political awareness .(28)

This rounded estimate could well be taken as an adumbration of that "right spirit and scholarly attitude" in which Sadler wanted the study of foreign systems of education to be conducted. And, in their common focus on national character, the two men are brought conclusively together when Mallinson, rounding off his chapter on The traditional elements in European education, selects a witty analogy from Sadler´s massive essay on the unrest in secondary education in Germany and elsewhere. Discussing aims and objectives underlying educational structures Sadler writes:-

> Different nations, of course, lay different stress on this or that outcome of secondary education. The German is apt to ask about a young man - ´What does he know?´ The American to ask - ´What can he do?´ The Frenchman to ask - ´What examinations has he passed?´ The Englishman´s usual question is - ´What sort of fellow is he?´

> All four, however, are tacitly referring to a current and rather vague idea prevalent in their respective countries as to whither a prolonged course of education should have led .(29)

NOTES AND REFERENCES

1.Mallinson,V. (1981): In the Wake of Sir Michael Sadler. Compare, Vol.II, No.2, pp.175-183.

2.Sadler,Michael (1916): An English Education for England. Contemporary Review. Reprinted in full pp.110-116 in Selections from Michael Sadler, ed. Higginson,J.H. (1979), published Liverpool, Dejall and Meyorre.

3.Mallinson,V. (1980): The Western European Idea in Education. Pergamon Press, Oxford.

4.Sadler, Michael: How far can we learn anything of practical value from the study of foreign systems of education? See p.50 Selections from Michael Sadler, op.cit.

5.Sadler, Michael (1902): Vol.IX Special Reports, p.167, H.M.S.O., London.

6.Sadler, Michael (1930): The Outlook in Secondary Education, p.16, Bureau of Publications, Teachers College, Columbia University, New York City.

7.Sadler, Michael: See reference 2, page 110.

8.Mallinson,V. op.cit, pp.153-163.

9.Ibid, pp.5-6.

10.Sadler, Michael: See reference 2, page 110.

11.Ibid, p.112.

12.Ibid, p.113.

13.Ibid, p.114.

14.Cook, H. Caldwell (1917): The Play Way: an Essay in Educational Method, Heinemann, London.

15.Sadler, Michael: See reference 2, page 112.

16.Sadler, Michael: The Outlook in Secondary Education, p.49, op.cit.

17.Sadler, Michael: See reference 2, page 115.

18.Sadler, Michael: Ibid, p.115.

19.Sadler, Michael: Ibid, p.116.

20.Mallinson,V., op.cit., p.246.

21.Sadler, Michael: See reference 2, page 113.

22.Sadler, Michael: Ibid, p.115.

23.Sadler, Michael: Ibid, p.114.

24.Anderson, Digby (ed) (1982): Educated for Employment? See Foreword by Lady Methven, publ. Social Affairs Unit, London.

25.Seaman,L.C.B. (1981): A New History of England, p.500. The Harvester Press Ltd., Brighton.

26.Mallinson,V., op.cit., pp.213-257.

27.Mallinson,V. (1975): An introduction to the study of Comparative Education, p.273, Heinemann, London.

28.Mallinson,V., Ibid, p.273.

29.Sadler, Michael (1902): Vol.IX Special Reports, pp.23-24. Also quoted in part on page 154 of V. Mallinson's The Western European Idea in Education.

Chapter Two

NATIONAL CHARACTER - CONCEPT, SCOPE AND USES

William Kay

One of Vernon Mallinson´s central concerns, was that of
"national character". This chapter seeks to examine the concept
critically in an attempt to clarify it and its uses as a tool
of comparative education analysis. The critique is written as a
mark of appreciation of many cheerful and informative seminars
that I enjoyed as one of Professor Mallinson´s students some
years ago, and because these seminars so fascinated me that I
was inspired to continue studying comparative education long
afterwards.

In dealing initially with Mallinson´s concept of national
character, it will probably be simplest to turn first to its
scope and definition, then to its formation and finally to its
function in comparative studies.

MALLINSON´S USE OF NATIONAL CHARACTER

An Introduction to the Study of Comparative Education (4th
edition) contains its main references to national character in
the early chapters and in appendix one. It is defined widely in
terms of "feelings and sentiments" (p.270), "semi-permanent
dispositions" (p.271), "a kind of fixed mental constitution"
(p.12), "relatively permanent attitudes - to these prime values
- common to a nation" (p.14) and "the modes of the distribution
of personality variants in any given society, a modal
personality structure being one that appears frequently and
which is recognisable as such" (p.271). We thus have a
description which includes mental and emotional features and
which gives rise to particular configurations of the total
personality system. Of special importance are the values around
which the personality is organised because these values serve
to guarantee the coherence of the nation which embodies them.

The formation of national character is interestingly linked
with the formation of the nation itself. In essence what
happens is that individuals combine in groups with common
interests - perhaps for the purpose of trade - and eventually
these groups themselves combine, despite clashes of loyalty

20

that may occur, into a higher conglomeration which comprises the nation. In a sense the suppression of individual desires and group self-seeking so as to rally round a national purpose is "an expression of faith" (p.267). Minor loyalties are put aside in order to serve the common values which then undergrid the nation.

The perpetuation of national character is achieved through the agencies of child-rearing, chiefly the family, and by means of the individual's search for personal identity which tends to find expression through the available cultural patterns - and these will involve "folk characters who are made to embody modes of response to life situations which are approved" (p.273).

There is an apparent ambiguity, however, surrounding the role of the so-called "determinants of national character" (p.28 ff). These are given as the social, the geographical and economic, the historical, the religious and the political factors. At first sight it appears that the effects of these factors are mediated through national character upon the educational system, but this cannot be correct because, for example, we are told that national character both is, and is not, the shaper of constitutions and forms of government. Rousseau, whom Mallinson quotes with approval, "reminds us that it is not the national character which shapes constitutions and forms of government" (p.268), while "it is from a people's character, and not from its intelligence, that stem its political constitutions, its social and cultural outlook" (p.5). Likewise there is some apparent confusion because national character "typifies those forms of cultural continuity which determine the social behaviour of the nation" (p.263) while at the same time the "social heritage" or "the social factor" (which presumably includes social behaviour) is listed among the determinants of national character. Which determines which?

We can postulate a reciprocal relationship here which will partly explain the difficulty. It may be that the various factors which are determinative of national character are operative in the early stages of a nation's life and that, after a while when the national character has been established, it acquires a momentum of its own and begins to influence the factors which helped it into existence; in the early years parents may influence their children, but later the children may alter the outlook of their parents. Attractive though this idea is, it would seem that it does not tell the whole story. One of the complexities the notion of national character needs to explain is that caused by a revolution. It would obviously be absurd to argue that the French national character changed overnight after 1789 or that the Russian character immediately altered when Lenin assumed power. The assertion that national character does <u>not</u> determine forms of government seems much more acceptable than its opposite. In other words, to be

theoretically valid, national character must be amenable to
change, but must be less amenable to change than those things
it is used to explain.

The function of national character in comparative studies
is threefold. First, as a basis for a proper appreciation of
foreign customs and cultures it is indispensable. "Students of
comparative education", Mallinson tells us, "must, therefore,
base their studies (if they are to be fruitful), on the potency
and workings of national character as reflected in the
educational system of various countries" (p.270). Students need
to learn to distinguish "the colour, shape and scent" of
different national mentalities so that they can come to
understand what makes a nation flower. Second, as an
explanatory concept enabling the analyst to see why certain
educational reforms failed and others succeeded. According to
Mallinson, French educational reforms after the Revolution
(p.5) and World War II failed (p.228) because they were out of
step with the overall character of the nation though it is
significant that since 1968 and 1977 they have been more
successful. Third, national character provides a synthesising
and linking entity which enables cultural patterns and
educational systems to be harmonised. If national character
typifies the "forces of cultural continuity which determine
social behaviour" (p.263) and if "educational systems are
determined by prevailing culture patterns" (p.273), we have a
model like that given in Figure 2.1.

Figure 2.1.

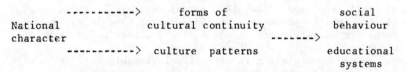

```
            ----------->     forms of              social
National                  cultural continuity      behaviour
character                                    ------->
            ----------->   culture  patterns   educational
                                               systems
```

National character is here anterior to culture, or cultural
patterns, and determines (a strong word) both social behaviour
and educational systems.

As "educational reform is the result rather than the cause
of changes in social perspectives" (p.273), we can elaborate
the model as in Figure 2.2.

Figure 2.2.

```
National       forms of cultural      change in     Educational
character---->    continuity;    -----> social ----> reform
               cultural patterns       perspectives
```

However, Mallinson is careful to delimit his claims for national character, calling it "imaginative rather than strictly scientific" (p.274) and "a valuable....tool of interpretation" (p.274). His own use of the concept is illustrated in the next paragraph. The point, though, of making models from his thinking is given at the end of this chapter.

To elucidate the function of national character, particularly as it relates to educational reform, one can look for examples of Mallinson´s discussion of French and Soviet education. He summarises the broad outlines of the Langevin-Wallon Reform Plan which was worked out when France was recovering from the last war. Having given a brief history of the struggle between the Catholic Church and the republican State, and having mentioned Jean Zay´s <u>orientation</u> principle which was designed to find out what kind of education suited the individual pupil, Mallinson showed how the mass gaining of a <u>culture générale</u> was not sacrificed to the production of an intellectual élite by the introduction of a common, and very French content, in the early years of secondary education coupled with, for pupils aged 13-15, specialist and trial options. The very scale of the plan and the "impetuous application" of its principles ran it into danger because it threatened to get "out of step with national character" (pp.226-228).

Soviet education offers a similar example. Peasant farmers resented the removal of their children for the purposes of education, and so the authorities circumvented their objections by a parody of Orthodox religious ceremonies and customs (p.20). A modification of a "harvest festival" celebration marked the departure of bright children for boarding education, and by this governmental sleight of hand parental acquiescence was obtained.

CRITICISMS OF NATIONAL CHARACTER

Jones(1) asks two pointed questions about national character which may be expanded as two criticisms:

1. National character can become a "catch-all" term: educational innovations which succeed can be attributed to their consonance with national character; innovations which fail can be equally easily attributed to the violence they do to national character. The weakness of national character as an explanatory concept rests on its inability to predict which changes will succeed and which will fail.

Halls(2) also mentions the Langevin-Wallon reforms and gives quite other reasons from Mallinson for their chequered history. He points to the perpetual instability of successive governments of the Fourth Republic, the pressure of other priorities of reconstruction, the rising birth rate and the elitist political views of some French politicians. It is a matter of opinion, but one can surely make a case for proposing that the points Halls raises throw altogether more light on the subject than a blanket reference to national character.

Similarly in the Soviet Union one can question the appropriateness of explaining peasant acceptance of boarding education by making a pseudo-religious ceremony of the departure of their children. The severe threat of Stalinist brutality coupled with the deliberate manipulation of the populace by Bolshevik leaders, whose ideological convictions justified any expediency, can account for the invention of secular ceremonies. A parallel situation exists with regard to Soviet weddings. The conduct of Soviet marriages apes the rites of the Church, but it would seem odd to suggest that such a state of affairs is a manifestation of national character. The Soviet authorities have designed their ceremonies in order to prise young people away from their ancestral faith: the notion is that a state wedding is as good as a church wedding.(3,4)

2. There is a greater variation in personality within cultures than between cultures. The subcultures that form such an important part of modern societies are more like each other than their parent culture. The French juvenile delinquent is more like the English delinquent than he is like the average Frenchman. An attempt to impose a unity on all subcultures which make up a modern nation-state is artificial. Additionally, can West Germans be said to be similar to East Germans, or does the Iron curtain have an influence on the character of Germanic people on either side of it? Are there specific Welsh characteristics that differentiate them from the English, or do the general characteristics of the British cover the Northern Irish, Scots and Welsh in one national type? These and similar questions have not been satisfactorily answered by proponents of the national character theory except insofar as the concept is claimed to be more illuminative and interpretive than precise and scientific.

3. A simplistic relationship between culture and personality is envisaged. All national cultures, from the most complex and variagated to the most primitive and monotone, are assumed to influence character formation in the same way. The possibility that the agents of character formation in advanced societies are different from the agents of character formation in simple societies is not fully discussed. The likelihood that the national character of the young north American is formed in the same way as that of the young Sri Lankan seems intrinsically improbable.

OTHER PERSPECTIVES ON NATIONAL CHARACTER

As Mallinson points out, mention of national character may be found as early as Heroditus in the fifth century BC. McDougall(5), one of the most influential psychologists in the early part of this century, posited the influence of racial and therefore genetic effects on national mentalities. Both he and the men cited by Ginsberg(6) - Schucking, Fouillée, Madariaga - attempted partly to explain large historical events by reference to basic conceptions of personality. McDougall postulated the existence of innate insticts which, according to their national distribution, affected characteristics of whole nations. Fouillée, by contrast, found the old theory of temperaments congenial and explained some national behaviours by the predominance of various combinations of these. Rousseau, too, by his discussion of the "general will" facilitated the consideration of nations in personal terms writ large. Likewise Hegel, by his doctrine of the state and his consequent belittling of the ordinary individual, propounded a view of history which matches national character. In Hegel, "the German spirit" may be understood to be almost synonymous with "the German national character". In the 20th century, anthropologists have adapted, utilised and tested the whole notion so that reviews of the literature (e.g. by Singer(7)) run to 60 pages. Mallinson's view must be considered not only in the light of its own probability and usefulness but also alongside variant expressions of the same idea.

Levine(8) notes a <u>reductionist</u> position which posits the influence of personality on culture. McClelland et al's(9) well-known thesis is that the literature or art of a culture can implant within its people a desire for achievement: before the flowering of British society in Elizabeth 1's time, there was a generation of preparation during which motives for achievement were instilled in the young. McClelland argued that all artistic, entrepreneurial and technological attainments on a large scale occur because the young have acquired a need to submit themselves to the self-discipline which is the precondition of realised aspiration. This position is reductionist in that it translates cultural progress into individual or collective motivations engendered by the kind of stories children hear and the kind of lives they learn to want. The sequence of events, then, is the formation of motives in children which, in later life, find outlet in creative use of extant cultural traditions and artefacts.

The <u>personality-is-culture</u> view is, Levine(8) suggests, especially associated with Margaret Mead(10) and Ruth Benedict.(11) Personality is thought of as an aspect of culture because personality could not exist without a pattern of behaviour by which to express itself. These patterns of behaviour, being culturally imposed, conjoin personality and culture indissolubly. The transmission of national character is by means of child-rearing practices and the agents of early socialisation, though Mead is careful not to presume too direct a relation between such behaviour as infant breast feeding and

the eventual mature character of the nation. The child learns
to internalise the dominant values and outlooks of his or her
culture. Thus national character can be thought of as cultural
character.

A more subtle view, that of <u>personality mediation</u>, proposes
"splitting culture into two parts, one of which is seen as made
up of determinants of personality while the other consists of
expressions of personality".(12) The "primary" institutions of
society, its child-rearing practices and socio-economic
structure are thought of as determining personality; the
"secondary" institutions of society, the folklore, art and
religion are thought of as being expressions of national
character. This view has been modified so that the "primary"
institutions are themselves split into two parts one of which
ensures the survival of the group while the other shapes the
personalities of the group, often against the needs of the
individual.

Strictly psychological views of personality are legion.(13)
In general they focus, of course, on its inner workings - the
internal relationships of motives, understandings, feelings and
so on, rather than on the world external to the individual
consciousness. Personality theory is extremely diverse and,
because the ideas generated within it are often not open to
empirical testing, such arguments as go on about the best way
of conceiving personality are more or less incapable of
solution. In England Eysenck,(14) however, has proposed a
method of describing personality based on traits whose
anchorage is in the physiological constituents of human beings.
His extroversion-introversion spectrum is explicable by
reference to the thresholds which people have to stimuli;
extroverts, for example, characteristically enjoy more intense
and more varied stimuli than introverts. When this information
is added to findings about conditioning, it is possible to
build up a picture of likely social behaviour in different
personality types: extroverts are more likely to be found in
the prison population because of their failure to succumb to
social conditioning in acceptable norms of behaviour.
Introverts, conversely, dislike demanding stimuli and therefore
tend to condition more easily and prefer occupations and
activities which do not contain risks or intense contact with
other people.

Needless to say, Eysenck´s views have been subjected to
various types of criticisms,(15) but, in the present context,
it is interesting to note that Eysenck has applied his
personality questionnaire cross-culturally and detected
differences in trait levels which roughly correspond to
national stereotypes.(16) There is therefore some empirical
evidence for the notion of national character, though Eysenck´s
descriptive system has only a small place for "attitudes and
values" which, in Mallinson´s scheme, are important in
initiating and maintaining national cohesion.(17)

CONCLUSION

If the concept of national character prompts comparativists to study the family, the folklore, the literature and the cultural patterns of any society before making pronouncements on its educational system, this can only be to the good. As an explanatory concept, by contrast, to explain why some innovations succeed and others fail, it lacks cogency and, indeed, because it could actually act to prevent further precise enquiry, there is a danger that it could stifle discovery.

As a bridging idea connecting cultural patterns and educational systems, however, it could open fertile fields of thought. There is certainly room here for socio-psychological investigation into the means by which certain types of behaviour, certain attitudes and emotions are assimilated by children and young people. In other words, the transmission and formation of the wider aspects of national character offer scope to empirical, multi-disciplinary work. If, therefore, an idea is to be judged by its potential usefulness and the insights which can derive from it, national character can be warmly commended.

Moreover, though Mallinson himself has eschewed too scientific an application of his idea, there is certainly the possibility of using the models based on his work given in Figures 2.1. and 2.2. for exploring educational reform. The hypothesis that educational reform arises out of changing social perspectives undeniably deserves careful scrutiny and empirical testing. What has to be asked, though, is whether the factors identified by Hans(18) - which correspond quite closely to the determinants of national character given by Mallinson, or the philosophical and historical method of Kandel, or the "problem(-solving) approach" of Holmes - can give a more convincing explanation of educational progress than one which includes national character. Whether or not this is so remains to be seen. It is interesting to note that Holmes´s latest statement of his position (1981) allows for residual values which he equates with national character.(19) Mallinson´s thought, nevertheless, is rich enough to be continued in several directions: in the tradition of lucid historical analysis or, breaking new ground, as the raw material for social science hypotheses. Such varying possibilities give an indication of Mallinson´s stature.

NOTES AND REFERENCES

1.Jones,P.F. (1971): <u>Comparative Education: purpose and method</u>, University of Queensland Press, p.82.

2.Halls,W.D. (1976): <u>Culture and Politics in Modern France</u>, Pergamon Press, p.19.

3.Smith,H. (1976): The Russians, Times Books.

4.Freeborn,R. (1966): A Short History of Modern Russia, Hodder and Stoughton.

5.McDougall,W. (1920): The Group Mind, Cambridge University Press.

6.Ginsberg,M. (1968): Essays in Sociology and Social Philosophy, Peregrine Books. Ginsberg's essay entitled "National Character" discusses continental writing on the subject between the wars, though Fouillee's Esquisse Psychologique des Peuples Européens was published in 1903.

7.Singer,M. (1961): "A survey of culture and personality theory and research" in Kaplan,B. (ed): Studying Personality Cross-Culturally, Row, Peterson.

8.Levine,R.A. (1973): Culture, Behaviour and Personality, Hutchinson.

9.McClelland,D.C., Atkinson,J.W., Clark,R.A. and Lowell,E.L. (1953): The Achievement Motive, Appleton-Century-Crofts.

10.Mead,M. (1971): Coming of Age in Samoa, Penguin. Mead (p.178) reported that Samoans, for example, took very little interest in individual personality and individual differences. Behavioural patterns are set by cultural expectations and their language contains insufficient vocabulary to discuss personal motivation properly.

11.Benedict,R. (1934): Patterns of Culture, Houghton Mifflin Co.

12.Levine, op.cit., p.56.

13.See, for example, Hall,S.C. and Lindzey,G. (1970): Theories of Personality; John Wiley and Sahakian,W.S. (eds) (1977): Psychology of Personality, Rand McNally College Publishing Company.

14.Eysenck,H.J. (1970): The Structure of Human Personality (3rd edition), Methuen.

15.Mischel,W. (1971): Introduction to Personality, Holt, Rinehart and Winston; and Mischel,W. (1977): "The interaction of person and situation" in Magnusson,D. and Endler,N.S. (eds) (1977): Psychology at the Crossroads, John Wiley and Sons contain some searching comments. Eysenck has replied in Eysenck,M.W. and Eysenck,H.J. (1980): "Mischel and the concept of personality", British Journal of Psychology, 71, pp.191-204.

16.See, for example, Eysenck,S.B.G., Adelaja,O. and Eysenck,H.J. (1977): "A comparative study of personality in Nigerian and English subjects", Journal of Social Psychology, 102, pp.171-178. Saklofske,D.H. and Eysenck,S.B.G. (1978): "Cross-cultural comparison of personality: New Zealand children and English children", Psychological Reports, 42, pp.1111-1116.
    Lojk,L., Eysenck,S.B.G. and Eysenck,H.J. (1979): "National differences in personality in Yugoslavia and England", British Journal of Psychology, 70, pp.381-387.

17.The IEA studies hold no brief for the doctrine of national character. The study of civic education in ten countries (Civic Education in Ten Countries by Torney,J.V., Oppenheim,A.N. and Farnen,R.F., Almqvist and Wiksell, 1975), however, did include scales to measure attitudes underlying widely held values. These attitudes, such as anti-authoritarianism could form descriptions of a personality system (as in The Authoritarian Personality by Adorno,T.W. et.al., Harper and Row, 1950). Such differences as the IEA study found were put down to educational or social rather than to psychological factors. Nevertheless, if pressed, the data could be interpreted as supportive of national character.

18.Hans,N. (1961): Comparative Education, Routledge and Kegan Paul, p.83.

19.Holmes,B. (1981): Comparative Education: some considerations of method, George Allen nd Unwin.

Chapter Three

THE PROBLEM (SOLVING) APPROACH AND NATIONAL CHARACTER

Brian Holmes

The message I received from Sir Karl Popper is that we are all fallible. If scientists are fallible how much more so are educationists? John Dewey's more optimistic message is that we should try to use our intelligence to solve problems which arise in a constantly changing world. Crudely, Popper's view is that scientists should try to refute hypotheses under specific conditions. Dewey thought that we ought to verify our hypotheses in order to resolve our problems.

For research workers in education one implication is that in considering alternative solutions to a problem we should reject those which are least likely to work (refutation Popper). A second implication is that as practising educators we ought to work out the conditions under which a favoured policy solution is likely to work (verification Dewey). As a comparative educationist I have drawn a distinction between my critical role as a pure scientist and my more constructive role as an applied scientist. As pure scientists or policy advisers, comparative eductionists should critically consider alternative policies (from wherever they arise) with the intention of saying which of them will not work in a particular context in the sense that stated aims will not be achieved. As applied scientists or technical assistants, comparative educationists should attempt to show how an adopted policy can be introduced effectively into a particular context. In the absence of experimental tests in education, comparative education research workers can contribute critically and constructively to the problems educational statesmen face.

Crucial to both tasks is our ability to predict what will happen if a new policy is put into practice. Humanistic and scientific approaches to education differ fundamentally. Vernon Mallinson tends to imply that those scientists amongst us who regard prediction (not prophecy) in the social sciences as important, disparage humanistic approaches to comparative education. In my case nothing could be further from the truth.

Humanists, however, tend to make unwarranted assumptions about the outcomes of policy. Conscious as they are of "values" and aims in education, they accept or reject normative statements by appealing to a political or ideological commitment and reject policies simply on the ground that "we ought to do this or that", e.g. punish young children. They confuse normative statements with empirically falsifiable (Popper) or verifiable (Dewey) statements. They assert for example that the consequence of "doing this or that" will be harmful either to a child or to society. Behind such statements of what will be the case are implicit beliefs which are neither refutable nor verifiable.

There is no reason, in an open society, why we should not accept or reject a belief or normative statement without reference to empirical evidence. To have one´s deeply held beliefs rejected by others does not imply fallibility. It is the possibility that our statements about what "will be the case" rather than what "ought to be the case" will be refuted by an appeal to empirical evidence which makes us fallible. It was with the intention of taking educational discussion and debate outside the realm of speculative philosophy and pure logic that I looked first at some of the methods used in the natural sciences and then tried to apply those which appealed to me to research in education. I may have been mistaken in my choice of "scientific method" and made errors in the way I have applied techniques appropriate to that method. As a scientist, I consider it important that I make my models, techniques and data as explicit as possible so that my fallibility can be revealed without using ad hominem arguments.

HUMANISTIC AND SCIENTIFIC EDUCATIONISTS

Far too often humanistic educationists work exclusively in the realm of normative statements within an ideological or philosophical position. They do not always acknowledge this. Philosophers of education, for example, all too often state what education "is" rather than what "it ought to be". In the same way, they make practical claims for education which should more properly be stated as hoped for outcomes. Under these circumstances the political strength of the protagonists determines which of alternative policies are accepted - and by the same token rejected. Perhaps we should accept that this is not only the case but that it ought to be the case. If so, we should abandon any hope that educational problems can be solved intelligently, in Dewey´s sense of the term, rather than politically. Perhaps educationists should restrict themselves to a discussion of "aims" and purposes, and should not attempt to plan the development of education because, in the end, it is not possible to plan adequately.

Vernon Mallinson, however, does not restrict himself to a discussion and comparison of aims, purposes and normative statements about education. He enters the field of social psychology when he writes about the constituents of "national character". He implies that in any nation there are serious constraints on the possible range of educational reforms and that these are determined by the "national character" of people. Consequently he does not turn away from the practicalities of development but is reluctant to accept that scientific procedures can add greatly to the approach of humanists.

Unfortunately, governments throughout the world are committed to planning and to a belief that it can be made reasonably reliable, if not scientific. Most of them have large planning departments. Many of them, anxious to improve standards of living, invite international agencies and other national governments to provide planning "experts" as advisers or technical assistants. Whether we like them or not, educational planners are members of a growth occupation, in spite of their dismal track record. Their major failure lies in their reluctance to admit fallibility. Technical failure stems from their unwillingness to subject educational policy solutions to critical testing with the intention of rejecting some of them. Theoretically, they want to verify an aim-inspired solution. In practice, they are likely to accept a host government's favoured policy. They are likely to go for panaceas which have received international political acclaim. They prophesy rather than predict.

Prediction is, however, necessary if we are to have any chance of anticipating the success or failure in practice of a proposed solution. The difficulties of predicting the outcomes of educational policies have been a major preoccupation with me for many years. I am still groping towards methods on which I can assert with some confidence that policy A is unlikely to work in country Y, although it has worked with some success in country Z. In my search for appropriate methods, I have remained faithful to Dewey and Popper in believing that general policy statements (hypotheses) should be tested by comparing (if possible directly, if not comparatively) logically predicted events with subsequently observed events in a given context. To describe a societal context I have proposed that data can be collected and placed in four patterns: (a) normative statements; (b) statements about institutions; (c) statements about the natural environment, and (d) statements about the mental states of the people who are to implement policy.

Vital to the identification of major problems is knowledge of "mental states". Important in assessing the possibilities of radical solutions being formulated and overtly adopted is knowledge of "mental states". Vital to any judgement about the future practical success or failure of a policy is knowledge of "mental states". In short, on our ability to identify and describe the permanent or semi-permanent "mental states" of people involved in the enterprise of education rests our success in identifying problems, and in anticipating a range of policy options which might be formulated, adopted and finally implemented in any society. It is this area of inquiry where Mallinson´s humanists and my scientists find common ground. We are both interested in identifying what persists in order to understand what is possible.

Consequently, I do not see Mallinson´s approach, and that of like-minded comparative educationists, as antithetical to mine. My ability to predict the outcomes of educational policy in any nation depends on the accuracy with which I can describe the constituents of its "national character" and the "mental states" of groups within a nation. Because the notion of "mental states" is so central to my methodology and the notion of "national character" is so central to Mallinson´s I make no apology for concentrating in this article on the two concepts and techniques which we may use to establish working models, in spite of the fact that, appropriately, there is in this Festschrift another article on "national character".

NATIONAL CHARACTER

Vernon Mallinson was not the first comparative educationist to use the notion "national character" as a methodological tool but he, more than anyone, persuaded me that it could be incorporated into my "problem solving" approach without violence to either his position or mine. His working definitions seem to me perfectly acceptable, if they are regarded nominalistically. "National character", he writes: "can finally best be described as meaning the totality of dispositions to thought, feeling and behaviour peculiar to and widespread in a certain people, and manifested with greater or less continuity in a succession of generations"(1) - a definition taken from Morris Ginsberg. He agrees with Friedreich Schneider that national character typifies "those forces of cultural continuity which determine the social behaviour of a nation as a whole". Finally, Mallinson quotes R.S. Peters with approval when he writes that: "A person is an individual who has a certain assertiveness in his point of view - his judgements, appraisals, intentions and decisions which shape events have a characteristic stamp, being determined by previous ones that have given rise to permanent and semi-permanent dispositions". Such dispositions, recognised as "common or standardised in a given society" may be regarded, according to Mallinson, as constituting "national character".

Permanence or semi-permanence is the characteristic of the various attributes identified in these various quotations. It is in the assertions that they are more or less permanent and that they determine social behaviour that the possibilities of predicting, with more or less success, the future behaviour of an identified person or an identified group of persons lie. Unless we assume that people will behave in the future in the same kind of way as in the present and the past we cannot, in my view, predict what is likely to happen under given circumstances. Thus Mallinson´s notion of "national character" is central to any attempt to improve the study of comparative education as a predictive science. From my own perspective, it is an assumption which facilitates the analysis of problems, in identified contexts, which educationists are striving to resolve. The possibility that some men and women can free themselves from these attitudes, dispositions and feelings which give rise to cultural continuity is an assumption which should be made if we are to assert, as surely we must, that social change is possible. It is the role of innovators, who are not constrained by the more widely shared "fixed mental constitution that guarantees a common purpose and a common effort from the whole group" which is of interest in any theory of social change.

THEORIES OF SOCIAL CHANGE

Indeed, many world renowned theorists have used the notion that a high proportion of individuals in any group are likely to behave in accordance with "difficult to change" attitudes, beliefs or sentiments. Among them nineteenth and twentieth century observers of the changing social scene in the U.S.A., William Graham Sumner and William F. Ogburn asserted, in their theories, that the majority of individuals, living in accordance with traditional folkways or mores, would be unable quickly to adjust to technological innovation. Ogburn´s theory of "cultural lag"(2) identified by observing the time interval between changes in the material, non-material adaptive and non-material non-adaptive cultures depends on his belief that men and women are slow to adapt to technological innovation, industrialisation and urbanisation. From another perspective, Vilfredo Pareto drew a distinction between people who, because they could see relationships, could be radical, and those, again perhaps a majority, whose "residues of persistence" made them unwilling to change.(3) Pareto was, of course, more interested than Ogburn in political change, and wishing to ensure that it took place in society without violent revolution, described the circumstances under which this could occur. Pareto also asserted that individuals rarely act, and are seen to act, in accordance with their public statements.

A similar view was central to the analysis made by a distinguished Swedish sociologist, Gunnar Myrdal, when he described "an American dilemma".(4) He suggested that individual, white Americans held at one and the same time two conflicting sets of values in relation to the negroes or blacks. At the level of general statements white Americans accepted, and indeed believed in, the high ideals expressed in the Declaration of Independence - that "all men are created equal" - and the Bill of Rights - that the rights of all men and women ought to be protected under the laws of the land. At the same time, and at another level of feeling, the same individuals held fast to beliefs such as "self-interest" and the legitimacy of pursuing it. Such beliefs, rather than their high ideals, Myrdal asserted, motivated their behaviour towards the black people of America.

The Marxist-Leninist view was not entirely different. Traditional Marxists assert that under-capitalism workers acquire a ´false consciousness´ which can be successfully moderated only after a Revolution has overthrown the capitalists and eliminated the economic basis of capitalism. For Lenin and his successors in the USSR, the educational task was to eliminate, as far as possible, the ´false consciousness´ which lingered on among an older generation and gave continuity to the Czarist tradition in older Soviet citizens, and to create among the new generation a ´New Soviet man´. Lenin consequently paid great attention to the young people of the Soviet Union not only as learners but as teachers who could be more easily freed from the ´false consciousness´ of Russian capitalism. Some neo-Marxists, incidentally, take a more optimistic view of attitude changes without a revolution but still recognise the persistence of ideologies in capitalist societies.

The groups of people identified by various theorists of social change vary considerably. Many nineteenth and twentieth century sociologists, for example, pointed to the differences between people living in rural areas and those living in industrial urban areas and were acutely aware of the emergence of more complex societies. Emile Durkheim, for example, drew a distinction between simple societies, in which mechanical solidarity informed behaviour, and complex societies which were formed by organic solidarity.(5) F. Tonnies identified the differences between Gemeinschaft (Community) and Gesellschaft (Association or Society).(6) Later theorists, such as R. Redfield and T. Parsons, made somewhat similar distinctions. Basically, the analysis made by Marx was that the characteristics of feudal societies were different from those of capitalist and, hopefully, socialist or communist societies. Pareto on the other hand was less interested in placing societies on a rural-urban or on a simple-complex continuum and adopted a social-psychological approach to the behaviour of people who seek to gain and retain power.

NATIONAL, SOCIETAL OR SOCIAL CLASS COMPARISONS

A major difference between these theorists lies in the kinds of people who they claim can, either explicitly or implicity, be compared in the light of societal dichotomies. Rural-urban societies; agricultural-industrial societies; capitalist-socialist societies: politically unstable - politically stable societies; each of these dichotomies is represented in the literature and would justify comparative studies based upon them. Certainly a classification of societies on the basis of one or other of these polar type models informs the approach of many comparative educationists today. Education in capitalist countries is frequently compared with education in socialist countries. Indeed, this is the position usually adopted by comparative educationists in the Soviet Union, the German Democratic Republic and other Communist countries. Neo-Marxists, on the other hand, often draw distinctions between neo-colonialist educators and their motives and educators in dependent countries, thus comparing central and peripheral societies. Perhaps equally widely used as a criterion of differentiation is that which distinguishes ´developed´ from ´developing´ countries. A considerable number of comparative studies have been based covertly or explicitly on this distinction.

In this paper attention will be paid to features which differentiate groups. While social scientists identify different groups of people and compare their institutions, attitudes and behaviour patterns, they have one thing in common, namely that in any group can be detected certain shared dispositions, residues, sentiments, beliefs and so on which are unique to members of the group and are semi-permanent. Mallinson therefore is in very respectable company when he makes a similar claim. His position, however, is different in that he claims that members of a <u>nation</u> share common characteristics which <u>determine</u> their behaviour. This assumption seems no more audacious than one which ascribes to members of under-developed societies, or to members of a social class in capitalist societies, or to politicians, certain unique persisting characteristics. Indeed Mallinson´s justification for assuming that members of a nation state possess a more or less "fixed mental constitution" is very plausible. He maintains that the dispositions which constitute national character are built up over the centuries. In so far as in any nation state its citizens can be located, the group to which he refers is accurately identifiable. If a nation state has existed for centuries it is possible to examine, in ways I shall discuss later, the attitudes and beliefs that citizens should possess if they are to be loyal and law-abiding. The history of nationalism reveals the determination of certain groups of people to ensure a commitment by the majority of citizens to nationally agreed goals.

Difficulties arise when attempts are made to identify people belonging to an ´ideal nation´. Only if Nicholas Hans´ factors are regarded as an ´ideal typification´ of a nation can they be said to be useful.(7) Unity of language, religion and race within a clearly delineated territory describes relatively few national groups of people today. Historically, and even now of course, there are examples of attempts made to ensure that all citizens satisfy one or more of the criteria laid down by Hans. American education in the nineteenth century was designed to ensure that all U.S. citizens were English speaking - a policy exemplifying the attention paid to language as a unifying force. Similar policies in France after the Revolution are less frequently mentioned. Language policy in newly independent India was also based on the assumption that Hindi could be used to give Indian citizens a sense of 'nationality'. Soviet policy has been rather different insofar as Russian has been used as a lingua franca rather than as a way of 'Russifying' members of a working class whose mother tongue differs. Official State religions are also frequently found. The established Church of England reflects views about shared religious assumptions. Pakistan was created on the assumption that all its citizens would be willing to accept Islam. Hitler's Germany was, on the other hand, based on the notion that all true Germans ought to belong to the same pure Aryan race. The full rights of citizenship in South Africa are allocated on the basis of racial criteria. The implications for education in each of these cases have been extensively studied. Failure to establish an 'ideal' nation on Hans' criteria has not been uncommon. Resistance to such attempts has frequently been fierce, either from within a nation state or from outside its borders. Present diversity within old and newly independent nation states therefore requires some modification to the notion of "national character".(8)

A Hansian 'ideal' typical model of a nation clearly facilitates comparative studies of problems in old or new legally constituted "nations" created by social class, religious, linguistic and racial diversity. Undoubtedly in most countries characteristics different from Mallinson's "national character" can be ascribed to different groups.

An appreciation of this possibility doubtless persuaded Pedro Rossello that intra-national studies were legitimate. His knowledge of Spain and Switzerland illustrated to him the value of comparative education studies between regions of a nation as well as between nations. Pierre Furter has indeed made analyses of Spain and Switzerland which brilliantly exemplify this approach.

Mallinson's assumption is, however, that it is possible to speak of French, Belgian, Spanish, Swiss and American "national characters". It rests upon the fact that these nations have a long history during which time educational policies have been designed in part to inculcate political sentiments ensuring loyalty not to family, class or tribe, but to the State. There is plenty of evidence, as mentioned, to show how these attempts have been and are being made.

The case of the Soviet Union, however, raises interesting questions about the possibilities of changing "national character". Theoretically, Soviet leaders had options from which to choose. The first, not entirely abandoned during the Second World War, was to unify Soviet citizens by appealing to the traditions of mother Russia - a low key approach now

37

because of protests from Ukrainians, Latvians, Georgians, to mention only some of the many possible objectors. The second option was to build up notions of Soviet citizenship and Soviet "national character". On what criteria, in such a vast and diverse country, could this be based? Religion? Race? Language? Class? The answer lies in the appeal to the unity of sentiments and dispositions which bring together and determine the social behaviour of members of an unexploited working class. It is on these sentiments that Soviet educators must build a Soviet national character. It is indeed hoped that on working class sentiments unity might be achieved in many newly independent territories in which on criteria of language, religion and ethnicity there are a multiplicity of "national characters".

To conclude this introductory section, in spite of the value of "national character" as a methodological tool, sovereign states are now culturally so very diverse, or have so short a history, that the concept is inadequate. The assumption that in a nation various groups of people possess different "mental states" is a more sensitive methodological assumption in problem solving studies in comparative education.

Let me summarise the major components of what I have chosen to call the "problem (solving) approach" in comparative education before discussing methods of establishing "national characteristics" or group "mental states".

THE PROBLEM (SOLVING) APPROACH

(a) Problem analysis

According to John Dewey, problems arise as a consequence of sudden or unexpected social change. How these are brought about in any society are matters for careful analysis and investigation. Clearly some individuals in a nation are not constrained by semi-permanent sentiments and dispositions and may propose radical initiatives in terms of new aims. The acceptance of new normative statements suggests that mental states have to be modified. Other reformers may invent new machines or new institutions. The introduction of technological or social innovations requires a modification of behaviour. Political agitators may precipitate a revolution. Subsequent success depends upon changes in "mental states". The persistence of sentiments, dispositions and ways of behaving (national character) may make it difficult for the majority of members of a society to adopt new norms or to adjust, on behavioural terms, to technological innovations and to new institutional arrangements.

The notion that within a society there are different groups of people - rural and urban, working and middle class, Christian and Moslems, English and Welsh speakers - implies that some members of the society, but not others, will be able to adopt new norms and respond, positively or negatively, to new institutions. Some groups, but not others, are likely to form the nucleus of a post-revolutionary political movement.

Changes of the above kind can, of course, be introduced into a society be people outside it because of the interdependence of societies and nations. Postwar technical assistance is a major example of deliberate attempts to introduce change into developing countries. Covertly, however, what goes on in the U.S.A. may change some circumstances in Europe, Africa, Asia or Latin America. The development of high level technology in Japan has undoubtedly had repercussions on Swiss watch makers and on car manufacturers in most other countries. In response to these externally induced changes, the sentiments, dispositions and behaviour patterns of recipients may change extremely reluctantly, slowly, or, in some cases, even rapidly.

Any logically identified gap between <u>desired</u> behaviour in response to a societal innovation and <u>persisting</u> behaviour patterns (based on group "national character") constitutes, in general, the source of major social problems.

(b) Policy solutions

Dewey suggested that in the light of identified problems individuals or groups of them propose possible solutions. The persistence of national sentiments and dispositions suggests that national solutions to worldwide problems are likely to be formulated within such constraints. Who can visualise that within the foreseeable future a majority of Americans would agree to <u>massive</u> Federal legislative or financial intervention to solve problems associated with, for example, the education of Roman Catholic children? Is it conceivable that in spite of Labour Party rhetoric in England, the majority of English men and women will agree to the abolition of prestige "Public" schools? How else can one explain the difficulties of introducing educational reform in France between 1945 and 1960 without the persistence of anticlerical attitudes? Novel solutions introduced into Japan after 1945 by SCAP officials were in a relatively short period of time transformed into policies and practices more in accordance with Japanese "national character".

The above questions and illustrations, themselves, are by no means rhetorical. The possibility that Federal money may be funded in the U.S.A. to Catholic schools exists under the 1965 Elementary and Secondary Education Act. With the strong support of de Gaulle, agreement was reached in France in 1959 and 1960 on the establishment of contracts making public funds available to Roman Catholic schools. Some proposals made by American members of SCAP to reform Japanese education were acceptable to liberal minded Japanese educationists. <u>Some</u> policies were overtly adopted by <u>some</u> educationists and rejected by others. The persistence of some elements of "national character" gave to the postwar conflict over educational policy in Japan a uniquely Japanese flavour.

Examples of radical solutions to radical change are found in the USSR. After the 1917 Revolution, as a result of which great economic and political changes were introduced, radical eductional policies were advocated by some Soviet leaders who were to an extent attracted by Dewey's educational theories. The radical nature of the early educational solutions points to the fact that not all members of a nation were constrained by "national character" and that in the USSR, as in Japan in the nineteenth century, some were prepared to adopt foreign solutions without taking fully into account the difficulties of implementing them. Violent or not, revolutions are accompanied by policy proposals in virtually every aspect of life. An analysis of "national character" and the "mental states" of identifiable groups helps comparative educationists to identify those who may adopt radical economic and political policies and those who may reject radical educational policies.

It is, of course, possible that against constructs of "national character" post-revolution educational policies may be regarded as very revolutionary. An assessment of the radical nature of policy solutions is more useful than immediately to judge whether they are good or bad, right or wrong, because it suggests the degree to which a solution will be accepted by all or some, and suggests what difficulties may be faced in implementing it.

(c) Planned reform

Both Dewey and Popper stressed the need to evaluate a solution or solutions in the light of the context into which it or they are to be introduced.

As stated, an important feature of any national context is the dispositions and sentiments of groups of inhabitants in that country. If we are unable to identify and systematically describe them we cannot predict how changes and proposed responses to them will be received and acted upon. Intuitively, we may guess that they will be welcomed by some and rejected by other participants in the process of implementing new policies. The balance of power between those with more radical sentiments and those whose persisting sentiments are conservative will influence the degree and speed and way in which any new policy is put into practice.

Examples can readily be drawn from the USSR and the Republic of China. In spite of radical political and economic change in both countries, and in spite of the attempts made to create, for example, a "New Soviet Man" or a "New Chinese", with new sentiments and dispositions, it has not been possible in either country to eliminate or substantially to alter the permanent attitudes of academics. Their resistance to change may be overt or, more likely, covert. The effective power of academics to resist institutional change is a common phenomenon and accounts in large measure for the apparent failures of planned educational reform, whether proposed by radicals within a social system or by external advisers.

In summary, I agree with Mallinson that on the whole national solutions to problems will be constrained by national traditions. Such a view justifies the establishment of "national character". On the other hand there is evidence to support the view that policy solutions have been and can be proposed which lie well outside what would appear possible in the light of "national" traditions. We therefore need to take into account the fact that some individuals in most societies will not be tied by tradition. We must recognise however that there will be different behavioural responses to proposed normative solutions corresponding to the "mental states" of those who can overtly adopt them and those individuals who cannot accept original solutions, much less implement them.

It is the unwillingness or inability of some groups within a nation either to accept certain policies or to put them successfully into practice that makes planning difficult. The political, economic and educational power of these groups and their predictable behaviour make it possible to assert with some confidence that policy ´A´ might achieve hoped for results, policy ´B´ will be so distorted in practice as to be unrecognisable, and policy ´C´ will be rejected in practice, even if it has been adopted in theory.

TECHNIQUES OF ENQUIRY

The "problem solving approach" requires that we know what may be regarded as conservative elements in a society, identified as "national character" and group "mental states". In some ways, the establishment of "national character" is less difficult than the establishment of relevant "mental states". Mallinson favours several approaches, which will be mentioned briefly. Personal experience is highly desirable. It should wherever possible be reinforced by knowledge of the national language. In other words, a comparative educationist should attempt to acquire knowledge of foreign countries similar to the knowledge he has of his own, by speaking their language. Theoretically, the replication of experience undoubtedly makes possible an understanding of more than one or even several "national characters". In practice, however, the number of languages a person can learn to speak, read and write fluently is limited, however gifted that person may be.

A second question is: How long must a person live in a country to acquire a worthwhile knowledge, based on experience of "national character"? Clearly, the answer is neither simple nor definitive. Trained and informed observers may well be able in a relatively short time to acquire knowledge not accessible to the less well-trained observer. Nevertheless, if the comparative educationist is to rely on close acquaintanceship of a country to know its "national character", he must be a mature scholar before he can know well more than a few countries other than his own. Indeed, it could be said that Nicholas Hans and Friedreich Schneider produced their most perceptive comparative studies towards the end of their formal academic careers.

Otherwise, comparative educationists must use vicarious experience. Several distinguished writers have written either about the "national character" of their own countrymen or about the "national character" of several nations. Lord Lytton in England and the English made brilliant psychological observations and David Hume, Sir Ernest Barker, G. Gover and A. Sampson are only some other authors who have provided accounts of British or English "national character". André Siegfried is one of the best known French writers to describe French mentality in France: a study of nationality. Siegfried was one of the most perceptive authors to compare "national characters" in The Character of Peoples(9) in which he drew brief sketches of the French, Italians, Spanish and Germans. An equally illuminating comparative study is provided in S. de Madariaga´s Englishman, Frenchman and Spaniards.

To these humanistic studies, which certainly cannot be replicated, should be added insights found in creative writing as Vernon Mallinson has shown so well. Kipling´s works portray archetypal British types. There is no better description of an aspect of English life in the thirties than that provided in A.G. Macdonell´s England Their England. Where else might we find Billy Bunter or Richmal Crompton´s William than in England of the same period? The contexts in which such characters performed are doubtless dated, but if there is anything in the notion of "national character" their behaviour should be recognisable in the present generation of boys. By the same token, Tom Sawyer, regardless of the historical context, remains an American character. Many examples could be cited of creative writings which illuminate clearly recognisable features of "national character" by observers and which through their popularity either reinforce existing dispositions or else influence the creation of new ones. Literary critics doubtless have views on the extent to which successful writers appeal to permanent dispositions and evoke favourable responses because readers are able to identify with these dispositions, or the extent to which the quality of the writing provokes more unusual reader responses. In either case, a research worker faces the dilemma of choosing which of many authors most faithfully or imaginatively exemplifies in their characters the most important dispositions which constitute "national character". Few workers would reject Shakespeare on either of these grounds. He indeed analysed English national characteristics in many of his historical plays and portrayed national patriotism perhaps no more stirringly than in

Henry V´s speech before Agincourt.

Vicarious experience through the writing of scholars, novelists and dramatists should not be rejected as either invalid or unreliable. Such works certainly throw light, not only on the characteristics of the nation as a whole, but on the "mental states" of groups within the nation. For example, in the last thirty years many works of fiction have centred on the lifestyles of members of the "working class", and in particular those associated with people from the north of England. The interest of novelists in the working classes reflects the willingness of sociologists in Britain to regard social class differences as most important and divisive. At the same time, they warn against stereotyping, which is rather strange in view of their commitment to class divisions as useful in sociological analysis. Working and middle class attitudes are frequently referred to. Attitude tests do not, however, penetrate to those deeply held sentiments which persist and motivate behaviour.

Consequently, if we are to use the latter in problem analysis and in predicting outcomes, we need techniques which are more capable of being replicated by research workers than those already used by humanist scholars and sociologists.

To analyse a problem it is necessary to identify not only persisting features of society, but change or changes which are the source of the problem. Some theorists of social change limit the kinds of change which they regard as real. Others assert that a certain kind of change precedes all other kinds. As stated, classical Marxists tend to argue that only economic change is important and can initiate a sequence of events. Neo-Marxists are inclined to argue that significant changes can be introduced into a society prior to an economic and political revolution.

I take the view that it is useful to identify normative change provided that it is not assumed that everybody in a nation accepts it or is willing or able to put it into practice i.e. institutionalise the novel idea. The research need is to identify the sources of normative change and to discover how it finds public expression. No doubt the pronouncements of the spokesmen of identified groups can be taken as suggesting normative innovations. The groups for which they speak may be any of those previously identified - churchpeople, politicians, the working class and farmers. How the views expressed become public knowledge can be investigated in various ways.

The advantage of taking nation states as the bases of comparison lies in the possibilities of examining and comparing the procedures for formulating local and national legislation. System analysis allows the mechanics of representative government to be thoroughly analysed. For this reason, recognising that pressure group politics play a part in the formulation of new normative statements and policies, I consider the comparative study of national policies useful in identifying normative change.

IDEAL TYPICAL MODELS

To meet the requirements that comparative educationists should describe normative patterns and "mental states", I have suggested that ideal typical models are useful.(10) It should not be assumed that ideal typical models correspond to reality. They help us to make sense of immensely multifarious subject matter of a certain kind.

In the case of ideal typical models of "mental states", the dangers of using them to stereotype people and their behaviour must be clearly recognised. It would be dangerous to assume that all Frenchmen, working class men and women, Muslims, Christians, Welsh speakers and members of other similarly identifiable groups act in accordance with an ideal typical model. With some justification, the use made of ideal typical models has been criticised by phenomenologists such as Husserl, Schutz and their present day followers. Yet it is not easy to see how the technical difficulties faced by Weber and modern comparative educationists can be met without resorting to ideal typical models. Useful as the techniques suggested by Mallinson are, I consider that in drawing up a construct of a "national character" or the "mental states" of a group, use should be made of ideal typical models in the way suggested by Weber.

According to Weber, any view of the world must be limited, partial and conditioned by the observer's point of view. These comments apply equally to creative writers and scholars who have studied carefully the history and culture of nations. Their views are subjective and selective. The establishment of ideal typical models, designed to make sense of many and complex data involves both selection and subjective decisions. The criteria on which selection is made and the sources from which the selection is made should, however, be made explicit. The sources of data should be known and open to third party inspection. It should be possible for subsequent workers who accept the criteria of selection and sources to replicate the model. Only then can ideal typical models of the kind proposed by Weber be established and used as logical rational constructs to examine "mental states", the ways in which institutions are run and social relationships.

In the case of ideal typical normative models, the model should offer a pattern of logically related normative statements - of the kind "this ought to be the case" - and give coherence to a multiplicity of views expressed by members of the society, or nation or group to which they refer. Conceptual clarity and simplicity, in the form of general statements relatively lacking in content, are gained in ideal typical models at the expense of accuracy and comprehensiveness. The more sharply and clearly constructed into a logical pattern these generalisations are, the more "unrealistic" the model is likely to be, because, at least in Pareto´s society, men and women rarely think and behave logically, and in Popper´s Open Society they are free to accept or reject, on whatever grounds, some or all the beliefs articulated in the model. The model, however, is useful because it permits the comparative educationist to make sense of debates and to identify normative initiatives in certain aspects of social life.

The distinction between these two types of model cannot be over-emphasised. According to Myrdal there are major differences between the very general statements of belief which people accept overtly and the much more particular beliefs which covertly motivate their behaviour. The former I have called their "higher valuations", the latter I have termed their "lower valuations" and correspond to their "national character" or "mental states".(11) The two ideal typical models for the same nation or society may well be very different. Ideal typical "normative" models relate to what people say they believe; ideal typical "mental states" models represent the dispositions which motivate people´s behaviour. While "higher valuations" may be revealed by attitude tests, it is unlikely that "lower valuations" will be reliably revealed by such tests. If psychological tests are to be used, Rorschach tests are the most likely, through interpretation, to penetrate behind what people say they believe, to what they truly believe. Given the difficulty of administering these kinds of test on a large scale and accepting Mallinson´s view that permanent or semi-permanent dispositions are the outcome of long historical processes, I came to the view that national "mental states" models could best be brought into coherent patterns by making a selection from historical documents. Ideal typical "normative" models can best be derived from current constitutions and legislation. The choice of documents, it might be said, is arbitrary. In the light of Weber´s view that any assessment of an ideal typical model should be in its usefulness, rather than in its accuracy or comprehensiveness, choices can be justified.

THEORIES OF MAN, SOCIETY AND KNOWLEDGE

In Comparative Education: Some considerations of method(12) I suggested that the criteria on the basis of which ideal typical normative and mental states models could be developed should be:

   1. the nature of man
   2. the nature of society
   3. the nature of knowledge.

In accordance with these criteria, normative statements about man, society and knowledge in the form of what "ought to be the case" can be detected in all the literature mentioned thus far. Not all authors, however, draw a sharp distinction between statements about what ought to be the nature of man, society and knowledge and psychological, political, scientific and epistemological theories which provide descriptions of what is the case. Such distinctions are important if we wish to differentiate between theoretic and mental states.

"Mental states" can best be derived from historical - philosophical and constitutional - legal documents. In several places I have suggested that Plato´s Republic offers a source from which can be selected the constituents of a European ideal typical "mental states" model. I have suggested that this model can be adjusted to take account of differences between the national character of Englishmen, Frenchmen and Germans by comparing it with the philosophical views (in terms of man, society and knowledge) of representative secular philosophers such as Locke, Descartes and Hegel.

The assumption I make is perfectly consistent with Mallinson´s. Over the years the normative statements, indeed theories, enunciated by philosophers have been incorporated into the sentiments and dispositions of regional (Europe) and national groups. Outside Western Europe, the works of Marx and Lenin may be regarded as legitimising new sentiments in Eastern European countries. In Western Europe through Marxists and neo-Marxists attempts are being made to revolutionise national aspects of education. It is important therefore to recognise that what is traditional in one context may be radical in other contexts.

Clearly, ideal typical models representing sub-group norms and sentiments are necessary. In Comparative Education: Some considerations of method I did no more than mention the need for them, if we are to make sense of diversity within national systems of education. Among the important sources are the religious traditions which clearly meet the same criterion of validity as secular philosophies. In Europe, as in the case of Plato and St Augustine and Aristotle and Aquinas, secular and religious philosophies are frequently brought together to reinforce religious dispositions and sentiments. An ideal typical model of Catholic mental states could be derived from Aquinas; a model of Protestant or Puritan mental states from Luther or Calvin. Such models would allow Christian denominational differences and differences between Christian and secular values to be analysed. Today there is need for non-European ideal typical models - the religious traditions of non-Christian groups need to be known if diversity in many European countries is to be more adequately analysed. Consequently, models based on one or more Islamic sources and on Hindu and Buddhist sources are needed. The choice of the Koran seems straightforward, and indeed Moslem scholars seem to have little difficulty in drawing up an Islamic ideal typical model based on the Koran and the Sharia.

In the U.K. today there is also need to represent Chinese

and Greek Cypriot thought. Out of the extensive works of Confucius may be drawn theories about the nature of man, society and knowledge for the Chinese. An older Hellenistic tradition is the source of Greek Cypriot "mental states". A selection from Greek literature would be needed to establish such a model.

Undoubtedly, a major task for comparative educationists is to discern among the peoples of a nation the dispositions and sentiments which unify them and those which are the source of diversity. Some of the sources in the light of which diversity can be examined have been mentioned. It simply remains now to justify the sources of a model exemplifying areas of agreement in a culturally diverse nation.

CONSTITUTIONS AND LEGISLATION

Ideal typical normative or mental states models can be derived from Constitutions and legislation. At a particular stage in the history of a nation, both are likely to represent normative change. In newly independent countries, constitutions are normally approved; in some cases having been formulated by former imperial advisers. Prior to independence, consensus on some very general propositions may reflect agreement in terms of independence and disguise reservations on the part of some indigenous people about some specific clauses in a proposed constitution. The U.S.A. exemplifies the agreement reached among its founders on the most general statements about the power of the Federal government. The amendments represent not only disagreement about the role of government, but the emphasis given to individual rights by Thomas Jefferson.

These differences of opinion at the highest level can be interpreted in several ways. They may be seen as representing clashes over normative changes, or as a clash between the new norms of a few pioneers and the "mental states" of others. In the event, clauses in the Constitution have been open to various interpretations.

At the same time, in so far as a Constitution or legislation includes normative changes, the latter may be designed to solve an existing problem. Consequently, normative changes may be regarded as problem creating or problem solving. If the latter, it should be recognised that they still have to be implemented in a certain way if they are, in Dewey's sense, to resolve a problem in a practical way.

Regardless of social and political diversity, national constitutions and legislation, whatever their purpose, are intended to establish a framework of beliefs in accordance with which citizens are expected to act. They may be formulated by a few representatives of a democracy or by an oligarchy. They may be put to the people for adoption or they may be accepted initially only by a power elite. The task of implementing constitutions and legislation is enormously facilitated if the beliefs and theories about man, society and knowledge implicit in them correspond to the deeply held sentiments and dispositions of all citizens. If they reflect the beliefs of only some citizens and are rejected by others, the seeds of conflict are sown. Only in the most simplistic sense is it true to say that a minority of powerful citizens can impose on all citizens unacceptable beliefs, i.e. beliefs which are contrary to their sentiments, dispositions or mental states.

In turning to constitutions as the source of ideal typical national models, it is necessary to decide whether partially or in toto they can be used to identify widely held "higher valuations" (normative beliefs) or widely dispersed "lower valuations" or "mental states". The hope of those who frame constitutions and legislation is that however radical when formulated, they will sooner or later be internalised. The Declaration of Independence of the U.S.A. was norm-setting, but the equality of master and slave was excluded from the "mental states" of all but a few white Americans when the Constitution was adopted. Even today, the rhetoric of the Declaration of Independence does not adequately reflect the "mental states" of some Americans. It is useful, however, because included in it is an ideal typical theory of individuality and the Constitution itself lays down a theory of society in which power and responsibilities are allocated to the judiciary, the executive and the legislature. The Bill of Rights spells out the rights of individuals and the States and how within the framework of government they should be protected. What is missing in the Constitution is a theory of knowledge. We have to look elsewhere for that. One source lies in the philosophies of the architects of the Constitution - Alexander Hamilton and Thomas Jefferson, between whom there were major differences of opinion about the political nature of an ideal society.

After two hundred years, it might be assumed that the ideal typical Constitution has been so widely accepted in the U.S.A. that it fairly represents American "national character". Certainly Federal and State legislation must be consistent with interpretations made of the Constitution by Federal Supreme Court judges. Citizens who feel that legislation is contrary to the Constitution may, and frequently do, appeal against it. Eventually, such cases come before the Supreme Court for decision. It could be said that built into Americans is a respect for the Constitution and a willingness to accept Federal Court interpretation of it. Over the years, interpretations have changed, notably in relation to segregated schools. As a result of a Supreme Court decision in 1896, the provision of separate schools for "negroes" was held to be constitutional, provided they were "equal". A 1954 Court ruling held that segregated schools were inherently unequal and hence unconstitutional. In spite of these changes, the Constitution remains a useful model in the light of which problems can be identified and the range of acceptable solutions assessed.

The Problem (Solving) Approach and National Character

The Constitution of the U.S.S.R. offers an appropriate ideal typical model of the government of Soviet society. In it the rights of citizens and the relationships between Federal, regional and local governments are spelled out. The role of members of the Communist Party is also laid down. Frequently, foreign observers ignore the ideal typical model and assume, or assert, how the system operates in the belief that it is monolithic and that no debate or dissent is permitted. It would be unwise, however, simply to observe or read about practice while ignoring the stated beliefs incorporated in a Constitution which, no less than any other, offers a useful model against which some of the problems of administering Soviet education can be judged. What is missing, of course, is a clearly articulated epistemology and again it is necessary to turn to Soviet authors to clarify the theories of knowledge which are assumed or debated within the U.S.S.R.

Communists in the U.S.S.R. always realised that Constitutional changes and even the overthrow of the economic and political sources of capitalism would not immediately change the semi-permanent sentiments of the Russian people. Under favourable conditions, it was the task of education to transform the "national character" of capitalist Russians into workers of the Soviet Union. The overt recognition of this long-term need exemplifies Mallinson's point in a very practical way.

Postwar changes in the Japanese Constitution are still in process of working their way into the "national character" of people who very systematically have resisted foreign influences likely to change their traditional value system and way of life. Indeed, very serious comparative education research was carried out by Mansura Hiratsuka and his colleagues to help them reconstitute the moral values in the light of which a new generation of Japanese children should be brought up. The new principles, which included a new concept of "man", were incorporated in <u>Dotoku</u> (course of morals) in 1966 to replace <u>Shushin</u>, a prewar moral code based on the Imperial Rescript of 1890. The normative changes involved appear to be more a matter of changed emphasis than a radical rejection of the earlier values, which stressed loyalty and obedience. Both before and after the publication of <u>Dotoku</u> there has been considerable debate suggesting that within the Constitutional framework it provides an important ideal typical model of what some Japanese educationists thought "ought to be the case".

Constitutional debates in France indicate the value of accepting constitutions as ideal typical models against which theoretical arguments can be judged and in the light of which persisting patterns of behaviour can be interpreted. The stability of the French system of government during a period (the 1950s) when governments were formed and fell very regularly is surprising only if the notion of a French "national character" within which Constitutional debates are welcome is rejected.

In the absence of a Constitution, major legislation can be taken as the source of English ideal typical models. Less comprehensive than a national constitution, each piece of legislation bears on a particular aspect of social life. The English 1944 Education Act should not be regarded as providing a general ideal typical model, although predictably in the way it was written and in its contents are found features common to much British legislation. In it, for example, are statutory provisions in line with assumptions about desirable relationships between the central and local governments. One such assumption is that local governments should formulate educational policy, the central government should adopt or reject it, while local governments should implement it.

Changes in constitution and legislation are likely, in accordance with Mallinson's theory, to take place within a framework of constraints established by the sentiments and dispositions of "national character". Specifically, in democracies the processes which are designed to facilitate normative and hence legislative change, are controlled by members of identifiable groups - some of which are part of the governing élite, while others may be located in the so-called masses. Pareto's theory suggests how change can be brought about without violence of revolution. Marx outlined the conditions under which change would be brought about by revolution.

Absent in most Constitutions and legislation is a theory of knowledge and how it can be acquired. In any ideal typical model such a theory is important because of its bearing on curricula and methods of teaching. An epistemology makes even mathematics and science education nation specific, even if the mathematics and science on which syllabuses are based are the same, or very similar, everywhere. In so far as mathematics is regarded as a vehicle for the training of logical thinking, French mathematics results in differences between French and British modes of argument. In so far as an aim of science education is to train young people to think scientifically British approaches to problem solving are different from American. The nationally negotiated nature of science and mathematics has been too little investigated even by science and mathematics educators.

To raise the question in the context of establishing nation specific ideal typical models brings us full circle. We are back not only to Popper's notion of fallibility but to a consideration of the different applications of science and mathematics in our social worlds. However "certain" scientific tests applied to the natural world may be, we have not yet reached the stage when, even if we can predict social outcomes, the empirical tests we apply in the social sciences will with the same certainty remove our doubts about the value of policy alternatives. Nevertheless, in making policy choices to reduce dependence on prejudice and long established dispositions and sentiments seems a worthwhile objective for comparative educationists.

Whether this hope lies at the heart of any disagreement there may be between Vernon Mallinson and me I leave readers to decide. Certainly, in this paper, I have done no more than suggest how techniques of arriving at "national character" and "mental states" can be made public and developed in ways that can be used by young, as well as mature, comparative educationists. In doing so, I have implied how change may take place and suggested that a theory of social change is a necessary constituent of the paradigm I adopt. The absence of a theory of social change in Mallinson's work has laid it open to the criticism of some comparative educationists. In this brief paper, intended as it is to celebrate Vernon Mallinson's contribution to comparative education, I have suggested how notions of "national character" and "mental states" can be incorporated into theories which account not only for the persistence of policies, but for educational change.

NOTES AND REFERENCES

1.All quotations from Mallinson are taken from Mallinson,V. (1975): An Introduction to Comparative Education (4th edition), London, Heinemann.

2.Ogburn,W.F. (1964): On Culture and Social Change: Selected Papers, Chicago, Chicago University Press.

3.Pareto,V. (1976): Sociological Writings, selected by S.E. Finer, Oxford, Basil Blackwell.

4.Myrdal,G. (1944): The American Dilemma: The Negro Problem and Modern Democracy, New York, Harper and Bros.

5.Durkheim,E. (1956): Education and Sociology, New York, The Free Press.

6.Tonnies,F. (1955): Community and Association, London, Routledge and Kegan Paul.

7.Hans,N. (1958): Comparative Education: A Study of Educational Factors and Traditions, (3rd edition), London, Routledge and Kegan Paul.

8.Holmes,B. (ed) (1980): Diversity and Unity in Education, London, Allen and Unwin.

9.Siegfried,A. (1952): The Character of Peoples, London, Jonathan Cape.

10.See Holmes,B. (1981): <u>Comparative Education: Some Considerations of Method</u>, London, Allen and Unwin.

11.Ibid.

12.Ibid.

Chapter Four

COMPARATIVE EDUCATION AND LITERATURE

Margaret Sutherland

Vernon Mallinson pointed out in 1968(1) the value of using
literature to enrich studies in comparative education.
Persuasive as his thesis was, its guidance has been less widely
accepted than one might have hoped: some comparativists
recognise that literature can be useful, but not all of them
get round to using it: some seem totally uninterested in this
approach: some have never heard of it. So it is worth while
considering what must reinforce, what must fight against the
inclusion of literature in comparative education studies. It is
particularly important to do so when many discussions of
comparative education methodology and the development of
empirical studies concentrate attention on statistical and
large-scale analyses and generalisations. Literature maintains
the individual, personal element, and since personal interest
and individual observation led to the beginning of comparative
studies, they are characteristics to be cherished.

We must of course consider what is meant by literature.
Here the interpretation can be generous. Reference will be
mainly to works of fiction, to novels in particular: but
autobiographies have special value for the comparativist and it
is always a moot point how far autobiographies are fiction,
though it is widely accepted that many novels are to some
extent autobiographical. Children's literature is an acceptable
sub-category. School textbooks used in other educational
systems would seem at first not to come into the category of
literature; yet - in so far as they contain semi-fictional as
well as documentary material - they may be included, though
they do not satisfy all the conditions which make literature a
valuable element in comparative education. Films and television
programmes are a fair extension of the category. For our
present purposes, some films and television programmes can
count as literature in giving an effective view of individual
experiences of education in other systems.

LITERATURE´S CONTRIBUTION

What then can literature contribute to comparative education? There seem to be four major contributions: (i) information; (ii) awareness of national characteristics; (iii) empathy; (iv) a fuller understanding of the process of education.

The first of these can be dealt with briefly. Literature conveys information about details of the system of education in another country or region: the selection of detail may well be incomplete but some details which would not be mentioned in official publications - e.g. the actual way of conducting a class, pupils´ activity during breaks, parent contacts with the school - can be realised while reading. We discover how dictation lessons used to be given in French schools, through Daudet´s La Dernière Class,(2) and countless readers have unwittingly picked up details of rural Canadian schools and teacher education in the past by their devotion to Anne of Green Gables.(3) Of course, such information has to be checked against the impersonal, wider information: the experience stated may be atypical. Yet details in the small-scale "case study" in literature complement the study of the whole educational structure.

Secondly, literature can produce awareness of the elements which give an educational system its distinctive flavour or ethos. It reveals national characteristics. Here we are in danger of running into the controversy about the concept of "national character" in comparative education, a controversy in which Vernon Mallinson has been much involved. Yet to emphasise the contribution of literature to understanding of different nationalities is not to indicate belief in national stereotypes. What is asserted is that in any educational system there is a distinctive personality which is manifest in the country´s policies, attitudes towards and intentions for eduction. This personality is expressed in the interactions of everyday life in the classroom, the relationships between teachers and learners, relationships among teachers and between teachers and those outside the school, parents and other authorities: it is found in the expectations and customs evident in all these interactions. Certainly something of this national personality shines through official legislation and statements of policy; but it cannot be comprehended simply by studying official documents. Its composite portrait is derived from the attitudes and behaviour of all concerned with the educational system. This personality ideed is the strongest element of continuity in education, one which links the generations and also, on occasion, offers a major obstacle to change in education when change has been proposed "from outside" and accepted cognitively but without understanding of its implications. Nicholas Hans indicated something of this in his tracing of the continuity between pre-Revolutionary and post-Revolutionary Russian education.(4) More simply, even the presentation of an academic paper can reveal some national traits, as can a teacher's classroom conversation.

So, while one notes the hard words published about the tendency of some British comparativists to reify (if not exemplify) national character - for instance, in a review article by Kelly(5) (oddly enough the charge there was with reference to Brian Holmes whom, earlier, one would scarcely have expected to find in this galère) - it is still to be asserted that different aspects of education within a country do add up to a distinctive entity, an entity also present in the interactions of life in the home and in other social groupings in the country. One of the major interests of comparative studies is precisely the appreciation of these distinctive characteristics: they give savour to the studies. If we are also concerned, as some comparativists are, to predict future developments in education, awareness of this national personality or "x factor" could well determine whether our predictions prove wild or accurate.

It could be alleged that this view is simply a survival of naive earlier approaches to comparative education, a regression to the child-like enjoyment of travellers' tales. But the interest is not trivial, child-like, devoted to the beads and baubles of education. It is an interest in a way of looking at life. To sit in a classroom in different parts of the world certainly means becoming aware of common factors - in some ways, one classroom is much the same as another, whether in Moscow or Montpellier. There are the problems of pedagogy which all teachers have in common. Yet to sit in a classroom also means to note not only the standard of equipment, the type and presence (or absence) of wall decorations (some systems allege they distract children's attention) but to perceive the numerous ways in which the situation in this classroom - the manner of teacher to children, of children to each other, freedom of movement, content of books - is not the same as in classrooms in other educational systems.

Indeed, in discussing such matters it is hard to know whether we should recognise a fundamental difference among comparativists, a difference equivalent to differences between those who are normal in perception of colours and those who are colour different or colour blind; or whether we have simply a pseudo-problem because of language usage and misinterpretations of words. All may be aware of national or regional flavours; some just don't think them worth talking about. Yet to throw students in at the structural or statistics end of comparative studies, with no glimpse of this aspect of educational systems, is to do them, and the study of comparative education, a major disservice.

Hence the advantage of reading literature which gives impressions of education in other places, impressions reproduced by those who absorbed and were part of the national system and so reproduce authentically the national or regional atmosphere.

A third contribution of literature is the stimulation of empathy. Not only can the reader become aware of differences in provision of education, but he/she may experience - to the extent possible in reacting only to words - the situation of being educated in another context. Granted, the memories of such vicarious experience are different from those of real experience. Yet they do affect attitudes. Comparative studies are thus part of a wider educational process, an enlarging of individual ability to understand people not only cognitively but emotionally. In meeting the products of other systems, the comparativist has - through literature - to some extent, the feeling of a shared background: though there are, of course, always dangers in trusting to empathy - the real experience and situation of others may be wrongly perceived.

A fourth value, linked to the preceding and essential if comparative education is not to cultivate cognitive qualities alone, is the recognition that educational systems affect individuals; that the official policies outlined in textbooks and in government publications are produced by real people and have real consequences for children and young people especially. This realisation is necessary if statements about other educational systems are to be properly understood. While there is fascination in noting wide general trends affecting otherwise different systems and intellectual delight in interpreting statistical data which show great educational movements from decade to decade and from system to system, yet the awareness that these changes are made up of the efforts of countless individuals and that they lead to change in the day-to-day experience of individuals and their children must not be lost. Generalisations must relate to realistic concepts if they are not to become superficial and misleading. For example, the Nazi government made great changes in education, as in society, over a period of time in the 1930s. But what did these changes mean for a child in a small German town? Reading Christa Wolf's Kindheitsmuster(6) reveals the process from the child's point of view, the personal interpretations of what teachers and relations said or hinted at. There is a new slant on ceremonies through the child preoccupied, during the endless verses of a patriotic song, by the sheer physical effort of keeping the arm properly extended for so long (teacher's eye lighting on her just as she improperly supports the tiring arm). There is the recall of emotional and physical unease when a classmate is subjected to group censure. And earlier, there are the specific and also the general problems of education - the child mind trying to cope with mysterious rules about types of nouns and words which have to be written with a capital; and the apparent arbitrariness of the teacher in accepting one answer and rejecting another. Literature, as in this most excellent book, shows how educational systems and social change work through and with individuals.

THE USE OF LITERATURE IN RELATED DISCIPLINES

These claims as to the contribution of literature to comparative education studies are reinforced if we note analogous claims in related fields. In the professional training of teachers, for instance, Professor Wragg(7) deplored the absence from the Top Twenty works most commonly included in reading lists provided for PGCE students of any reference to good fiction. He suggested such reading could lead to a better understanding of pupils - A Kestrel for a Knave(8) throwing light on adolescence and A Portrait of the Artist as a Young Man(9) serving as deterrent from corporal punishment. On a similar line, P. Abbs(10) has experimented with the study of autobiographies in teacher education. He considers that such study extends a student's perception by letting the individual benefit from the educational experience of others in the same or another system, contemporary or in past times. He cites as examples Jean-Jacques Rousseau, J.S. Mill, Edmund Gosse, Gorky and Herbert Read. His main purpose, however, is to help students appreciate their own individuality from an understanding of their own educational experiences.

For a form of international education, Renate Anders(11) has pointed out the value that can be, and has been, found in using books of one country to educate children in another. She outlines the use made of Soviet books in the D.D.R. and the resulting development of friendship between children of the two countries. The German children, she asserts, acquired through their reading not only political insight into the day-to-day life of a socialist state but an appreciation of the beauties of Russian and Soviet folk tales which "leads to a reinforcement of friendship". Obviously, there were sound practical reasons to use translations of Soviet books in the post-war period when Nazi-influenced books had to be eliminated: but a continuing value for this kind of reading is also claimed. In books and plays which present contemporary situations and problems, young people of the D.D.R. "experience extracts from the daily life of the Soviet girls and boys" and this "understanding of the other with one's heart ('mit-dem-Herzen Begreifen des anderen')" is the best pre-condition for a firm friendship.

Possibly more unexpected is reference to the use of literature as background reading in higher education. Wolfgang Arnold(12) has stressed the value of such reading in fields as diverse as technology of food production and methods of higher education: "Belleletristik" can evoke animated discussions of political and cultural issues: "schöngeistige" literature can provide emotionally impressive perceptions and thus stimulate thought.

Comparative education has a strong component of history: the past must be known if the present system is to be understood. So it is not surprising that historical and comparative studies share a common interest in the insights to be achieved through fiction. Many history teachers in fact encourage the reading of historical novels and of novels written at different periods in the past as a method of arriving at greater empathy with past generations and as a method of enabling learners to understand more fully the events they learn about from other historical sources. The history teacher does have to exercise care in deciding which novels to recommend. Patricia Lawes(13) for example, deplores the kind of fiction which attributes sayings to "real" historical characters, sayings which may be totally inappropriate or involve them in events "which may or may not have happened". (This danger seems less great in comparative studies). She notes also that "it is very difficult for anyone to ´think´ themselves into a different period of time; we tend to superimpose our own patterns of thought and experience". Hence the value for the historian of books written as fiction at some time in the past: they naturally give information about the customs and attitudes of daily like at the time they were written. Similarly, we note, for comparativists, the contemporary account - to be accurate, more frequently the remembered account of early childhood - gives this sense of realism.

Sociology also closely approaches comparative and historical studies in some respects. Here two major functions for literature have also been noted,(14) that of holding a mirror up to society and that of offering material for study of the social situation of the writer. The reliability of the mirror is not, of course, beyond question; but the material remains valuable. "Literature clearly reflects norms... it reflects, too, values in the sense of the writer´s own intention".(15) "The task of the sociologist is not simply to discover historical and social reflection (or refraction) in works of literature, but to articulate the nature of the values embedded within particular literary works".(16)

LITERATURE AS MATERIAL FOR COMPARATIVE ANALYSIS

Using an approach like that stated for sociologists, we move to a different aspect of the use of literature in comparative education. Works of fiction can be useful not only as background reading but as the substance of serious comparative analysis. This technique is demonstrated in an analysis by Berkenkopf and Rüttenauer(17) of Zwei Schulgeschichten aus der Sowjetunion, (two school stories from the Soviet Union) by V. Tendryakov. In one story ("Die Nacht nach der Entlassungsfeier"), the pupil giving the valedictory address at the ceremony marking the end of her class´s school years unexpectedly departs from the normal style of discourse to say that "In fact, I love nothing. Nothing beyond my parents and the school. These I love - yes, as a young wolf loves its lair.

A thousand ways lie before me - all the same, with nothing to choose among them. Don't think me happy. No, I feel afraid! (Ich habe Angst!)" This outburst is followed by recriminations among staff as to what has really been intended or achieved by the school and by disputes among the pupils who say harsh and hurtful things to each other. The other story, "The Reckoning" (Die Abrechnung) similarly presents a crisis situation: an adolescent has killed a drunken father who mistreated him. Again, there is self-questioning among those who know or feel responsible for the culprit. Analysis of the stories is developed to elucidate the way of thinking of Soviet educators. Scrupulously, Professor Ruttenauer reminds us that this is fiction: we cannot assume the author to be representing an actual situation or situations. But the value judgments uttered by those discussing the events and what the school has done or should do reveal common pedagogical problems as well as a distinctively Soviet way of thinking about education. In the second story, for example, there is the teacher's belief in the moral effects of literature on pupils and his belief in the strength that the school collective ought to have - even though, as Rüttenauer points out, the story indicates the school environment to have been inferior in influence to a bad home. Yet the teacher holds to the belief that collective action, more effective support by classmates might have prevented the tragedy, a belief which overlooks the fact that the class collective in the day school is united for the purpose of learning and cannot have the completeness of the collective in the residential Makarenko-type community. Thus literature, especially school stories which aroused great controversy in the home country too, can be used to learn not about the externals of another system but the explicit or implied value judgments.

In passing it should be noted that this approach through literature is also recognised by Ruttenauer as a specially useful technique when the possibilities of direct observation of an educational system at work are limited.

THE PRACTICAL PROBLEMS

(a) Language

Given these manifold advantages, why is literature still relatively neglected in comparative education?

There is, obviously, the language factor. Students can much more easily gain impressions from literature if they can read the language of the country in question. One can understand why (for other reasons also) some teachers of comparative education require students to be competent in at least one or preferably two foreign languages - but these are seldom English-speaking teachers. Even so, there are many translations available and while translations may not give the full flavour of the original, some are highly effective - and there is, after all, a limit to the number of languages of which one can acquire even a reading knowledge. Yet we might consider, incidentally, whether those nationalities which learn many foreign languages and read many foreign books in translation become much more widely understanding and empathetic than other, culture-bound, monoglot nationalities. In countries which cope with many languages readers have a much wider educational experience; they must know more about how people elsewhere live and are educated, what the different circumstances of everyday life are. On such a supposition, nations like the Finns, for example, would be among the most highly educated in the world, as indeed they probably are.

Nevertheless, those whose native language is English have a considerable - and most unfair - advantage in that they do have wide access to documents, factual and fictional, about many other systems. Many ministries of education are obliging enough to provide at least some official publications in English. And the range of literature written in English is immense. There are not only the U.K. products (offering comparisons of neighbouring systems) but the whole wealth of books from North America, Australia, New Zealand, some African countries and India. From the United States certainly, as Vernon Mallinson pointed out,(18) has come a fair number of masterpieces of fiction which give enlightenment both as to educational systems and the reactions of individuals to them. Vernon mentioned Up the Down Staircase(19) as a notable example and The Catcher in the Rye,(20) which has become almost over-exposed as an educationally illuminating book. But there are so many others. Television and the film industry have likewise co-operated in offering portrayals of school and college life in that other environment, so that the average viewer must feel, however unjustifiably, fully conversant with American college or school experience.

The eductional systems of various African countries have perhaps been less easy of access until fairly recently; but now a number of paperbacks offer glimpses of education at least in anglophone areas. Camara Laye´s The African Child(21) has been used by many comparativists as background reading. Ezekiel Mphahlele provided autobiographical views of one form of South African eduction in Down Second Avenue.(22) Chukwuemeka Ike´s works(23) - Toads for Supper, The Naked Gods, The Potter´s Wheel, The Chicken Chasers - offer sometimes startling insights into other forms of elementary and higher education in West Africa while Expo 77 depicts an ingeniousness in pupils´ plotting to gain access to examination questions and a seriousness of approach to passing examinations which put European pupils´ exam-cramming to shame. Allowances must of course be made for writing for comic effect: but something of the Nigerian way of life and education does come through.

Oddly enough, books giving insight into educational

experience in Australia seem less widely known in the United Kingdom, possibly because of some neglect of Australian authors by readers on this side of the world. It has apparently been easier to find works indicating what education was like in the past in Australia: such a glimpse came in the film of <u>Picnic at Hanging Rock</u>. But for more recent times Clive James´ <u>Unreliable Memoirs</u>(24) depict hilariously aspects of school and university education in the 1940s and ´50s in Australia.

Native Indian education too seems rather neglected in fiction. Many novels of course show the problems of colonial education and the effects of English-type education (Paul Scott´s <u>The Jewel in the Crown</u>(25) offers a notable example - with a slight component too of native education). Narayan´s(26) <u>The English Teacher</u> does however give some useful insights into the other system: and impressions of the out-of-school, informal educational processes are widely accessible, for example in writings by Ruth Prawer Jhabvala(27).

Language is not therefore as much of a barrier as might have been supposed. There are also occasional windfalls of writings about systems not thought of as anglophone: for instance, Lionel Davidson´s <u>Smith´s Gazelle</u>(28) provides a fascinating, if offbeat, impression of kibbutz education. In addition there are, as we have noted, translations. Russian education of the past has long been accessible through the works of the classical Russian writers as well as through autobiographies: for more recent times, translations such as Solzhenitsyn´s <u>For the Good of the Cause</u>(29) also provides interesting insights.

School books, too, can overcome the language barriers when they are books used in other systems to teach English. In so far as these give "typical" accounts of school life and attempt to appeal to the interests of children in their own system, they can be remarkably revealing. Yet they do lack the emotional impact and realism of the true literary work. They give useful material for a comparative study of teaching methods and the rationale of choice of content of books in a foreign system, but they do not necessarily convey effectively the true feeling of being in that system.

(b) Time and Assessment

Language therefore does not emerge as an insuperable barrier, the more so as the alternative sources of insight, foreign films, are frequently dubbed - almost invariably (and infuriatingly) so on television. Is the neglect of literature quite simply due to problems of time and assessment?

Looking at courses of study in comparative education, we find few students who are devoting themselves exclusively to this one area. The fortunate few research students can certainly afford the luxury of reading literature and can be strongly urged to acquire this enrichment of thinking about their topic. If the research student is doing field work in a foreign country, the chances of discovering literature written from within the foreign educational system are so much the greater. But for the typical undergraduate or postgraduate on a taught course there are competing claims on time and attention. Reading during the course tends to become strictly utilitarian, confined to prescribed books and works "recommended" for special essay topics. If a modular course is being followed, all the greater will be the drive towards concentrating on what seems directly relevant to the course. The student may well feel there is no time for "relaxation" by indulgence in reading light literature. This is the more likely as in any one piece of fiction the total amount directly concerned with education (especially formal education) may be limited: education may form only a relatively small part of the content. While the rest of the book serves to give more general information about circumstances in which the educational system functions, much of the book could thus be regarded as not clearly useful. On the utilitarian standpoint, should a book be read for only part of its contents? Novels - unlike textbooks - do not offer the easy solution of consulting the index and looking at only those pages which bear on the topic of interest to the reader, so reading a novel may seem to a student to be a lot of effort for a comparatively small usable return - however enjoyable the novel as a whole may be.

A possibility in these circumstances could be to recommend background literature for reading <u>before</u> the course begins. In one instance certainly, students embarking on studies of education in developing countries have been provided with a reading list including a section on "atmospheric" reading, works of fiction concerning African educational experiences, in an attempt to help to disengage them from their own background of education in a developed system. This would seem a constructive way of using the enthusiasm normally felt before beginning a course: students are likely to be highly receptive at this point.

But students' minds rapidly turn to immediate problems of assessment. What work <u>has</u> to be done in order to meet course requirements? The values to be derived from the kind of reading we are concerned with do not lend themselves easily to assessment. It is a problem common to other aspects of learning, that affective responses and attitude formation are not easily measured by our normal procedures. One would hope that background reading would lead to more balanced and realistic writing about other educational systems. More directly, students can be invited to write essays reviewing an appropriate novel or novels: or they can make an analysis of books for children in another system. But while these are useful exercises in some ways, they would not necessarily give proof of enhanced awareness of the characteristic personality of another educational system. This awareness is something which builds up gradually, even if one powerfully written book may make a considerable contribution to it. To comment effectively on the impression conveyed by a book may demand a degree of literary skill which the average student is - unhappily - unlikely to possess. Appreciation of literature is notoriously hard to measure: attempts to assess it tend to evoke a considerable amount of reproduction of others´ ideas, of "faking" and the worser horrors of "Inglit" answers. It would be a pity to introduce these into comparative education studies. There is, admittedly, also the possibility of the in-depth analysis exemplified by Berkenkopf and Rüttenauer´s work but such analysis may call for complementary knowledge of the foreign system which the student may not yet have acquired: and it may well call also for foreign language skills. In any case how does one measure empathy?

As the students assess their own progress too, there may be a bias towards the other aspects of study. There is a considerable amount of factual data to be learned in comparative education, detail about the structure of systems as well as formation of an appropriate conceptual framework. Students are aware of the need for this factual basis - or at least most of them are - and may also feel more confident as to whether they are making progress in acquiring it. It is also relatively easy to assess by the traditional methods. So while discussions or essays may contain welcome reference to insights obtained from literature, it is probable that assessment will concentrate on what is clearly measurable, that is, knowedge and analytic competence. Thus the literature approach to comparative studies may sink into the limbo of aspects of education which are non-examinable.

CONCLUSIONS

Even if one takes the pessimistic points made in the last few paragraphs the cause is not lost. It remains important that students of comparative education should know of the existence of literature which, as well as being an enjoyable way of occupying leisure, can contribute vitally to the understanding of other systems of education. Some such reading can be made to co-exist with their other studies from the beginning: they can enjoy it in the present and now it is there to be further enjoyed once the hassle of course work is past. Comparative studies make it clear that education continually changes; this fact at times brings despair to the earnest student. Knowledge has to be continually revised, reinterpreted. No one can fully appreciate an educational system all at once or even in a year or so. Its subtleties reveal themselves gradually, as study continues over a number of years. As the individual reads more, travels more, compares more, comprehension of the real nature of other systems is consolidated and sometimes considerably modified. We find repeatedly something we had not known before about our favourite system.

If students can early acquire awareness of literature as access to other systems, it will greatly assist their gradual and continuing development in comparative education. Or, putting it from the other point of view, being a comparativist will give an added dimension to their future reading. Comparative interests will remain alive and be strengthened as they read for enjoyment. Literature in comparative studies is thus not something to be added simply as a short-term interest: it is rather a part of the lasting, long-term process of learning. For those who become specialists and research workers in comparative education it is especially important that work they may do with "objective" data and in large-scale studies is balanced by insights they will derive from literature, but, of course, the literature must be worth reading in its own right.

NOTES AND REFERENCES

1.Mallinson,V. (1968): "Literary Studies in the Service of Comparative Education", Comparative Education, 4, 3, pp.177-181.

2.Daudet,A. (1910): "La dernière classe" in Lettres du Lundi, Nelson.

3.Montgomery,L.M. (1925): Anne of Green Gables, Harrap.

4.Hans,N. (1963): The Russian Tradition in Education, Routledge and Kegan Paul.

5.Kelly,G.P. (1982): "Methods in Comparative Education: New Trends or Old Wine in New Bottles?", Comparative Education Review, 26,2, pp.292-294.

6.Wolf,C. (1976): Kindheitsmuster, Aufbau-Verlag Berlin und Weimar.

7.Wragg,E.C. (1982): "Education's top twenty: an alternative view", Times Educational Supplement, 2 July 1982, p.21.

8.Hines,B. (1969): A Kestrel for a Knave, Penguin.

9.Joyce,J. (1952): A Portrait of the Artist as a Young Man, Cape.

10.Abbs,P. (1974): Autobiography in Education, Heinemann Educational Books.

11.Anders,R. (1981): "Die Schuljugend der DDR und die USSR: Sowjetische Literatur und Kunst im Dienste der Erziehung zur

Comparative Education and Literature

Freundschaft mit der Sowjetunion (1945-1952)", Jahrbuch für Erziehungs - und Schulgeschichte, 21, Volk und Wissen Volkseigener Verlag, pp.81-96.

12.Arnold,W. (1982): "Rolls und Wirkung der Literatur im Ausbildungs - und Erziehungsprozess", Das Hochschulwesen, 30, 7, pp.177-180.

13.Lawes,P. (1977): "The Use of Fiction in the Teaching of History", History in School, 3, pp.50-53.

14.Laurenson,D. and Swingewood,A. (1971): The Sociology of Literature, MacGibbon and Kee.

15.Swingewood,A. (1971): "Introduction: Sociology and Literature", op.cit. supra, 15.

16.Ibid., 16.

17.Berkenkopf,G. and Rüttenauer,I. (1982): "Zwei Schulgeschichten aus der Sowjetunion", Neue Sammlung, 22, 2, pp.201-220.

18.Mallinson,V. (1968): Op.cit. supra.

19.Kaufman,B. (1964): Up the Down Staircase, Prentice Hall, (Avon, 1972).

20.Salinger,J.D. (1955): The Catcher in the Rye, Hamilton.

21.Laye,C. (1964): The African Child, Collins (and Fontana).

22.Mphahlele,E. (1959): Down Second Avenue, Faber and Faber.

23.Ike,C. (1965, 1970, 1973, 1980, 1980): Toads for Supper, The Naked Gods, The Potter's Wheel, The Chicken Chasers, Expo 77, Fontana/Collins.

24.James,C. (1981): Unreliable Memoirs, Picador.

25.Scott,P. (1966): The Jewel in the Crown, Heinemann.

26.Narayan,R.K. (1978): The English Teacher, Heinemann.

27.Jhabvala,R.P. (1975): Head and Dust, John Murray Ltd.

28.Davidson,L. (1971): Smith's Gazelle, Jonathan Cape.

29.Solzhenitsyn,A. (1964): For the Good of the Cause, Pall Mall Press, (Sphere Books 1971).

Chapter Five

CHOICE AND REFORM IN BELGIAN EDUCATION

John Owen

INTRODUCTION

The Belgium of which Vernon Mallinson wrote so eloquently in his "Power and Politics", known affectionately as "la Belgique de grandpère" - "grandfather's Belgium" - ceased to exist between 1968 and 1971. This period marks a turning point in the history of Belgian affairs which is probably more important than anything which has happened since the Revolution of 1830. Long-awaited constitutional reforms changed a unitary state into one which is divided into semi-autonomous Cultural Communities but which is yet not federal. Although some of the reforms of that period still await implementation, and some of the more recalcitrant problems, notably that of the status and future of Brussels, still await solutions, it is nevertheless clear that Belgium will never be the same again.(1)

At the same time, sweeping educational changes, involving nothing less than the "renewal" of secondary, and later of primary education, have been put in motion. The major objectives set out for the new education are threefold. First and foremost it should work towards the fullest possible personal development of the individual. Secondly, it should seek to help that individual to integrate harmoniously into society. And thirdly, it should aim to secure for him vocational capacities which will allow him to face tasks which confront him.(2)

In attempting to realise these objectives, and particularly the first of them, it works from some important assumptions. In the first place, personal autonomy should not be thought of as an option but rather as a normal and necessary social requirement without which the individual cannot hope to realise his potential.(3) In addition, practice in decision-making and evaluation are necessary for the development of the autonomous person. These assumptions, together with those implied by the existence of a free, democratic state, suggest that the school system needs to offer a wide range of choices.

If these objectives and assumptions seem familiar, it must

66

be remembered that Belgium has long been one of the most
dedicatedly European members of the European Community and its
educational thinking, though often in the past astonishingly
innovative, has in recent years been much influenced by the
ideas of the Council of Europe, the European Cultural
Foundation and UNESCO.(4) Furthermore, one must not suppose
that either the "new" Belgium or the "new" education appeared
fully-formed, like Minerva from the head of Zeus, as a result
of political or pedagogical planning; rather they represent a
particular stage of development in reforms which have been
taking place gradually since the end of the Second World War
and which have their roots both in much earlier Belgian events
and ideas, and in ideas which originated outside Belgium.

The present essay will attempt to consider some of the
educational choices available to individuals in Belgium, the
way these choices have changed and developed, and some of the
limitations and problems which have been encountered.

CHOICE IN EDUCATION

For the idea of choice in a modern school system always
involves a certain amount of conflict. The system itself is
normally compulsory - compulsory for children between certain
ages to receive schooling and compulsory for their parents or
guardians to see that they do. As Wallace has pointed out, all
societies demand from their members certain cultural knowledge,
skills and behaviour which cannot be optional.(5) Choice, on
the other hand, implies that options are permitted. Mass
schooling was in the first place set up and paid for by
societies to see that these cultural imperatives, and
especially the knowledge, skills and forms of behaviour
demanded by the Industrial Revolution, were transmitted, and
that certain characteristics, such as social strata, were
constantly reproduced and renewed.(6)

However, the effects on Western nation-states of what
McNeill calls the "Democratic Revolution", that change of
historical direction characterised by the Enlightenment and the
American and French Revolutions, were also extremely
powerful.(7) Schooling can very easily become education, and
education of the masses can, as we all now know, have
unexpected or undesired side effects. Eventually the masses,
enlightened by education and influenced by democratic thoughts
and writings, begin to demand things other than those which
they are offered, and are even prepared to seek political power
to get them.

In order to accommodate these demands, changes have to be
made in societies, and especially in the educational systems
which serve them. Clearly, some changes are made simply with
the object of achieving existing aims more efficiently. But
others, especially those concerned with demands for freedom and
equality, involve modifications of society's aims for

education. There has been a gradual shift from seeing these aims as being only concerned with cultural transmission and vocational needs towards an inclusion of the demands of personal development and social integration. As we have seen, these demands involve an extension of the opportunities for personal choice in education.

However, choice will always be limited by certain demands of society. It must always be confined to what is culturally acceptable; there will be economic limitations; and sometimes the whole society will demand that choices offered to one group do not disadvantage members of another group. The last point becomes increasingly important in societies such as Belgium, which recognise themselves as multicultural.

CHOICE IN THE BELGIAN CONTEXT

The events of the Counter-Reformation left Belgium as an ultramontane Catholic enclave within a strip of Europe with mixed religious feelings; while the latter part of the Democratic Revolution produced an independent country where the differences between Catholic and freethinkers and between Walloons and Flemings were regarded as less important than freedom itself. Nevertheless, the potential for religious, linguistic and cultural conflict was considerable.

The idea of individual choice in Belgian education is consequently by no means recent. Certain aspects of it were already deep-seated when in 1831 the National Congress approved the Constitution, whose Article 17 stated that education should be free of all restraints except when given at State expense. From the beginning there has been a strong tendency in Belgium to think of choice for the individual child as being the prerogative of the père de famille. This derives from the Catholic tradition, reinforced by the fact that in the earlier days of the new state the first educational choice to be made was whether the child should go to school or not. It was not until 1919 that the Poullet Law of 1914 was implemented. This finally deprived parents of the right not to send their children to school by making education compulsory but free of cost for children between the ages of six and fourteen.

The most important choice, however, has always been whether the education should be Catholic or not. The various "school wars" which raged through the first 128 years of the new state's existence were basically about the right of the père de famille to choose whether his children received Catholic or lay education. Many Catholics believed that the ultimate choice was the renunciation of choice; while extreme Liberals could not see that "neutral" schools were no choice at all for devoted Catholics. Also, as the Liberals were not slow to point out, for many of the working class the school they chose was determined above all by economic considerations.(9)

The early legislation, such as the first organic laws on

primary and secondary education,(10) created schools most of which were basically Catholic in character; but, since the Constitution guaranteed religious freedom, pupils were permitted to opt out of any actual religious teaching. Gradually, in the latter part of the nineteenth century, the realisation began to grow that choice for everybody was a reality only when there existed a number of available schools and courses to choose from, and when economic, cultural and social pressures were eliminated, or at least reduced to a minimum. Most of the reforms which took place up to 1958 concentrated on improving availability.

On the whole, however, progress was very slow. The process of actually creating schools was left largely to the communes, which tended to create only schools which accorded with their own political beliefs. The minorities, especially non-Catholic minorities in Flanders, were subjected to what Lord Acton called "the tyranny of the majority".(11)

It was not until 1958 that the Pacte Scolaire, an agreement concluded between all three major political parties, resolved to a major extent the conflict between Catholic and lay interests and thus eliminated most of the social and religious pressures attending choice of school. As the Report of the School Pact Committee to the Senate said: "La préoccupation essentielle a été d'assurer à tous les chefs de famille la libre choix de l'école à laquelle ils entendent confier leurs enfants".(12) An important measure was that forbidding what it called "pratiques déloyales". Chapter IX of the law of 29 May 1959 explains that this means any sort of attack against the principles or practices of any other school or type of school, and provides for sanctions against offenders, including withdrawal of subsidies.(13)

The Pacte removed an economic barrier to choice by subsidising all schools which conformed to certain mutually agreed standards on condition that they charged no fees. Practical barriers were removed by Article 4, which stated that the right of parents to choose the sort of education their children has implied that the sort of school they would choose existed within a reasonable distance. The State recognised the right of parents to have access to a confessional or "neutral" school either by opening one or by providing free transport. Later, the Standing Committee of the Pacte Scolaire in an extensive declaration on 8 May 1963 established the principle of "neutrality", which is described as perfect objectivity in the way of expounding facts and ideas, and absolute respect for the religious and philosophical convictions of the pupils. The staff of a neutral school must include at least three-quarters of teachers who have been trained in State (i.e. non-Catholic) establishments. Any parent is entitled to demand neutral education for his children.

Although three languages are officially spoken in Belgium, the communities who speak these languages are on the whole geographically separate. Flemings have fought for, and gradually obtained, the right to be taught in their own language; but the question of choice has rarely arisen, except in Brussels, where Flemish-speakers with aspirations for their children often choose to have them educated in French.(14) The question of co-education or segregation is also one which is not usually open to choice. Recent schools are normally co-educational, while older ones, especially Catholic ones, are often single-sex. What is available is a question of historical accident.

A final important choice is concerned with the content of education. At first, this simply meant choosing between different types of secondary school, and religious considerations probably predominated. But after the law of 1850 a more coherent structure began to appear, with choices between the athénée and the école moyenne, and even between sections within these schools, being made for socioeconomic reasons.

It eventually became apparent that making such educational choices had practical vocational consequences as well, and from this point of view it was desirable that choice should be well-informed. The first service to help parents and children make these choices had been set up in Munich in 1902. Boston followed in 1908 with its "Bureau for Vocational Guidance" and in the same year the Société belge de Pédotechnie was formed, to concern itself with questions of vocational education and apprenticeship. In 1911 the Société set up an employment bureau for adolescents, which became the following year the first Belgian office for vocational guidance. Its director, A.Christiaens, made it clear from the beginning that its function was to inform and advise parents and children, not to tell them what to do.

With the advent of the First World War, and the economic crises which followed, only slow progress was made; but in 1928 La Jeunesse syndicale, with the help of Christiaens, set up the first Catholic office and organised a peripatetic guidance service.

It was not until 1936 that a reforming coalition government of all three major parties, concerned with the problems of young people, decided to set up the first official guidance centre called the Centre national de l´Orientation professionnelle. This laid the foundations for a network of offices, both public and private, subsidised by the State, which gradually grew, even during the Second World War, until by 1948 there was a total of 78 offices, 43 in the Flemish region and 35 in the Walloon region.

In 1949, partly in an effort to alleviate the overcrowding in certain secondary schools, and partly to improve the service to middle and technical schools, the Director-General, Vandenborre, created a new type of institution, the Psycho-medical-social Centre. This was staffed by a psychologist, a social worker, a nurse, and a doctor. Initially, two of these

P.M.S. Centres, as they became known, were set up, one at
Etterbeek in the Brussels agglomeration, one at Charleroi, for
a trial period of three years. In fact, the trial period was
soon extended to six years, and by 1972 the number, including
Offices O.S.P., had grown to 263, 145 in the Dutch language
region and 118 in the French; and by 1977 the latter figure had
increased to 162.(15)

Research in the late forties and early fifties, much of it
carried out by the P.M.S. Centres, led to some seminal
conclusions regarding choice of content. The first was that
important choices were being made too early. It was shown, for
instance, that verbal maturation in children from socially and
culturally underprivileged backgrounds occurred later than
normal. These children were therefore likely to perform poorly,
especially in the first year of secondary school, and
especially in their mother tongue and in Latin. Another study
indicated that vocational interest tests given to twelve year
olds were 80% invalid when the pupils reached the age of
eighteen; on the other hand, those given to fifteen year olds
remained 80% valid. The effect was intensified for brighter
pupils whose later choices were less likely to be affected by
earlier failure. Yet other studies indicated that choices of
secondary school were often made for socio-economic reasons
rather than reasons based on pupils' educational needs or
aspirations. Furthermore, the structure of the school system
was such that choice prematurely forced upon children at eleven
was irrevocable.

School reform in the post-war years has therefore been
directed mainly towards creating structures or situations which
delay choice, often by making it possible to modify choices, or
which improve the quality of choice by means of guidance or
participation.

The first step in delaying choice occurred when the law of
14 August 1947 on the confirmation of the certificat
d'humanités (equivalent to the French baccalaureat) allowed a
pupil to qualify for homologation after spending the last three
years, the upper stage, in the same section instead of the six
years previously demanded. This allowed, and could even be used
to encourage, the possibility of changing direction in the
lower stage without compromising the pupil's future.

At about the same time, to take advantage of these new
opportunities of choice, a number of middle schools added
technical sections to their Latin and modern sections, thus
producing what were in effect multilateral schools.

In the fifties some twenty-odd schools experimented with
school records, class councils, complementary activities and
other ideas inspired by the classes nouvelles of France. The
main object was to find ways of getting to know pupils better
in order to help them to adapt to school and make more suitable
choices. Since the experiment appeared to work, it was
generalised to all lower secondary sections in 1956.(16)

Reforms up to and including the Pacte Scolaire of 1958, however, still distributed choices unequally in social class terms. Because of great differences in the content of courses, habit and prejudice saw to it that changes from one section to another were based on failure rather than success, and only in one direction, from classical to modern and from modern to technical courses. This "negative orientation" further depreciated the value of the technical courses.(17)

Another experiment was therefore initiated with the object of improving choice: the observation and guidance cycle. This started in six schools in 1957 and was extended to a further six the following year. Mixed-ability groups followed a common-core curriculum with classical, modern and technical options, mixed-ability classes, and a number of complementary activities geared to observation of the pupils' interests and abilities.

The experiment was regarded as sufficiently successful to justify making the school "avec cycle d'observation et d'orientation" the norm, and a Royal Decree of 10 June 1963 therefore stipulated that all new general secondary schools should be of this type from 1 September 1963, and all new technical schools from 1 September 1964, with the intention of eventually extending the reform to the whole network. This was followed by a law of 8 June 1964 which allowed certain further choices to be made within upper secondary education and, more importantly, established the principle that all upper secondary certificates, general or technical, and in whatever subjects, gave access to higher education and, provided the candidate obtained a diplôme d'aptitude à l'enseignement supérieure, often referred to as the "Maturity Examination", to all University faculties except Civil Engineering.(18)

From this point on there has been a continuous monitoring of secondary education, with a view to ensuring that distinctions between various forms of secondary education are based on the need to specialise, rather than on a hierarchy of supposed value.(19)

This monitoring soon led to the conclusion that there was still plenty of room for improvement. Whether the reform succeeded or failed in particular schools depended a good deal on the attitudes of the teachers. Many of these were unable to accept or operate the teaching of mixed-ability classes, and techniques of selection were often more prominent than the elements of observation and guidance which had been intended. Others felt that the reforms did not go far enough, in that the options merely perpetuated the older system, without materially changing it. The Secrétariat-Général de la Reforme de l'Enseignement Moyen et Normal, which had been set up at the same time as the guidance courses under the joint leadership of Yves Roger and Professor J.-J.Van Hercke, was soon thinking of more drastic reforms.(20)

Choice and Reform in Belgian Education

EDUCATIONAL AND CONSTITUTIONAL REFORMS

As we have seen, by 1968 the time was ripe, both politically
and educationally, for some of these reforms to be implemented.
The voting public, traditionally much more stable than in the
U.K., suddenly showed its desire for change, both in the 1968
and 1971 elections, by voting for small, ethnonational parties
such as the Volksunie, the FDF, and the Rassemblement Wallon.
Street fighting broke out over the fact that the University of
Louvain, which was located on Flemish territory, taught partly
in French.

The government led by Gaston Eyskens, formed in 1968 after
seventy-nine days of difficult negotiations, was only too well
aware that the world was rapidly changing, and Belgium must
change with it. But as well as the familiar problems which were
facing all developed Western countries, the explosions of
population, knowledge and communications, coupled with changes
in the occupational and social structure of the country, and
exacerbated by the speed of change, Belgium had an extremely
complex community problem.

Wallonia, which had for the last two hundred years been in
an economically superior position because of its coal and iron
deposits and its industry, which regarded itself as culturally
superior, and which believed itself to have political
superiority because of the ascendancy of French, found, after
the Second World War, that things were changing. The coal
deposits were running out and traditional industry was in
decline. Wallonia, like England, was suffering for being one of
the first runners in the race to industrialise. At the same
time, the Flemish part of the country was thriving. Not only
had fresh coal deposits been found in the region, but
international investors, attracted by the better work record
and industrial relations of the Flemings, were setting up
modern industries. The Flemings themselves were learning to use
their newly-found political strength and linguistic rights.

The tensions resulting from this change of fortunes were
further increased by the question of Brussels. Traditionally
the capital of Flanders, and firmly located in Flemish
territory, it was becoming increasingly "frenchified" as a
result of business and international connections. Francophone
demands that it should be allowed to grow were met with Flemish
accusations of cultural and linguistic imperialism. Proposals
for dividing the country into autonomous regions foundered on
the cultural and linguistic status of Brussels.(21)

Some solution had to be found, however, and the government
announced in its programme:

> We believe that the maintenance of a Belgian nation
> founded on the union of the communities is our only
> chance of achieving progress for all in a strong
> Europe...... But this Belgian nation must at the same

time be more regional and more European in character.(22)

It was therefore necessary not only to embark upon a programme of constitutional reform which would change the basic political structure of the country and give the communities a considerable degree of cultural autonomy, but also to develop an educational system which would support a more regional but more European Belgium at the same time as preparing the young people of Belgium for the world of the future. Both Constitutional and educational reform have been taking place progressively over the last fourteen years. Neither is yet complete.

But there were also other compelling reasons for educational reform. The situation in the secondary school system was anarchic. There were middle schools from the nineteenth century, technical and vocational schools, multilateral schools and schools with observation and guidance courses. There were various types of establishment: athénées, lycées, middle schools, technical schools, vocational schools; some of these had primary sections, and even nursery sections, attached, others not. Some schools were co-educational, others segregated by sex. In at least one town, girls could attend the co-educational Athénée from the age of three until they were twelve. They then had to transfer to the girls´ middle school until they were fifteen, transferring back to the Athénée if they wished to complete upper secondary education.(23) There were four main organising powers running schools: the State, the provinces, the communes, and the Catholic Church. Some Belgian villages had schools organised by all four.

The private, Catholic sector was also adding its voice to the calls for educational reform. "L´Enseignement Secondaire Rénové", a brochure of the Fédération Nationale de L´Enseignement Catholique, said:

If the job of education is to contribute towards taking its place in a society in order to transform it, the best system - or the least bad - is that which adapts itself to the realities of a given era. In a sense, consequently, the renewal of education should be permanent since every society develops and - in any case - ought to develop. There are, however, moments - and this is the case today - when the development of the society becomes so radical and so rapid that everybody agrees that they are at a turning point, a real mutation in the sense in which in biology one talks of a mutation of a species.(24)

The events of May 1968, although they had been less spectacular in Belgium than in many countries, were widely interpreted as indicating that young people felt that they were being faced with a new world for which their education had prepared them badly.

In the face of all these demands the government therefore declared that:

> Having decided to observe and carry out the School
> Pact so as to work out a balanced educational
> programme guaranteeing free choice to parents, the
> government also affirms its wish to adapt our school
> system to the realities of our times, and to re-
> examine its spirit, its programmes and its
> methods.(25)

Among the immediate consequences of the Constitutional reform and the creation of two Cultural Communities was the setting up of two separate Ministries for education: the Ministère de l'Education Nationale et de la Culture Française and the Ministerie van Nationale Opvoeding en Nederlandse Cultuur. National educational policy was still laid down by fundamental legislation approved by Parliament, but each Ministry had a separate budget and autonomy over those things not decided at national level.

One of the new Ministers of Education, Abel Dubois, who believed that Belgium should place itself once more in the van of educational progress, was made responsible for the execution of the reform of the secondary schools. The reform, which had been sketched out earlier by Ministers Janne and Van Elsland, drew heavily upon current European ideas and indeed Dubois himself described the proposals as "largely in accordance with international recommendations".(26) He believed that the school was still the corrective and normative influence par excellence and that its role should be strengthened. "Je crois à l'éducation et à la perfectabilité de l'homme, par l'éducation......", he wrote in 1970.(27)

An important feature of the reform was that it involved a revision not only of the school system but also of the whole area of parental involvement. The educative process itself, with the child at the centre, was to be seen as a partnership between school, P.M.S. Centre, and family; and parents were also to be involved in the management of schools.(28) Within the school, examinations, competition and selection were to be abolished. One Belgian commentator on this reform claimed that "Avec l'enseignement secondaire rénové commence l'histoire de l'enseignement francophone de Belgique".(29)

Dubois asked for secondary schools to volunteer to try out the new ideas. Instead of the expected fifteen, eighty schools volunteered. Twenty-four establishments, twenty-two of which were run by the State and two by communes, were chosen, and the experiment began in September 1969.

The new system was given legal existence by the law of

1 July 1971. As well as passing through Parliament, which had
to take into account the separate points of view of the private
and official networks operating under the <u>Conseils de
Perfectionnement</u>, the <u>Conseil de l'Enseignement de l'Etat</u> and
the <u>Conseil Supérieur de l'Enseignement Technique</u>.(30)

The intention of the law was to provide a flexible
framework, acceptable to all the organising powers, without
lapsing into bland ineffectuality, within which all forms of
secondary education might adapt to the needs of the times and
evolve as times changed. Thus, Article 4 stated that programmes
"may include cycles, sections, options, and all other
subdivisions determined by the King, including certain forms of
reception and adjustment".

One of the important structural changes introduced by
Article 2 of the law was that it abolished the old pattern of
dividing secondary education into lower and upper cycles of
three years each and replaced it with three cycles of two years
each. This pattern had to some extent been foreseen by the law
of 8 June 1964, which treated the last two years of secondary
education as a whole. Since research had indicated that for
two-thirds of pupils it was impossible to determine the levels
of particular aptitudes before the age of thirteen or even
fifteen, the change was seen as an important step towards
delaying, and thus improving, choice.(31)

In effect, the new school is "comprehensive" in that all
children go to the same school instead of choosing a technical,
vocational or general education. The three two-year stages are
devoted respectively to observation, orientation, and
determination.

The first year of the Observation stage has a single
programme for all pupils. Twenty-six periods a week are devoted
to a basic common training or "<u>formation de base</u>" while eight
are spent on compulsory trial activities or "<u>activités
d'essai</u>" in the various disciplines which will be the objects
of later choice. The purpose of these activities is to discover
aptitudes rather than to measure acquisition.

At the end of the year the <u>Conseil d'Observation et de
Coordination</u>, which includes teachers of all the disciplines
along with representatives of the P.M.S. Centre acting in
collaboration with the families, advises the pupil on a first
choice, which is in no way definitive, to be made at the
beginning of the second year.

In addition to the set programme, pupils may attend school
on Wednesday afternoon or Saturday morning, for not more than
two hours, either for free activities, which are either sociocultural or sporting, or for <u>rattrapages</u>. The latter are
remedial, or "catching-up" classes for those who are having
temporary difficulties with important parts of the programme.
About half of all pupils take advantage of the free activities.

In the second year the basic common training or "common
core" is increased to twenty-eight periods by the addition of

one period of musical education and one of plastic art. The trial activities now become options, of which the pupil must choose a basic option, to be studied for four periods, and a different, complementary option studied for two. The choice of option may be modified during the year or at the begining of the next stage. Observation continues during this year.

The second, or Orientation, stage offers a basic choice between transition courses in general, technical or artistic education for those who wish to continue to the third stage or to higher education; courses giving technical or artistic qualifications which allow entry to work without prejudicing the possibility of continuing to study; and vocational courses for those who definitely wish to leave school. Pupils taking either transition or qualification courses may obtain a Certificat d´Enseignement Secondaire Inférieur at the end of the third year; those taking qualification or vocational courses may obtain a Certificat de Qualification at the end of the fourth year.

The third, or Determination, stage again offers three choices. These are: (1) transition courses in general, technical or artistic subjects. These are available to pupils who have successfully completed a second stage transition course and intended as a preparation for higher education, while at the same time allowing access to employment; (2) qualification courses in technical or artistic subjects. These are available to pupils who have successfully completed either a transition course or a qualificaion course at the second stage, and are intended as a preparation for employment, while at the same time allowing access to higher education; and (3) vocational courses, available to pupils who have successfully completed any type of second stage course. At the end of the sixth year pupils who have taken either transition or qualification courses may obtain a Certificat d´Enseignement Secondaire and a Diplôme d´Aptitude à Acceder à l´Enseignement Supérieur. Those who have completed qualification or vocational courses may obtain a Certificat de Qualification.

Further modifications to the reform of secondary education were made by the Royal Decree of 30 July 1976 with some very minor amendments by the Royal Decree of 1 April 1977. The new education became known as "Type I", while the traditional arrangement of lower and upper secondary stages of three years each became "Type II". The implications of Article 4 of the law of 19 July 1971 were made clear. The first year, now known as année A, was to be supplemented with an adaptation year (année B, année d´adaptation or enseignement d´accueil) for those pupils who had either reached the age of twelve without successfully completing primary school, or who in some other way had not adapted to primary education. It was essentially a part of normal education, not of special education, being intended for the retarded, not for the handicapped.(32)

The situation regarding retardation was obviously causing concern. A Ministerial Circular of 9 January 1978 pointed out that during the 1975-76 school year 24,139 pupils, representing 37.4% of twelve year olds, and 2,319 pupils, representing 3.75% of fourteen year olds, were still in primary school. The continuation of this situation was considered as unacceptable, since most of these pupils were likely to finish school only to be faced with unemployment and living on social security.

The basic programme of the adaptation year is similar to that in the observation stage, but teaching is more individualised and much more use is made of projects and group work. Every effort is made to give pupils confidence in their own abilities and to compensate for fundamental shortcomings, especially in the mother tongue and mathematics, with the intention of reconciling pupils with school and reintegrating them into the mainstream of the system. Academic subjects are omitted from the trial activities; the emphasis is on artistic and technical subjects and environmental studies of all sorts.

For those unable to make enough progress to reintegrate, there is a second year where the essential disciplines are still studied, but twelve to sixteen hours a week are spent on practical, vocationally-oriented courses in technical, artistic, economic or agronomic studies. Pupils are given career information in the first year to help with initial orientation, and contacts are made with local establishments and organisations. Observation, of course, continues.

Clearly a major purpose of these changes of structure was to modify the situation regarding choice. Premature choice was to be eliminated in favour of progressive choices leading gradually to more and more specialised training in the second and third stages. Choice was to be made on a basis of observation, rather than on the subjective views of pupils or parents. Choices were not to be irrevocable, but could be modified and followed by reorientation. Furthermore, given that the realities of modern life demand certain basic tools to be supplied by education, the pupils were to be offered a choice of activities which would effectively adapt the education to the aspirations of the pupil, rather than the reverse. It was hoped in this way to give everyone an equal chance to study and to provide the maximum possible access to all sorts of studies and occupations. Everyone would be given the opportunity and the means to learn to live a full life in a society in which differences of sex, social class, and so on would cease to be important.(33)

For a while, at least, many parents had a choice between Type I and Type II schools, though the French-speaking sector, with a secondary school population only a little more than two-thirds that of the Dutch language community, had, by the 1977-78 school year, made considerable progress in changing over to Type I education. Overall, just under 40% of the children were in the éducation renové. This mounted to 54.88% in the State

schools, and 26.14% in the private schools. A study based on
1974 figures indicated that the higher the social class of the
child, the less likely it was to be in a Type I school.(34)

The Dutch-speaking sector, not surprisingly, has been much
slower to change. During the 1977-78 school year just over a
quarter of all pupils in secondary schools were receiving Type
I education. Although the State schools had 83.15% of pupils in
Type I, the private sector, which educates 71.71% of all
secondary pupils, had 92.48% of those in Type II schools.(35)

OTHER DEVELOPMENTS

Although secondary education has been the main target of recent
reforms, it has also been thought necessary to revise preschool and primary education and teacher education, each of
which has necessary and formative connections with secondary
education. The main purpose in both these areas has been to
improve efficiency and reduce waste, and considerations of
space do not therefore permit any detailed examination of the
reforms which have taken place.(36) It may be hoped, however,
that the reforms in the primary school aimed at producing more
autonomous individuals will eventually lead to better use being
made of choices already offered at secondary and tertiary
levels.

One reform which will actually reduce parental choice is
the lowering of the starting age to five proposed in February
1980 and postponed several times. It is intended that the first
year will still be a nursery year and in future children will
not be allowed to enter first year primary until they are six.
This should effectively retard entry by four months, which it
is hoped will help to reduce the number of failures at the end
of that year.

In the early seventies it was felt that some areas of
discrimination still existed between the private, local and
State networks. Heads of political parties therefore met in
April 1972 to discuss revision of the <u>Pacte Scolaire</u> with a
view to solving this problem. The Committee had realised for
some time that the concept of neutrality was unrealistic in
demanding "perfect objectivity" on the part of the teacher and
the pluralist school was therefore put forward as a more
practical solution to the problem.

After a period of discussion and trial, Parliament passed a
law defining the characteristics of the pluralist school, which
came into force on the 1 September 1975. This stated that they
would be run by the local community in collaboration with
delegates from the organising powers. All the main local
beliefs would be represented on the governing body, with none
in a majority. This would decentralise the administration of
education and lead to more flexible management. Since in most
cases the local people would be either Catholic or free-
thinking, staff should consist normally of 60% of the former

and 40% of the latter. All staff were to sign an agreement to the principles of the pluralist school, which must:

Be accessible to all, without discrimination.
Offer a free choice for parents between the various religious courses and moral education.
Recognise and appreciate that there can be a diversity of opinions, while stressing common ground.
Allow all members of staff to make known their own personal beliefs, while refraining from proselytism and respecting the development of the personality of the pupils.(37)

In common with other Western countries, Belgium during the last ten years has been faced with the problems of economic recession, a falling birth rate, and unemployment. Considerable efforts have been made to deal with these problems by reducing waste and inefficiency without seriously reducing the choices available.

The first warning note came in January 1973 from the new Education Ministers, M. Michel Toussaint and M. Willy Calewaert, who stated that government expenditure on education must be rationalised and more strictly controlled and could not go on increasing indefinitely. In the primary sector this has mainly meant closing down schools which were insufficiently attended, though schools as small as eight may still be subsidised in rural areas. Pluralist schools were immediately seen as a way a of preserving parental choice without continuing the wasteful and expensive practice of offering choice by duplicating schools.

In secondary schools the first effects were a suspension of State grants for sporting and sociocultural activities; a freeze on new allowances for teachers, which reduced the opportunities for "rattrapage"; an increase in minimum class size, which reduced the number of options available; and the introduction of a "numerus clausus" in teacher-training courses.(38) Proposals made in the summer of 1978 to reduce the weekly hours of secondary and vocational courses were greeted with protests and strikes, as a result of which the organisation of "rattrapage" classes was actually increased to cover all subjects and opportunities for learning foreign languages were improved. Class sizes in nursery and primary schools were reduced.(39)

In July 1980 all the major political parties agreed to plan for the further rationalisation of secondary education. The first stage, starting in September 1980, was to close down or regroup very small establishments. The second, to be completed by September 1984, involved a new idea, the "centre d'enseignement secondaire", or C.E.S.

Although traditionally schools are classified by their organising powers (State, provincial-communal or private), they may also be divided according to whether they give confessional, non-confessional, neutral, pluralist, or "unclassifiable" education. Using this form of classification, a C.E.S. is a school or a group of schools of the same character, which offer education at all stages from 12 to 18. Unclassifiable schools may be included in a centre if all the organising powers agree. There will be a maximum of 285 centres in the French community and 340 in the Flemish community. Minimum numbers of pupils are laid down for each stage, which give a minimum size for each centre of about 280 pupils.

One of the objects of this reform, which was intended to come into force in September 1981, is to effect economies by eliminating unnecessary duplication of courses. In future, any stage which does not have the requisite number of pupils will be progressively closed down. No new Type II schools are to be created, subsidised or recognised; and all new Type I State schools must form part of a C.E.S. and be either confessional, non-confessional or pluralist. Progress has been greatly hampered by lack of funds.(40)

The same is true of reforms in vocational education and plans to raise the school leaving age.(41) Although both of these interconnected changes are thought extremely desirable in view of the high rate of unemployment amongst those educated in vocational schools, plans for reform remain in the experimental stage and the raising of the leaving age has consequently been postponed several times. However, éducation de promotion sociale, the old evening classes, intended to allow changes of career or second chances, have recently been reorganised on a modular basis.(42)

Criticisms of the rénové reveal again the "double bind", the conflict referred to earlier, in which the Belgian education system, along with all other educational systems in democracies, finds itself with regard to choice. On the one hand the very idea of a free, democratic western European country seems to demand freedom to develop one´s potentialities, with open choice. On the other hand, the stratified, capitalist society which is Belgium must, for its own preservation, prevent more than a token development of this freedom, except along approved lines.

Javeau, arguing mainly from a theoretical and philosophical standpoint, claims that both the doctrinal bases of the new education and their practical extensions are pernicious. Analysing an article by Dupont on the general objectives of the educational system,(43) he concludes that, far from liberating the citizen of the future, it is likely to produce a race of conformists, "bien dans leur peau", but slaves of the State in a sort of Brave New Belgium.(44)

This conclusion is to some extent supported by Billiet, who sees the orientation and guidance processes as subtle and effective means of social selection which are made acceptable to the pupil because he believes he has made the choice

himself.(45) The view seems to be taken that freedom is
impossible when the framework of the educational system is laid
down by the State. Subscribers to this view, among them
Javeau(46) and the Confédération générale des enseignants,(47)
demand more autonomy for schools, more decentralisation, more
democratisation, and the depoliticisation of education. What
they appear to be asking for is freedom to decide what choices
will be offered. They would perhaps do well to ponder
Lacordaire's dictum: "Entre le faible et le fort, c'est la
liberté qui opprime et la loi qui affranchit". It seems
unlikely that most pupils would come into the category of "le
fort".

DISCUSSION AND CONCLUSIONS

Part of the process of reform has been a continuous evaluation
of results. All the official studies carried out have pointed
to disparities between theory and practice in the rénové.
Difficulties are still being caused by conservative teachers,
often the products of inadequate university training courses;
by restrictive legal prescriptions for certification; and by
the limiting demands of higher education.(48)
    Several commentators have pointed out that some of the aims
of the rénové are in fact impossible of realisation. Billiet,
for instance, makes it clear that while the school claims to
offer limitless possibilities of social mobility, these must in
reality be very restricted. Moreover, a "democratic illusion"
has been fostered by confounding the improvement of social
mobility with the destruction of social stratification.(49)
    Pirson de Clercq believes that the most important aim of
the rénové, to produce people who can think for themselves,
will always be regarded in a capitalist society as subversive,
and therefore can only be allowed to succeed if the structure
of society is changed.(50) Nevertheless, a number of studies
seem to indicate that changes which may profoundly affect the
future Belgium - what one might call la Belgique des petits-
enfants - are taking place.
    One study, for instance, has found that the products of the
new schools are more concerned about freedom and social
justice, more tolerant of cultural and racial differences, more
flexibly-minded and less materialist than those of the
traditional schools.(51)
    Another, concerned with the Determination Stage of the
rénové, found that student criticisms were often "both highly
relevant and extremely sound", which the researchers regarded
as an indication that the schools were succeeding in their aim
of producing critical and analytical attitudes.(52)
    Some destratification of choice is indicated by a study
carried out in 1977 at Ghent University, which found that
curriculum choice in the new schools, unlike that in the
traditional schools, was not particularly dependent on status

origins. Moreover, the innovations exerted a moderate but statistically significant positive influence on the pupils' attitudes to study, especially on girls' attitudes.(50) The new schools have, of course, done nothing to destratify society itself; but they may, as Nizet has suggested, have altered the process so that in the future the function of the school will not be to reproduce the social order, but to produce "nouveaux rapports de classe".(53)

Billiet has pointed out that the reforms have been accompanied by a great deal of mystification. A school system is really incapable of equalising chances or of destratifying society, and it is misleading, or even dishonest, to suggest that it can. Nevertheless, she sees other aspects of the rénové as having democratising potential. The unification of the early years and the changes in teacher-pupil relationships may well result in the elaboration of a new mode of non-authoritarian relationships outside school. Undoubtedly, pupils are beginning to behave and to think differently; but what effect this will have on society it is as yet too early to tell.(54)

One can only conclude, as Billiet does, that there is reason to be cautiously optimistic that the country which Mallinson regards as "possibly the last true democracy to flourish in western Europe"(55) may, with the help of its educational system, continue to make progress towards a more democratic and just society. Perhaps the rest of us may learn something from their progress.

NOTES AND REFERENCES

1.See Senelle, Robert (1978): The Reform of the Belgian State. Memo from Belgium No.179. Brussels: Ministry of Foreign Affairs, External Trade and Co-operation in Development, for an account of the Constitutional reforms.

2.Roger, Yves (1976): "L'enseignement rénové". Les Amis de Sevres, Vol. No.81/1, entitled "La Renovation Pedagogique", March, p.87.

3.For a discussion of personal autonomy in education see Blackham,H.J. (1978): Education for Personal Autonomy: an enquiry into the school's resources for furthering the personal development of pupils. London: Bedford Square Press.

4.Owen, John (1982): "Teacher Education in Belgium: Towards Practopia?" in Changing Priorities in Teacher Education, ed. Goodings,R., Byram,M. and McPartland,M. London: Croom Helm, gives further details.

5.Wallace, Anthony F.C. (1973): "Schools in Revolutionary and Conservative Societies" in Cultural Relevance and

Educational Issues: Readings in Anthropology and Education, ed. Ianni, Francis A.J. and Storey, Edward. Boston: Little, Brown and Co.

6.Bourdieu,P. and Passeron,J. Cl. (1970): _La Réproduction_. Elements pour une theorie du systeme d´enseignement. Paris: Editions de Minuit, Le Sens Commun.

7.McNeill, William H. (1965): _The Rise of the West_: a History of the Human Community. London: New English Library, pp.811-819.

8.An international project, "The Politics of the Smaller European Democracies", has examined this question in great detail. Amongst publications derived from the project, see Rokkan, Stein, et.al. (1970): _Citizens, Elections, Parties_: Approaches to the Comparative Study of the Processes of Development. New York: McKay; Lorwin, Val R. (1972): "Linguistic Pluralism and Political Tension in Modern Belgium" in _Advances in the Sociology of Language_, ed. Fishman, Joshua A. The Hague: Mouton, Vol.II, pp.386-412; and Lorwin, Val R. (1974): "Belgium: Conflict and Compromise" in _Consociational Democracy_: Political Accommodation in Segmented Societies, ed. McCrae, Kenneth. Toronto: McClelland and Stewart, pp.179-206.

9.Lorent, Henri (1954): _Les Guerres scolaires en Belgique_. Document No.143. Bruxelles: Ligue de l´Enseignement; Roy, Albert du (1968): _La Guerre des Belges_. Paris: Editions du Seuil.

10."Loi organique de l´instruction primaire. 23 septembre 1842", _Pasinomie_, 3e.serie, Vol.12, pp.463-468; and "loi sur l´enseignement moyen, 1 juin 1850", _Pasinomie_, 3e.serie, Vol.20, pp.145-153.

11.Many examples of this problem are recorded in Houvenaghel,H.L. (1935): _L´Enseignement Public en Flandre Occidentale_. Rapport presenté au Conseil general de la Ligue de l´Enseignement. Document No.95. Bruxelles: La ligue de l´Enseignement.

12.Houben,R. and Ingham,F. (1962): _Le Pacte Scolaire et son Application_. Bruxelles: Centre d´Etudes Politiques, Economiques et Sociales, 2e. edn., p.70.

13.The organisation of free school transport by any body other than the State is regarded as a _pratique déloyale_, according to a Ministerial Circular of 17 August 1960.

14.Louckx, Freddy (1978): "Linguistic Ambivalence in the Brussels Indigenous Population". _International Journal of the_

Sociology of Language, Vol.15, pp.53-60; Swing, Elizabeth Sherman (1974): "Separate but equal: an enquiry into the impact of the language controversy on education in Belgium". _Western European Education_, Vol.5, No.4, pp.6-33.

15. Pasquasy,R. and Siron,R. (1972): _L'Orientation Scolaire et Professionnelle en Belgique_. Bruxelles: Editest, pp.7-12. The later figures were supplied by the Service Statistiques et Programmation of the Ministere de l'Education Nationale et de la Culture Francaise.

16. Roger, Yves (1967): _The Observation and Guidance Period_. (Education In Europe, Section II, No.7). Strasbourg: Council for Cultural Co-operation of the Council of Europe, pp.70-77.

17. Dubois, Abel (1972): _L'Enseignement Secondaire Renové_. Paris: Fernand Nathan; Bruxelles: Editions Labor, 3e. edn., p.19.

18. Owen, John (1967): _Belgian Education_. Particularly as manifested in the Schools of Dinant. Oxford: Unpublished paper, p.44.

19. Vanbergen,P. (1972): "Educational Reform - the State of the Question". _Western European Education_, Vol.IV, No.3, Fall, p.168.

20. Owen, John (1967): op.cit., p.7.

21. See Scheinman, Lawrence (1977): "The Interfaces of Regionalism in Western Europe: Brussels and the Peripheries" in _Ethnic Conflict in the Western World_, ed. Esman, Milton J. Ithaca and London: Cornell University Press, pp.65-78, for an account of the Brussels problem.

22. Coppieters, Franz (1974): _The Community Problem in Belgium_. Brussels: Institut Belge d'Information et de Documentation, 2nd. edn., p.30.

23. Owen, John (1967): op.cit., p.32.

24. Dubois, Abel (1972): op.cit., p.37. The English translation of this and the two following citations are by the present writer.

25. Ibid, p.16.

26. Ibid, p.25.

27. Ibid, p.51.

28.Direction Générale De L'Organisation Des Etudes (1974): La Gestion Associative. (Ser. Faire le point sur....) Bruxelles: Ministère de l'Education Nationale et de la Culture Française, contains the texts of Ministerial Circulars and many articles on the subject of co-operation between teachers, parents, pupils and guidance services.

29.Vanbergen,P. (1972): "Où en est la réforme scolaire?" Information, April. The article referred to in Note 19 is an English translation of this article.

30.Direction Générale De L'Organisation Des Etudes (1978): L'Enseignement secondaire rénové: organisation générale. (Ser Faire le point sur....) Bruxelles: Ministère de l'Education Nationale et de la Culture Française, 2e. edn. This volume contains the texts of all relevant legislation on secondary reform up to February 1978.

31.Dubois, Abel (1972): op.cit., p.39.

32.Ministère De L'Education Nationale Et De La Culture Française (1978): Aux Parents. Bruxelles: Ministère de l'Education Nationale et de la Culture Française, 3e. édn., passim.

33.Dubois, Abel (1972): op.cit., p.47.

34.Nizet, Jean (1976): "Position sociale et fréquentation de l'école rénovée". Recherches Sociologiques, Vol.7, No.1, March, pp.86-104.

35.Data are calculated from figures published in Effectifs Scolaires 1977-78 des regimes linguistiques français et allemand, Bruxelles: Ministère de l'Education Nationale et de la Culture Française; and in Onderwijs Statistieken Schooljaar 1977-78, Brussel: Ministerie van Nationale Opvoeding en Nederlandse Cultuur.

36.For the theory and practice of primary reform, see Ministere De L'Education Nationale Et De La Culture Française (1973): Eduquer pour le monde de demain: la rénovation de l'enseignement primaire. Bruxelles: Ministère de l'Education Nationale et de la Culture Française. Owen, John (1982): op.cit., gives further details of the reforms of teacher training.

37.Documentation Centre for Education in Europe (1972): "La revision du Pacte scolaire - vers l'école pluraliste?" News-Letter/Faits Nouveaux, 2/72, p.5; Documentation Centre for Education in Europe (1975): "Réforme scolaire et rationalisation". News-Letter/Faits Nouveaux, 3/75, pp.5-7.

38. Documentation Centre for Education in Europe (1976): "Compressions budgétaire et dénatalité". News-Letter/Faits Nouveaux, 3/76, pp.10-12.

39. Documentation Centre for Education in Europe (1979): "Aménagement des horaires dans l'enseignement". News-Letter/ Faits Nouveaux, 2/79, pp.7-8.

40. Documentation Centre for Education in Europe (1979): "Plan de rationalisation du secondaire". News-Letter/Faits Nouveaux, 5/79, pp.6-7; Documentation Centre for Education in Europe (1980): "Plan de rationalisation de l'enseignement secondaire". News-Letter/Faits Nouveaux, 3/80, pp.8-9.

41. Raising the school leaving age to 15 or 16 was first mooted in 1935. A decision in 1979 to extend compulsory education in three stages by lowering the starting age to 5 in 1980 and extending the leaving age to 15 in 1981 and to 16 in 1982 still awaits implementation. See Documentation Centre for Education in Europe (1980): "Prolongation de la scolarité obligatoire". News-Letter/Faits Nouveaux, 1/80, p.8. For information on and discussion of earlier projects, see Jacquemyns, Guillaume (1952): La Prolongation e la Scolarité Obligatoire. Bruxelles: Institut Universitaire d'Information Sociale et Economique.

42. Documentation Centre for Education in Europe (1980): "Plan d'action contre le chômage". News-Letter/Fair Nouveaux, 1/81, p.7.

43. Dupont,M.J. (1979): "Les objectifs généraux du système educatif". Revue de la Direction générale de l'Organisation des Etudes, 14e. année No.2, February.

44. Javeau, Claude (1979): "L'Education malade du systeme ou la trahison des pédagogues". Revue de l'institut de sociologie, Université Libre de Bruxelles, Nos.1-2, pp.137-154.

45. Billiet, Cécile (1974): L'Enseignement Secondaire Rénové et la Démocratisation. Louvain: Institut des Sciences Politiques et Sociales, Université Catholique de Louvain.

46. Javeau, Claude (1970): Essai sur la réforme administrative des écoles. De l'empirisme a la rationalité. Bruxelles: Editions de l'Institut de Sociologie, Universite Libre de Bruxelles.

47. The Confédération général des enseignants published a document in January 1974 entitled "Pour une libéralisation de notre système scolaire". For details, see Documentation Centre for Education in Europe (1980): "Pour une libéralisation du

système scolaire". <u>News-Letter/Faits Nouveaux</u>, 1/74, pp.6-7.

48.Pirson-De Clercq, J. and Pirson,R. (1979): <u>La renovation scolaire</u>: réalités d'une theorie. (Ser. Recherche en Education, Nos.12-14). Bruxelles: Direction générale de l'Organisation des Etudes, Ministère de l'Education Nationale et de la Culture Française, 3 Volumes.

49.Billiet, Cécile (1974): op.cit., p.100.

50.Pirson-De Clercq, Jacqueline (1979): "Le rénové analysé au travers du discours de ses élèves". <u>Revue de l'institut de sociologie</u>, Université Libre de Bruxelles, Nos.1-2, pp.123-136.

51.Violon, Jacques and Skinkel, Raymond (1978): <u>Opinions et attitudes des jeunes sortis de l'enseignement secondaire rénové en 1975 et en 1976</u>. (Ser. Recherche en Education, No.11). Bruxelles: Direction générale de l'Organisation des Etudes, Ministère de l'Education Nationale et de la Culture Française.

52.Pirson-De Clercq, J. and Pirson,R. (1979): op.cit.

50.Brutsaert,H. and Cooreman,G. (1979): "Empirical Evaluation of Educational Innovation in Belgian High Schools". <u>Urban Education</u>, Vol.14, No.3, October, pp.359-366.

53.Nizet, Jean (1974): "La fonction sociale de l'école rénové", <u>La Revue Nouvelle</u>, September.

54.Billiet, Cécile (1974): op.cit., pp.101-103.

55.This intriguing suggestion comes from Professor Mallinson's own Preface to Mallinson, Vernon (1969): <u>Belgium</u>. (Ser. Nations of the World). London: Ernest Benn.

Chapter Six

THE STATE - A MAJOR ELEMENT IN WEST GERMAN EDUCATION

Kenneth Smart

INTRODUCTION

The first need for the student of German education is to decide
what he understands as Germany. It is convenient nowadays to
use "Germany" as a shorthand for the Federal Republic, and
occasionally expedient to refer to "the two Germanies", but
both these expressions beg the long-standing basic question -
what is Germany? The search for an answer to this question may
be illuminating, even though we may not succeed in avoiding the
need to indicate a geographical idea by using a phrase like
"the territory now designated as the Federal Republic" or to
indicate an ethnic idea by something like "native speakers of
Hochdeutsch".
     If we go back far enough into history, we find ourselves in
a period when most of the territory now occupied by "the two
Germanies" fell within the Holy Roman Empire. The eventual
disintegration of the Empire saw that territory fall into the
hands of a multitude of rulers, many connected with each other
by bonds of kinship or feudal allegiance or treaties in ways
which varied in their levels of strength or permanence. By the
seventeenth century, marriage, conquest or treaty had reduced
the vast number of rulers to a mere three hundred or so, a
process which continued up to the nineteenth century, when
Prussia brought about enforced unification after the wars of
1864 (against Denmark), 1866 (Austria) and 1870 (France).
However, in order to see how artificial was and is the unity of
"Germany", we have only to look at maps showing the evolution
of the railways, or to recall the origins of the postal service
(in a private enterprise by a minor nobleman) or to consider
the location of some major cultural institutions (Hamburg
Opera, Stuttgart Ballet, Leipzig Gewondhaus, Dresden Art
Gallery, Weimar Theatre). We refer to the period after 1871 as
"the Empire", but it should not be forgotten that the states
which made up that Empire retained responsibility for
education, culture and religious affairs,(1) and that these
states consisted of four kingdoms, three free cities and

nineteen other minor political entities. The Weimar Republic had a constitution which contained numerous possibilities for centralisation, but significantly not in connection with education, local administration and religion, concerning which the central government could legislate only as regards basic principles.(2) Only during the period 1933-1945 was there a central legislative body laying down detailed policies for education, culture and religion in the whole territory, with a centralised machinery for execution of those policies. The nature and outcomes of those policies were the reasons for the rejection after 1945 (both by the victorious Allies and by many Germans) of a centralised republican constitution of the French type in favour of a federal structure based on regions which might be imagined to bear some resemblance to the kingdoms and dukedoms of yore and might even in one or two cases correspond to some extent with the old geographical boundaries. This basic idea held good for only a short time in the Russian Zone, which evolved on other lines.

If we look for a German identity along different avenues, we continue to encounter difficulties. If we hypothesise that "Germany" means the areas where German is spoken, we find that for a long period the most important German-speaking area (politically, economically and militarily) was in fact Austria. "Germany" is very diverse in its demographic and economic structures - a patchwork including densely populated urban industrial areas and thinly populated rural agricultural areas. Political outlooks vary between extremes of radicalism and conservatism, and religious affiliations likewise, from Schleswig-Holstein (88% Protestant) through Rheinland-Pfalz (56% Catholic) to Bavaria (70% Catholic).

The purpose of the preceding paragraphs has been to establish that the Federal Republic is an artifical creation held together by considerations of political expediency within territories the peoples of which may well have an interest in collaboration for common defence and the sharing of certain resources and services, who speak a common language (but are not the only speakers of it), but who do not necessarily have common views on the goals, methods and structures of education, religion and culture. From this it follows that the use of the words "centralised" and "decentralised" will beg the question: from whose point of view, within what context? Similarly, the use of the word "state" will beg the qustions: where do policies originate, to whom are those who execute policies accountable, what are the conditions and limits to "democratic participation"? In these connections, the British student in particular is in danger of falling into the trap of inferring that because the Federal Government has relatively few educational functions, therefore the system is "decentralised" ("like ours") or into the other one of supposing that because educators are civil servants, therefore curricula and methods are all under rigid control by bureaucrats. If we can grasp the implications within the German use of the word "state", and if we can understand the defects and advantages of the status enjoyed by teachers and educational officials throughout the Federal Republic, we shall start to understand the nature of the problems encountered in German attempts to make the system work and evolve, and shall be able to sympathise with the frustrations of the many parties involved, all of which may base their attitudes on plausible, but incompatible, principles. Also, of course, we can perhaps see a logic in a situation where political education has been considered necessary and desirable, whilst educational establishments and those working in them have to be constantly on their guard against any action or stance susceptible of the label "partisan".

THE CONCEPT OF THE STATE

The most important of the words to clarify is the word "State", which (when spelt with a capital letter) will be used throughout the remainder of this essay to mean the abstract idea. We are all members of a community, which devises rules for its own smooth functioning and perpetuation and also imposes obligations on its members - either negative, to avoid breaking the rules, or positive, to make contributions, either financially through taxes or in other ways such as by service on a jury or a committee or council. The State is the formal expression of cohesion and political identity. It also becomes concrete as the mechanism whereby we procure and ensure both physical goods such as defence, communications, health services, and also intangible goods such as educational, cultural or recreational provisions. The State, therefore, makes provisions and also makes demands.

For an Englishman there is no question about what he sees as the formal manifestation of the State (the British Government) but we also frequently use the word "government" in a way which would seem loose in the German context, where the term "local government" is self-contradictory.

> Government is essentially a policy-making activity; it lays down the lines within which the administration is carried out. It is a task, therefore, which can be exercised only by the juridical persons in public law which are the repositories of sovereignty, or state power, namely the Federation and the "Länder". All subordinate authorities are "administrations", not governments... Public administration is the day-to-day exercise of state power in order to carry out the ideals and principles of the laws by the use of all the spiritual, technical and economic means permitted by the law.(3)

The State - A Major Element in West German Education

In the German context, the State´s formal manifestation may be either the Federal Government or the Land Government or in some instances the Land Government acting as the agent of the Federal Government.(4) It may be worth commenting that the word "State" frequently has a vaguely pejorative undertone in Britain because of the numerous ways in which we relate to local rather than national authorities and because of the extent to which the national Government is associated with negative experiences such as taxation, conscription, incomprehensible documents or sheer inaccessibility. This pejorative undertone is not necessarily present in those countries where numerous people in socially well-regarded occupations are national rather than local authority employees.

This brings us to another important element: the role of the official. The German word is "Beamte". The prefix "be" implies an imposition upon the bearer of the title (cp. "belastet" - burdened; "beauftragt" - mandated) - "endowed with office" perhaps. On the one hand, the official is regarded as not merely representing the State - he actually embodies the State, and has all the powers the State has, with all the duties and responsibilities pertaining to his specific sphere of action (as one of the "juridical persons" mentioned by Chaput in the quotation above). On the other hand, he has all the State´s rights to expect co-operation and support from all citizens, including children, students, parents, teachers. Not only support - but also respect: "Beamtenbeleidigung" (insulting an official) is a criminal offence in the Federal Republic, and one could never imagine a German judge telling a teacher he or she might expect physical assault from time to time as a normal occupational risk!

In the Federal Republic, the State may be either the Federal Government or a Land Government. From the point of view of legal interpretation, it is important to note that the Federal Government and the Government of the Länder do not stand in a superordinate-subordinate relationship. Each Land has its own Constitution and passes its own laws relating to matters within its competence, and the Federal Republic has a constitution incorporated into the Basic Law of 1949,(5) which also defines the areas of competence of Federal and Land Governments. Every Federal and Land law is tested for compatibility with the Basic Law by the Constitutional Court, which also issues a ruling on any occasion when a Land law and a Federal law are seen or thought to be in conflict. Since responsibility for education is vested in the Länder, there is no reference to education in the first text of the Basic Law of the Federal Republic, but (as in the United States of America) the courts have had to work energetically to keep up with a never-ending stream of questions arising from the evaluation of laws, regulations and procedures in the light of the Basic Law´s general dicta on human rights.

The State - A Major Element in West German Education

THE STATE AND EDUCATION

In Germany the notion of the State´s responsibility for education is deeply rooted, and is also probably related to the idea of the ruler having power to impose his religion on his subjects ("cujus regio, ejus religio"). In most of the Länder the minister for education is called "Kultusminister". As may be inferred from the earlier discussion, as far as education is concerned, the State in question is the Land and not the Federal Government. Historically, the origins of educational provision lie in the creation of educational systems embodying the dual concept of the State´s responsibility to provide and the citizen´s responsibility to make use of the provision made, for his own and the community´s benefit. The outstanding example is of course Prussia, where Frederick II laid foundations, on which Hardenberg, Humboldt and Fichte etc. built, to arrive at a system which was considered eminently worthy of study by foreign visitors (including Victor Cousin, Horace Mann and Michael Sadler) seeking to clarify their own philosophy and to draw up plans for their own countries. As a further (typical) example one may quote from the 1860 Constitution of the Free City of Hamburg: "The State exercises supreme conduct and supervision of the whole provision of instruction and education".(6)

This long tradition of State involvement in education has combined with the Federal Government´s lack of historical legitimacy to give rise to the powerful, indeed almost insuperable principle of "Kulturhoheit der Länder" (cultural sovereignty of the states) which has delayed and almost even frustrated attempts to move towards any policy and planning for education over the whole of the Federal Republic. Space does not permit a detailed narrative of all the ramifications of this problem area or of the movements towards its solution, but some examples may be mentioned in a general way.

The traditional cornerstone of German educational systems has been the university - a state-established institution for the creation and propagation of intellectual achievement, but based on the ability and effort of individuals.(7) The prestige of a university was based on the stature of its professors, and on the prestige of their researches rather than of their competence as teachers. Admission to the university itself was not based on a selection process conducted by the university itself, but on possession of the "Abitur", a certificate acquired on completion of studies in a "Gymnasium", the only recognised form of secondary school. Entry to the Gymnasium was a self-selection process in which family tradition, socio-economic status and life expectations could play a more important role than academic potential (the tools for measuring which did not formerly exist, anyway). The standard represented by the Abitur was guaranteed by the Gymnasium teachers (themselves university-trained) and some of the weaker students could be brought up to standard by private coaching and by being allowed to repeat a year. Once in the university, the student was presumed to be capable of largely self-directed study at his own speed and towards his own goals.

The post-war economic miracle of West Germany combined with the world-wide explosion of educational expectations and pressure for democratisation of the educational process gave rise to two large problem areas. First, the quantitative problem - increasing numbers entered the universities, to the point where there were manifestly not enough places and where the deficiencies (in both their numbers and their teaching effectiveness) of the professors became visible. Second, there was a need for reform of curricula, of structures of governance, and of career patterns for non-professorial teaching personnel. Many students faced both material difficulties (especially cash to live on) and also problems of orientation. At the secondary level, the curriculum of the Gymnasium was clearly in need of modernisation, and its assumption of some kind of guidance role was desirable. There was also pressure (not, of course, from the Gymnasium teachers) for the creation of new school types with diverse curricula, enjoying a status comparable with that of the Gymnasium and likewise extending to their students the opportunity of progressing to higher education. During the late 'fifties and 'sixties all these matters gave rise to a massive literature of controversy and in due course to German education's own "events" in 1968.(8)

As late as 1967 it was possible to describe the Federal Government's responsibility as being limited to academic research and cultural foreign policy.(9) Co-operation between the states was sought through the Standing Conference of Ministers of Education (since 1949) and reform proposals were drawn up by the German Committee for Education (1955-1965) and by the more formal and prestigious German Education Council (1965-1975), but strength and ingenuity were needed to avert the "educational catastrophe" which loomed. A kind of legal sledgehammer was brought in, in the shape of a supplement to the Basic Law. Article 91 provided for Federal action to avert national emergency, and to this were now added in 1969 Article 91a, which inter alia defined universities as being of national significance and authorised the Federal Government to contribute to the planning and the enormous costs of university expansion; and Artible 91b, which provided for Federal and state Governments to collaborate in the planning of education generally.

Major steps could now be taken to expand the provision of university places, and the Federal Law for Educational Promotion (Bundesausbildungsförderungsgesetz, or BAFoG, 1969) became a systematic vehicle for the provision of Federal finance in support of students' living costs according to a national formula. A joint (Federal + states) Commission for

Educational Planning was set up, and a first Overall Plan was published in 1973,(10) but the execution of the plan remained a matter for the individual states to pursue to whatever extent their governments thought appropriate. At secondary level, neither structural change nor curriculum reform could become an area of considerable Federal action, and the best that could be achieved was a benevolent interest, backed up by the Federal financial support offered to experiments or projects initiated by individual "Länder".

In consequence we now see, for example, a wide disparity in the extent to which "comprehensive" secondary schools have been developed, between the extremes of West Berlin, where an all-comprehensive secondary system has long been a formal long-term objective, and Bavaria, where the few comprehensive schools set up are still (1981) officially stated to be experimental. Curriculum development appears patchy and unco-ordinated, with, for example, an expensive Curriculum Centre at Bad Kreuznach in Rheinland-Pfalz (with an adjacent vineyard as some compensation for its not very convenient location) contrasting with the one in West Berlin, urban in both location and pedagogic outlook. The obvious questions will continue to be: how cost-effective are these scattered projects and how rapid and thorough can be the lateral percolation of their research reports and new curriculum materials?

When we look at vocational education, the situation is seen to be even more complex, since craft-level training has long been seen as a dual responsibility anyway, with employers providing skill training and the State both obligating and providing further education in part-time vocational schools, final trade testing being under the control of the Chambers of Industry and Commerce. The 1960s again were a period during which there was widespread interest and discussion. The importance of technical skills for economic well-being was accepted, with the corollary that the transmission and development of those skills was a matter of national concern which could not be left to employers alone. In Britain this line of thought led to our Industrial Training Act of 1964, the Employment and Training Act of 1973, and the present major significance of the Manpower Services Commission. In West Germany, the Federal Government has undertaken a total overhaul of the craft-level training system, especially the rationalisation of the guidelines for skill training in the 400-odd recognised trades, under the Vocational Training Act (Berufsbildungsgesetz) of 1969. A Federal-financed research institute for vocational education was set up in Berlin in 1970, and the Federal Government has given financial support for the establishment of centres for full-time craft training in the late seventies. The Educational Promotion Act (BAFoG) of 1969, originally aimed at supporting university students, has been extended to several other categories of beneficiaries, including those in many full-time vocational courses and in particular the "basic" vocational educational year (Berufsgrundbildungsjahr) which is comparable to some extent, at least in its objectives, with the English UVP and ABC courses. In the late seventies, any attempt at extension of the Federal Government´s interest in vocational education was met with some suspicion and resistence. A move towards further legislation was delayed by conflict between Bundestag and Bundesrat; state Governments have resisted encroachment on their "cultural sovereignty" as regards vocational schools; and employers have reacted fiercely against any move seen as potentially coercive.

These two examples - secondary and university education and craft-level vocational education - may suffice to illustrate the nature of the problem. To repeat, the State has an obligation to provide education, and it is the Federal Government which has the data needed to form an integral view of the country´s manpower requirements, and can develop unified policies in this respect and also in relation to such matters as secondary curricula, the education of children of foreign (especially Turkish) origin, and educational guidance, though the Federal Government cannot proceed very far in any active role before coming up against the question of how far its executive powers are constitutionally permissible. As regards higher education, costs are so great that the Federal Government probably alone has the financial resources to give it flexibility in either expansion or contraction, and in a time of rising youth unemployment it is the Federal Government which can set in motion appropriate vocational education programmes to provide skills for better times to come and keep the young people off the streets now.

In 1978 the Federal Government put forward a report embodying these arguments in favour of a strengthening of Federal powers in educational policy-making. On the other hand, the "cultural sovereignty" of the Länder is a firmly entrenched constitutional and legal principle, and the state Governments are averse to any departure from this principle as long as they remain convinced that diversity and healthy rivalry are conducive to the maintenance of quality and progress. It has been argued authoritatively(11) that there is a de facto uniformity of practice as regards teachers´ salaries and service conditions, involvement of parents and pupils in school governance, exemption from tuition fees, and many other matters, but there are still structural and curricular differences between the states which are important in the eyes of many parents and teachers and continue to be a fertile source of political controversy. As Christoph Führ coolly puts it: "In view of the present state of discussion, a change in the Basic Law with the objective of increasing Federal powers over education is not to be anticipated within the foreseeable future".(12)

THE STATE AND THE EDUCATORS

The previous section has attempted to show that whilst the State's role as the provider of education may be generally accepted as being in conformity with tradition, ambiguity or even conflict may arise when the State (abstract) is seen as embodied in more than one policy-making authority. In this section we shall look at the ambiguity or even conflict which may arise when professional people see themselves in a close relationship with the State embodied in an organisation governing their employment, career, job discipline etc. and simultaneously with a society or community embodied in parents, children, cultural goods and behavioural norms. The first relationship is that of the official, the second that of what we may call the educator (embracing not only teachers but also educational researchers, inspectors, welfare workers, psychologists and some categories of purely administrative staff in the education service).

The actions of any public official whilst on duty are governed by regulations and formal guidelines, and when not on duty may be influenced by less specific guidelines (for the avoidance of certain forms of "unsuitable" action, e.g. acceptance of generous hospitality or gifts). Since it is not possible to draw up regulations and codified instructions to cover every single aspect of the work of every official in every public service, a large proportion of every official's tasks is based on his own judgement and experience. He is constantly aware of his relationships with immediate subordinates, whose actions he has the duty of supervising and for which he is responsible, and with his immediate superior, to whom he is accountable and to whom he must turn for guidance or instruction when his course is not clear. Theoretically, the level of accountability and competence of any individual official is identical with his level of fitness (qualification and experience). Hence the essential hierarchical structure of any public service and the important role played in practice by considerations of seniority. However many links may intervene, it is a direct chain which binds an official to the State, to which he is responsible and from which he derives authority. All this is generally acceptable, as long as the State is taken to be morally unimpeachable, as is guaranteed in West Germany by the Basic Law, in the U.S.A. by the Constitution or in England by the Monarch. The Nuremberg trials after World War II were of course the classic case of a questioning of this doctrine, but Nuremberg was unprecedented and has, in any case, remained controversial.

A member of a "free profession" is in a different set of relationships. A profession may be defined as an autonomous, self-educating and self-perpetuating body. Admission to membership follows a selection process, a training process (often embodying an "apprenticeship") and an assessment of qualification, all under the control of existing members and none of which may be replaced by a purely administrative decision. Membership involves commitment to an ethical code including the strict confidentiality of professional action and the paramountcy of the relationship with clients as individuals. In the case of educators, there are a few weaknesses in this doctrine: a mathematics graduate without training may be a teacher in England (although the teaching profession is not happy about this); some categories of workers in the education service are not members of the teaching profession (but tacitly adhere to the ethical code of their colleagues who are). Nevertheless, most of the generalisations about "free professions" hold good for education. The relationships between members of this profession is collegial rather than hierarchical.

In any country, therefore, where the education service is a State function, any member of it finds himself in an unavoidably ambiguous situation. To a large extent the ambiguity may be resolved by postulating that the State's moral unimpeachability applies simultaneously to its roles as the source of power and authority for the official and of protection for the professional's clients. In the case of West Germany, the Basic Law lays down fundamental human rights, including, for instance, that of freedom from physical assault, (Article 2), which effectively outlaws corporal punishment, and the right to defence against State power (Article 19). Nevertheless, the predominant impression will probably be that educators are first and foremost part of the State's machinery.

As soon as a new teacher joins his professional association (e.g. for a Gymnasium teacher, the "Philologenverband") he will be given a 300-page vademecum giving the texts of the School Law of his state and of all the laws and regulations and prescribed procedures to which he is subject - not only as a teacher, but also as an official. Here he can ascertain what committees must exist in the management structure of a school, what is his career structure, how many lessons a week he must teach, or how to ask for leave to attend a funeral. If he later wishes for a move, he finds out where vacancies exist by referring to the "Amtsblatt" (official gazette). Promotion prospects are extremely limited, as there are only four salary scales for secondary teachers (Studienrat, Oberstudienrat, Studiendirektor, Oberstudiendirektor). Staffing levels are laid down strictly according to numerical calculations in relation to actual classes to be taught, so in practice a head has little or no flexibility in the allocation of duties. If a bright young teacher wishes to do something new, he will have to do the extra preparation involved in his own time, with no expectation of recognition, and in any case must take care not to depart from the syllabus. The syllabus is an official document with statutory force, and the procedures for conduct of examinations are published as State decrees. If he hopes for promotion, he will see that the salary scale is attached to the individual and does not necessarily or invariably correlate with the duties. It would not be surprising to discover a strong tendency for teachers to accept the probability of their remaining in their "career grade" (for secondary teachers, Oberstudienrat), and for the whole profession to be relatively lacking in mobility. At worst, the pressure is on a teacher to do exactly what is required of him, no more; to adhere to the syllabus; and, as far as possible, to avoid frictions with colleagues, students and parents - in other words, to be the alleged stereotype civil servant, plodding along on a steady salary towards a peaceful pension.

Mention has been made in the previous section of the effect on curriculum development nationally of the ambiguous relationship between Federal and state Governments. Let us look at the same subject again from the point of view of the practising teacher especially at secondary level. Since his relationship with colleagues is basically a hierarchical one (rather than the informal and flexible collegial relationship one frequently finds in an English school) he will find it difficult to muster support for interdisciplinary experimentation. Since his immediate superior may well not have the function of "Fachbereichsleiter" (head of department) the teacher cannot count on support for any movement in a direction which could make the mandatory supervisory task more complex. Budgets are normally drawn up and resources allocated by traditonal government-department methods; the head has little or no discretion for virement; and technical assistance is virtually non-existent anyway. It is not surprising then that grassroots initiatives for curriculum reform are relatively few and far between: curriculum development projects are normally initiated from the top, and are regarded with a touch of cynicism by many teachers. The same mild cynicism may also be found in the attitude of teachers to subject advisory committees or the committees which prepare lists of authorised text-books.

TEACHERS AND TEACHER TRAINING

As another example of the impact of what may be called the bureaucratic approach, let us look at teacher-training. Traditionally, secondary school teachers are trained in the university, and primary teachers in non-university institutions ("Pädagogische Hochschulen"). This is not universally true and the situation is changing, but the generalisation is largely valid. They are on different status and salary levels, and there is no machinery to enable a primary teacher to rise to a secondary teacher´s level. The budding secondary teacher will have studied certain educationally relevant subjects at the university, but will not have had any significant practical experience. He will become a "Studienreferendar" (probationary

teacher) on the lowest scale of what is called the "higher
service" (an indication already of his civil service status)
and will start teaching immediately, but with a reduced
teaching load to enable him to attend a "Seminar" thirteen
hours a week and to prepare a dissertation on a relevant
educational topic. The structure of studies in the seminary is
laid down by law. The formal assessment of his teaching
capability will be based in due course on one lesson, on a
topic of his choice, to a class of his choice. Success in the
Second State Examination brings confirmation in the service, as
Studienrat, and within four or five years he may expect to have
the title and salary of Oberstudienrat. The traditional view
would appear to be that if a teacher knows his subject, he is
capable of teaching it, at least to the well-motivated students
found in the Gymnasium. In those places where the two basic
categories of teacher (Lehrer trained for primary work and
Studienrat trained for secondary) find themselves side by side,
e.g. in a comprehensive school, morale will be affected by
their difference of salary and status. Only modest success has
so far attended the pressure of the "Gewerkschaft Erziehung
und Wissenschaft" (roughly comparable with the English National
Union of Teachers) for teachers to be given status and salary
according to the level of work they do, rather than according
to the way they embark on their training and career.

The work of every teacher is reported on in a prescribed
manner and at prescribed intervals, but he is entitled to ask
for sight of what is written in his personal file. It is an
explicit part of a teacher's obligation, that he engage in
further education and training, through courses and
conferences, but clearly the extent to which this obligation
can be carried out will depend on the kind of opportunities the
Ministry provides in the state concerned.

As a Land civil servant, the teacher is liable to transfer
"in accordance with the exigencies of the service". He is
pledged to obedience to all the rules and regulations and to
instructions issued by his superior. In his job, he must be a
model of cleanliness, tidiness, punctuality and courtesy. In
his personal life, he must avoid frequenting any dubious place
or having any irregular liaison, and he must ensure that all
his family does likewise: failure in these respects could lead
to disciplinary action or ultimately to compulsory transfer.

Much has been made by radical groups of the so-called
"Dienstverbot" (prohibition of career) whereby an intending
teacher is refused entry to that career because of his
adherence to an extreme political group, especially one of the
several Communist parties. By definition, a member of such a
party is committed to rejection of the "bogus" or "bourgeois"
constitution, so is unable to pledge loyalty to the State,
whilst seeking to enter its service.

In addition to his teaching duties, the teacher is obliged
to serve as a member of various relevant councils or

committees, to participate in the drawing up and execution of syllabuses and examination procedures. He may also be obliged to accompany students on excursions or periods spent in the country under the aegis of the school. Some of these duties may be tedious or onerous or entail personal inconvenience, and may more than offset what may by English standards appear to be a relatively light teaching load.

It may be appropriate to this argument to indicate the amount of detail in the examination regulations. As an example, the ordinance governing the final examination for bilingual secretaries in Berlin runs to thirteen pages, not including the syllabus or the marking scheme, which are separate documents. It covers the composition of the examining board, registration procedure, grading system, recording procedure, duration and nature of every paper, discipline, procedures for oral examinations, moderation and publication procedures, provisions for referrals, and conditions for award of certificates. An unsuccessful or (in his own view) inadequately rewarded candidate may go through all this with a fine-tooth comb in search of a basis for court action to give success on the ground that the examination was conducted improperly. Heads of institutions usually take out insurance against risks they incur by involvement in such proceedings.

In the last few years there has been concern over the possibility that the situation may become even more oppressive to professional educators, owing to the increased politicisation of educational debate in certain areas (e.g. in the state of Hessen). Hitherto, the State's provision of education has largely been assured by means of a school law passed by the "Land" Government (e.g. the School Law of Rheinland-Pfalz consists of only 30 pages) which becomes the enabling act for all the detailed regulations and procedures, which are worked out by permanent administrators and professional educators. Public concern over education has led politicians to give attention to more and more of the detail, including ultimately possible parliamentary control over school structures, curricula, management processes etc. This trend would appear to be supported by the views expressed in 1976 by the legal profession: the German Conference of Jurists passed a resolution maintaining the legitimacy of legislators' "normative declarations and regulations" in a wide range of detailed concerns hitherto left to the professionals.(13)

All this may sound as though the individual educator is only a cog in a large bureaucratic machine, and indeed he must be aware constantly of his status and of the limits to his effectiveness. There is, however, another side to this argument: that if the State controls the machine it is nevertheless benevolent, and that if the educator's role is defined, it is not defined out of existence - quite the reverse. If the syllabus for a course of study, the content of an examination, and procedures for the examination are all laid down in a statutory document, that document has been drafted by the teachers involved, with the aim of making the course as relevant as possible and of ensuring that assessment is fair and consistent. The system is fallible to the extent that those operating it are fallible, and the internal checks and balances go a long way towards elimination of foreseeable defects and anomalies. It is open to question whether the British reliance on external examinations and externally devised syllabuses produces a smaller total of defects and anomalies, although it probably costs less than this German system in which large numbers of people are devoting large amounts of time to devising, operating and monitoring a relatively rigid, complex and cumbrous machine. It may also be open to question whether more than a modest proportion of teachers have a passionate desire to become innovators in curriculum or teaching or assessment methods.

Similarly, in Britain we have long prided ourselves on the manner in which parents and other lay people were involved in educational decision-making, especially through school boards of managers and governors. No doubt since the Taylor Report of 1977(14) there has been welcome progress towards more balanced representation of parents, teachers and students. In West Germany, several states have legislated for the establishment of school councils and committees with the explicit aim of facilitating (and in the case of teachers, compelling) democratic participation in policy-making at school level.(15) The wording of some of these recent statutes makes it clear that the objective is not a further bureaucratisation of education, but the reverse - to enhance the professional consciousness of teachers by increasing their opportunities to ventilate professional concerns and contribute their skills and insights to a co-ordinated evolution of educational provision.

In general, as Heckel and Seipp point out,(16) the accommodation of the ethical attitudes and interests of professionals with the obligations and constraints of a State servant is a matter which has been receiving attention for some time both from lawyers and from the Study Commission on Reform of the Public Service (under the aegis of the Federal Ministry of the Interior). They also quote instances of positive discrimination in favour of women in the public service, based on the Basic Law's stipulation of equality of the sexes (Art.117). Membership of the public service brings with it protection against insult, assault and unfair treatment (all the states have laws governing "Personalvertretung" - representation of the individual in his relations with the service). However, what is perhaps most important is that the official's duty of obedience is not a duty of blind obedience: his professional code is conceived as being in accord with the basic human rights inherent in the Basic Law, to which he may refer in case he has doubts about the ethical acceptability of any action the service may enjoin upon him.

There are the Constitutional Court to study laws and proposed laws in the light of the Basic Law, and Administrative Courts (to some extent comparable with our Ombudsman) to look at the execution of procedures from the same viewpoint. As far as the rights of students are concerned, for example, the Federal Constitutional Court handed down a detailed opinion, including some injunctions, on the conception and operation of the "numerus clausus" for places in certain university departments.(17) Some states have set up standing committees to hold a watching brief on the rights of children (e.g. in Rheinland-Pfalz, the "Children's Attorney" Committee). In a less formal way, but often working in the same direction, there are parents' associations in individual states, co-ordinated under the Bundeselternrat (Federal Parents' Council) which enjoys Government support and encouragement.

CONCLUSION

The purpose of this essay has been to focus attention on the significance of the State for education and to bring out the two areas of inherent ambiguity: what is the "State" in question? and is service to the State compatible with the educator's duty to his charges? Both these ambiguities have not only been brought out in numerous studies by German and other scholars and in official reports, but were explicitly emphasised ten years ago in the OECD review of German Education.(18) In the intervening decade it cannot be said that much progress has been made towards resolution of the ambiguity which is deepseated and perhaps inherent in the German people themselves. On the one hand, there is pride in tradition, history, orderliness and explicitly in recent years in West Germany as a Rechtsstaat (a State where law prevails). It is almost a cliché that "Germans like to be regimented". On the other hand, there is a striving towards democracy, participation, individual freedom, self-expression, unfolding of the personality, many of the things conventionally regarded as contained within the basic aims of education and basic necessities for educators themselves. If we read again the words written by Thomas Mann in 1939, we are reminded that the power of the State in education was the means whereby the Nazi régime brought about the corruption of academics and the perversion of young minds towards support of "national pre-eminence and warlike preparedness".(19) The fact that Thomas Mann's words now sound grotesque in the context of the present-day Federal Republic may encourage us to believe that although progress may be slow, progress there is towards a fostering of the desirable elements in a situation containing diverse and often mutually incompatible potentialities.

NOTES AND REFERENCES

1.Lindegren,A.M. (1957): Germany revisited - education in the Federal Republic (US Dept. of Health, Education and Welfare).

2.Die Verfassung des Deutschen Reiche vom 11 August, 1919, Art.10.

3.Chaput de Saintonge,R.A. (1961): Public administration in Germany, (Weidenfeld).

4.There are eight "Länder" and two "free" cities (Hamburg and Bremen) plus West Berlin. In this essay they are referred to as Land/Länder or as states.

5.Grundgesetz für die Bundesrepublik Deutschland vom 23 Mai, 1949.

6.Verfassung der Freien und Hansestadt Hamburg, Art.111, quoted in Wagner,O. (1965): Hamburg berufsbildendes Schulwesen 1865 - 1965, (Gewerkschaft Erziehung und Wissenschaft, Hamburg).

7.Scott,D.F.S. (1960): Wilhelm von Humboldt and the idea of a university (inaugural lecture, University of Durham).

8.Perhaps the most notorious polemic of the period was Picht,G. (1964): Die deutsche Bildungskatastrophe (The German education catastrophe).

9.Knoll,J.H. (1967): Aufbau und Struktur des deutschen Bildungswesens, (Inter Nationes, Bonn).

10.Bildungsgesamtplan (1973): (Bund-Länder-Kommission fur Bildungsplanung).

11.Heckel,H. und Seipp,P. (1976): Schulrechtskunde (Luchterhand).

12.Führ, Chr. (1979): Education and teaching in the Federal Republic of Germany, (Inter Nationes, Bonn).

13.Becker,H. (1976): Zum Problem der Schulaufsicht, in Schul-Management, Dezember, 1976.

14.HMSO: Department of Education and Science (1977): A New Partnership for our Schools, (The Taylor Report), London.

15.For example: <u>Landesgesetz uber die Schulen in Rheinland-Pfalz</u> (1974), Art.22: "Participation in meetings of the school council is obligatory for all full-time teachers, participation in class conferences is obligatory for all teachers".

16.Heckel und Seipp (1976), op.cit., Chapters 18-22.

17.<u>Recht der Jugend</u>, März/April 1977, pp.132-133.

18.Review of National Policies for Education in Germany (1972), (OECD).

19.In his Introduction to Mann,E. (1939): <u>School for Barbarians</u>, (Lindsay Drummond).

Chapter Seven

THE WESTERN EUROPEAN IDEA IN EDUCATION*

Sixten Markland

THE WESTERN EUROPEAN IDEA IN EDUCATION

Is there a "Western European Idea in Education?" If there is,
how is it to be defined, described and analysed? Can it
actually be subjected to an evaluation?

An ambitious attempt to do all these things is presented in
a book by Vernon Mallinson, former Professor of Comparative
Education at the University of Reading, England. It is entitled
precisely The Western European Idea in Education, and is
extremely rich in content, with perspectives in both time and
space.

The writer follows what he calls the Western European idea
in education from the dawn of our civilisation in classical
antiquity, through the Middle Ages, the Renaissance and the
Enlightenment, to the point at which we now stand. This is a
huge, one would have thought practically impossible task. It is
thus all the more of a pleasure to note that Professor
Mallinson has succeeded. His presentation is both rich and
stimulating. He has been obliged, naturally, to select among
the almost incomprehensible volume of relevant arguments,
events and facts. His aim has been to organise these into
surveyable units, bringing system and order to the apparently
unsystematic and chaotic. His presentation is lucid both in
style and analysis, which makes this book highly readable in
spite of the vast scope and complexity of its material.

In the introductory chapters he describes the cultural
heritage of Western Europe and the traditional elements of
European education. The classical heritage of Greece and Rome,
the role of Christianity, and the influence of Western
commercialism are painted with broad strokes of the brush. He
further portrays the development of the education system from
one designed to serve a social élite to one providing a basic
schooling for everybody. "How comprehensive?" he asks in one
chapter, in which he describes how education, previously
strictly compartmented by class, has become common to different
social strata, and the problems involved in this re-evaluation.

Via the demands currently being made in Western Europe for reforms in teacher training, and the ever clearer trend towards recurrent education, he then arrives at what are now in Western Europe the particularly acute problems relating to the organisation and function of higher education and research. Consistently with his generally optimistic view of the future and development of Western European education, he describes in his closing chapter a number of recent attempts to bring Western Europe towards a policy of harmonisation.

Professor Mallinson's analysis leads to the conclusion that Western Europe is a family of individual cultures, and that these cultures are mutually different, but that they nonetheless have something in common. They constitute a unit, and that unit is reflected in the "Western European idea in education" that is the theme of the book. Characteristic of European man, according to Mallinson, is "his unquenchable passion for arriving at the truth and the tremendous importance he attaches to man's worth, man's dignity, man's place in the universe". From these, he says all else stems. This is what conditions the shape of Western European education.

The task of reviewing this book did not, initially, seem likely to present too much difficulty. But the further on I read, the harder my task seemed. If Mallinson's intention has been to generate thoughts and questions concerning the origins and nature of our education, and the status and future of our educational system, then he has most certainly succeeded. And below I shall consider some of the reflections and questions to which his book has led me. I myself have two main starting-points. The one lies in my experience, over a period of years, of international collaboration in education and educational research in UNESCO, the Council of Europe and the OECD, and in various joint Scandinavian bodies. The other lies in my strong association with specifically Swedish educational reforms in recent decades. As a result of the latter - and in spite of the former - I do read Mallinson's description of the Western ideas in education essentially as a Swede. My view of this idea thus acquires its own colouring, and that view I should like here to describe. I frequently asked myself while reading the book whether we Scandinavians are Western Europeans. Is it possible that Austrians, Italians, Hungarians, Greeks and Spaniards will ask themselves a similar question? And perhaps also the Yugoslavian, Finnish, Irish, Bohemian and Swiss readers? How large is Western Europe and what educational ideas does it contain?

WESTERN EUROPEAN UNITY

Mallinson's Western Europe as described in his introductory chapters seems to me somewhat on the small side. Its centre of gravity is in an area situated geographically by the Rhine, the Mosel and the Schelde, and by the North Sea and the English

107

channel, on both sides of these waters, which is to say in
England, Northern France, Holland, Belgium and Luxembourg. Is
this not far too small an area to be designated "Western
Europe?" And even if the centre of gravity lies there, this is
surely not to be interpreted as meaning that the ideas about
education, and about culture at large, are to be found there
and there alone? (We know from mechanics that the centre of
gravity of a ring is in the middle, where there is in fact no
matter). If therefore this "Western Europe Minor" has been a
spiritual centre, this need not imply that the ideas, the
culture, flourished there exclusively: it may be, rather, that
this was where forces from the north, the south, and the east
met. That I find this likely stems from the fact that I
consider - as I suggested just now - that Scandinavian ideas on
education (and thus probably also Italian, Bohemian, Austrian,
and Hungarian ideas, and those from the other peripheral areas)
have been too summarily dismissed in Mallinson's monograph.

I am aware that I am here not only making enormous demands
on the writer, but also lapsing into the sin, so common among
reviewers, of criticising a book for what it does not contain
rather than for what it does. My criticism of too narrow a
Western Europe will thus be justified only if educational ideas
and their significance have as a result been too imperfectly or
one-sidedly treated to afford us an understanding of the
educational problems at large that face Western Europe today.

The first two chapters of the book, which are devoted to
what is specifically Western European in our cultural heritage,
stand as an excellent digest of current educational thinking,
cultural goods in stock, and attitudes towards science from
Aristotle, via Descartes, Newton and Darwin, up to the
Positivist and post-Positivist epistemologies and scientific
methods of our own century. Mediaeval scholasticism is
described, with its heritage from Abelard and Thomas Aquinus.
And how the concept of education was developed in France
through Montaigne and Descartes, acquiring its characteristic
seal in the French educational ideology, according to which
knowledge is achieved by reasoning.

Over against this we have the English idea of knowledge
being acquired by experience, as put forward by John Locke and
others, and the German idea of knowledge developing as a result
of an intellectual and dialectical process, as according to
Kant, Fichte and Hegel etc.

The countries whose cultures fall outside the sphere of the
world languages are here doomed to remain forgotten in the
shadows, not so much because ideologies and cultural debate are
there lacking as because that debate remains an exclusively
domestic affair owing to their linguistic isolation. Particular
versions of the French, English and German educational
ideologies have emerged, for example, in a country like Sweden.
Uniquely Swedish ideologies have also been developed. It seems,
however, inescapably the case that these should remain unknown

in the great "cultural languages". It is little help that ideologies and arguments may subsequently be translated into these languages: by that time the debate there will often have moved on to new fields.

This harsh fate my own country shares with many others. We have frequently spoken, with mild resignation, of a "language imperialism" also within the sphere of European culture. A country like Finland is in practice left entirely out of the discussion, owing mainly to its unique language. Mallinson´s book does not even mention Finland. And yet that country, above all in the nineteenth century, has had a number of very distinguished educationists (including, for example, Uno Cygnaeus). Finland is <u>not</u> an Eastern European country, as one might imagine from Mallinson´s presentation. In its educational ideology, Finland is more Central European that Sweden, Norway and Denmark. This is just one example of how easy it is to define Western Europe too narrowly.

An excellent section of this book is that describing the emergence of the bodies handling European co-operation. Although I have worked a great deal with some of these, I have not previously seen any authoritative and fairly exhaustive description of all the stages comprising the prehistory of such bodies as the Council of Europe, the OECD and the EEC, of the role played by the European Coal and Steel Union, and of the development of a European "baccalauréat" and the various European institutes for research and information.

Also of great value are Professor Mallinson´s descriptions of how the education systems of individual Western European countries have developed up to our own day. In its wealth of dates, statistics on students, and descriptions of the institutions concerned, Mallinson´s account differs favourably from the majority of studies in comparative education, which tend to dwell on great thoughts about education, seldom or never getting down to the actual education provided. His presentation of the preschools is of particular interest, in that the role of these differs so widely from one cultural area to another. In Sweden the preschool is not even a "school", but an institution run by the central and local health and welfare authorities, with groups that are seldom in excess of 20 children, supervised as a rule by two preschool teachers, often with one or two assistants, i.e. with a very high teacher-pupil ratio (6-7 children per adult). Sweden has preschool facilities for only half of all children between the ages of 3 and 6. Belgium has facilities for almost all children over the age of 3, but at the price of large groups, 25-30 children per teacher, which in Sweden has been found entirely unacceptable. Clearly ideological differences thus prevail.

HOW COMPREHENSIVE?

A question of method that arises is whether the Western

European idea in education can and should be described, analysed and evaluated exclusively from within. If it is to stand out as something unique, as a unit, must it not be related also to Eastern Europe, and to North America? Mallinson makes certain comparisons between Western Europe and the USA, the Soviet Union and China, but these are brief and superficial. They fail to illustrate how Western European education has been influenced by these cultures. This is particularly evident with regard to the emergence of the comprehensives during the past fifty years. The idea of the comprehensive is nothing new in Western Europe, but it was first applied in practice in the USA and the Soviet Union. At the beginning of this century, when education increasingly came to involve "parallel" schools, with one system for compulsory education and another for so-called "higher" education, the USA was the first country to react to the parallel system and the degree of social stratification involved. With a view to democratising education, the US Government appointed in 1913 its Committee on the Reorganisation of Secondary Education, which submitted its final report ("Cardinal Principles of Secondary Education") in 1918. By the terms of this report, the parallel system of Elementary Schools and High Schools was to be abolished. Secondary education was to be organised for all young American people until the age of 18. Development of the education system along these lines started in 1925, with Federal support for slow learners even at the upper secondary level. The great expansion occurred in the 1930s, during the Depression, when the period of schooling was prolonged with the use of both State and Federal funds. Here, as was so often to be the case, it was essentially the lack of jobs for young people that prompted the extension of schooling within the compulsory system. Work camps for young people were organised (the Civil Conservation Corps, or CCC). Practical schools for young people were set up (by the National Youth Administration, or NYA). The main objectives laid down in "Cardinal Principles of Secondary Education" were said to apply to the entire system of education, not just the secondary level. These related to the individual in respect of his "health, command of fundamental processes, worthy home membership, vocation, citizenship, worthy use of leisure and ethical character". Compulsory schooling, which in the majority of states commenced at the age of 6, was extended to cover 9 or 10 years, for the majority of students. In some states it was extended to 11 or 12 years. The report on "Cardinal Principles" provided the basis for a number of other reports, including "Education for ALL American youth", by the NEA's Education Policies Commission. This led in its turn to a major evaluative report, the "Eight Year Study", published in five volumes in 1942.

Various other evaluative studies were also performed in the USA, including "Youth Tell Their Story" (1943), by the American Youth Commission. This reproduced the attitudes of over 13,600 young people, and their experiences of different types of extended education and the co-ordination of education and practical work. The result was the "Prosser Resolution" (C.A. Prosser being the man charged with the task of summarising these views), the gist of which was that the 20% of students who were well equipped to benefit from a theoretical education should be given their own, specially geared programmes, that the 20% with a clearly vocational bent should similarly be given their own programmes, and that new programmes for "life adjustment training" should be designed for the remaining 60%. In the latter 1940s, this gave rise to what was termed in the USA the "life adjustment movement", which in its turn became the subject of various evaluations. These, published mainly in the 1950s, were in some cases highly critical. This criticism subsequently culminated in the so-called "Sputnik psychosis" which involved various kinds of soul-searching as America suddenly saw itself overtaken in its technological development by the Soviet Union.

Basically, the subject of all this evaluation and criticism was quite simply various practical applications of the "Cardinal Principles" of 1918, or in other words what I have pointed to as the American comprehensive. There is no doubt whatsoever that these various applications have had their importance for at least some Western European champions of the comprehensive system.

The development of a comprehensive school in the Soviet Union subsequent to 1917 has certain features in common with events in the USA. The foundations were laid by a Declaration concerning a united labour school, adapted by the Council of People´s Comissars in 1918. By the terms of this Declaration, all schools were to be state-operated and open to all Soviet citizens, regardless of sex and nationality. No distinctions were to be made on grounds of social status, teaching was to be free, and grants were to be made available to those in need of them. Textbooks and school meals would also be free. Teaching was to be given in the pupil´s native language, and the different peoples within the union would have school systems of the same type.

This was a comprehensive school programme as clearly formulated as one could wish for. An intensive phase of development commenced. By 1930 the number of schools and the number of students had more than doubled. That year also saw the first comprehensive Act concerning the Public and Compulsory Teaching of Beginners, introducing compulsory schooling for at least four years from the age of 8. From 1938 compulsory schooling in the towns was extended to seven years, starting from the age of 7. The 7-year school (in some cases it was in fact longer) has a 4-year primary stage, followed by a secondary stage with specialised teachers that was common to all students. In 1949 it was ordered that compulsory schooling even in the country should be extended to at least seven years.

In the towns it has subsequently been extended to ten years, between the ages of 7 and 17. In 1958, a minimum compulsory schooling of eight years was introduced in the country districts. At the same time, it was stipulated that all students should participate in regular work outside the school on two out of the six school-days in the week. This rule, the "Khrushchev school reform", has since been modified to apply only to certain types of education.

The important aspect for our purposes is that these comprehensive movements in the USA and USSR were prior to and influenced the comprehensive school movement in Western Europe. Particularly the "cardinal principles", known in the USA as the "Magna Carta" of education, have been of great importance in Western Europe, via the various forms in which attempts were made in America to apply them. I myself can testify that these American experiences were of major importance in the case of Sweden. The proposals concerning comprehensives put forward by Government committees in the 1940s, and the political decisions which followed them, were inspired more by American than by Western European ideas and experiences.

There were, however, parallels to the "Cardinal principles" in Europe. In England we find them in the Spens Report of 1938, and in the 1944 Education Act. In France, the Langevin-Wallon Report of 1948 gave rise to a series of reforms tending in the direction of a comprehensive school, the most recent of these being the "Haby reform" of 1975.

Mallinson has described the development of ideas and the course of events in Western Europe, but fails - in my mind - to indicate the extent to which Western Europe has been influenced by other areas, primarily the USA. Within Western Europe, however, it is not the central areas but the Scandinavian countries that have come furthest with the "comprehensivisation" of their education. They have thus, naturally, been the first to encounter the really large problems, for example, the transformation of university-level education into a "mass education" while at the same time training an élite. (Mallinson's description of Sweden's difficulties, pp.308-312, I find, however, excessively negative; he does not discuss at all the value of the new opportunities for increasing numbers to study at a university).

The comprehensive school movement is thus an almost global phenomenon in the industrialised world, with Western Europe as a whole not taking any kind of lead, but reacting to influences from both west and east.

One is tempted to wonder whether some kind of correlation might not be traced between this movement and economic development. From the Alps to northernmost Europe, through Switzerland, West Germany, Denmark, Sweden and Norway runs an "axis" of high material welfare. The standard of living in conventional terms (e.g. GNP per capita) is twice as high in these "axis countries" as in Western Europe at large. However,

the correlation between standard of living and
"comprehensivisation" is not a simple one:
"comprehensivisation" has come 20 years later in West Germany
and Switzerland than in Scandinavia. What has characterised
Sweden and its neighbours more than Western Europe as a whole
is the development of the Western European welfare state, with
increased social as well as economic equality. Here, the
comprehensive system has been one of the important instruments
in a broadly planned movement towards class equalisation. Here,
too, the traditional "People's Movements" of the Nordic
countries have played a major role in the past 100 years - the
labour movement, the women's movement, the consumer co-
operative movement, the temperance movement, the sports
movement and the free church movement. All these "People's
Movements" have organised popular education of different kinds.
At present, 2 million out of the total Swedish population of 8
million participate each year in different kinds of "study
circles". This is one Swede in every four, an impressive figure
in both absolute and relative terms when compared with what is
offered by the Open University in England, and the zweite
Bildungswege in West Germany.

THE DIGNITY OF MAN

Mallinson returns on several occasions to the "dignity of man"
as the essential aspect of the Western European idea in
education. I can agree that the European, even the more
narrowly defined Western European, differs from the African,
the Indian, and the Chinese, and, indeed, from the Russian and
the American. But does the characteristic stamp of the European
really lie in this "dignity of man?" If we try to answer this
question, we find outselves confronted by some difficult
problems of definition and appraisal. What sort of "dignity"
and what "man?" Even if we early on abolished slavery in
Europe, and later also (against some resistance) the serfdom of
the peasant classes, I think we should be careful about posing
as the upholders of human dignity. Major population groups in
Europe have long since been reduced to proletariat status, and
have hardly lived lives of any dignity. According to Thomas
Hobbes, the one man's dignity stops where the other man's
starts. Man at liberty, he says, only leads to the warring of
all against each other, and a strong government is therefore
necessary. Even if we have not held these views in Europe in
the past few centuries, it is only very recently that we have
begun to approach a situation in which the "dignity" is shared
by more than a handful of people. The famines and the plagues
are no longer with us, but Western Europe still has a long way
to go in achieving any very general application of "man's
dignity". The efforts made to achieve equality encounter
constant resistance. And I would venture to suggest that this
resistance is stronger in the French, the English and the

German cultures than it is in Scandinavia. It is strong, in
other words, in what Mallinson sees as Western Europe proper.
It is this that provokes my earlier question. Who are the
Western Europeans? Do we Scandinavians belong? I suppose, after
all, that we do, with certain reservations. But what, for
example, do the 9 million Western Europeans currently
unemployed feel about "man's dignity?"

This brings me to the Western European ideology to which
Karl Marx gave rise, an ideology that for the space of a
century has exercised a very strong influence on both Eastern
and Western European thought. One need not be a Marxist to
admit this influence. Even if one questions the fruitfulness of
Marxism's critical social and historical research, even if its
conflict theories do not offer the best understanding of social
development, and even if its catastrophe theory has failed to
function in Western Europe, it is unreasonable not to
acknowledge that Marxism and its successors have had a major
impact on contemporary political thought and action, even among
non-Marxists. That the ideas and theories of Karl Marx have
acquired their special application in the Socialist states of
Eastern Europe, and in Yugoslavia, Albania, China and Cuba
hardly prevents Marxism from belonging, also, to the Western
conceptual world. Karl Marx lived and worked in Western Europe,
he is buried in London. That Mallinson has excluded Karl Marx
from his otherwise excellent survey of ideas (he mentions Marx
in a couple of lines, but does not discuss him) is a paradox of
considerable interest. The spirit of Marx hovers, invisible,
between many of Mallinson's lines. And if, as a reviewer, I
were forced to answer the question "This book has one weak
point, what is it?" I should be bound to say it was the
omission of the writer to discuss the influence of Marxism on
the Western European idea in education, not only in Scandinavia
but also in France, England, Germany and other countries in the
west. Such concepts as democracy and the democratisation of
education have a very different meaning now than during the
breakthrough of liberalism.

PSYCHOLOGY AND EDUCATION

Mallinson's book also lacks a section discussing how the
Western idea in education has been influenced by the advances
made in psychological research during the last hundred years.
The pre-psychological era was strongly characterised by formal
thought and formal education. Euclidean geometry, Latin
grammar, logic, rhetoric and dialectics were studied at an
early stage to "train the mind" and "sharpen the mental
apparatus". Right up until our own day, education has been
characterised by formal theories of this kind. A hundred years
ago, when scientific psychology began to detach itself from the
embrace of philosophy, it was found to afford but scant support
for this sort of formal thinking. Here, again, it was mainly

American researchers who offered new findings to Western
Europe. Psychologists, such as W.J. James (1842-1910),
presented new theories of learning and development. An
iconoclast on the grand scale was John B. Watson (1878-1958),
the father of behaviourism, who actually denied the existence
of the free mental life on which all humanistic theories of
education had been based. In the wake of the new psychology
followed a new theory of activity learning or "learning by
doing", as put forward by John Dewey (1859-1951) and William
Kilpatrick (1871-1965).

Nor were European psychologists slow to contribute to a new
view of man and of knowledge. Examples include L.W. Stern
(1871-1938) in the field of perception psychology, above all
through his journal, the Zeitschrift für angewandte
Psychologie, and Alfred Binet (1857-1911) through his early
studies of intelligence (Les idées modernes sur les enfants,
1909). Depth psychologists like Sigmund Freud (1856-1939) and
C.G. Jung (1875-1961) published theories suggesting strong
subconscious drives in upbringing and learning. Differential
psychology was developed and led to sophisticated testing
techniques, through psychologists such as L.M. Terman (1877-
1956). The 1930s and 1940s saw the entrance of social
psychology, the 1950s and 1960s the appearance of an
educational technology.

Of particular interest was the polarisation in educational
psychology between two main pictures of the human being. In the
one view, the human being - including the student in school -
is active, and learns as a result of his own drives. In the
other view, man is reactive, and his behaviour is determined by
exclusively external stimuli. The former view found support in
such researchers as Sigmund Freud, Jean Piaget (1896-1980) and
Jerome Bruner (born 1913). The latter was supported by such men
as the Russian reflexologist Ivan Pavlov (1849-1936), the
behaviourist John B. Watson and the stimulus-response
psychologist F.B. Skinner (born 1904). Quite obviously, these
two views of human nature lead not only to different
educational ideologies, but to different teaching matter,
different methods, and a different sort of school organisation.

These are only a few names in a long row of influential
scientists. They were followed by practitioners with various
views on education. It took time for the new ideas to acquire a
foothold in the education system (and the process is still
continuing). Two observations should be made at this point,
namely that these influences have come to a certain extent from
outside, and that they have had an essential bearing on the
development precisely of the comprehensive idea, with a
prolonged schooling and - above all - a postponed
differentiation of the students along different paths of
education.

The role played by modern psychology, it is true, would be
worth a book of its own. The same might be said of the

influences from other disciplines, such as sociology and anthropology. I am aware that I am here getting into what Mallinson´s book does <u>not</u> concern itself with, and that I should have restricted my remarks to what he actually discusses. Professor Mallinson has correctly and consistently limited his presentation to ideas within Western Europe as he had defined it, and to how these ideas have emerged, developed and been applied. And that, as a subject, is large enough.

NOTE

* This is reprinted from the European Journal of Education, Vol.16, No.1, 1981, pp.121-128, by kind permission of the editor.

Chapter Eight

A COMPARATIVE POLITICAL AND SOCIOLOGICAL ANALYSIS OF
EDUCATIONAL OPPORTUNITY IN WESTERN EUROPE, 1960-1980

W.D. Halls

INTRODUCTION

Education is peculiarly subject to the vagaries of fashion.
Themes such as "participation" and "accountability", thrown up
by events such as May 1968 in France and Mr. Callaghan´s Ruskin
College speech in 1976, are debated, theorized about, half-
heartedly acted upon, then die away and are quietly pigeon-
holed. However, one such theme, equality of educational
opportunity, has occupied the stage for a score of years and
refuses to die. Educationalists, those committed idealists,
have kept the theme alive. Parents, although their faith in
education has now been rudely shattered, still cling to it as a
precept for justice for their children. Even today no
politician in Western Europe could afford not to pay at least
lip-service to it as an ideal.

This paper takes a deliberately pessimistic view - if only
to counterbalance past euphoria - of the way the concept has
developed. What is remarkable is that, often working
independently, politicians, sociologists and educationalists
from many different parts of Western Europe have provided
parallel evidence and taken parallel action to realise
educational opportunity, and in the end have experienced the
same frustration. It is therefore, in a Durkheimian sense, a
proper subject for comparative study. It is hoped that the
final conclusions regarding what is one of the failures of
education may nevertheless stimulate fresh efforts to realise
the ideal.

Firstly, however, in what does that ideal consist? The
principle of equality is usually held to mean that in matters
that are public everyone should be treated identically, except
in situations where there are good reasons for treating certain
individuals or groups differently. The exception, of course,
begs the question: is education, or certain levels of
education, or certain options within it, an exception or not?
Political theorists state that within a democracy, in the
sphere of social interests, the individual must not be excluded

117

through lack of education from prosecuting his own interest to the utmost.(1) On the whole, since 1960 this more "liberal" interpretation of opportunity has prevailed, with the result that educational policies have attempted to minimize differences in treatment of pupils and students. Thus in Western Europe grouping of children in primary schools has been abolished, secondary education generalized. With the notable exception of West Germany, the lower secondary school has become a non-selective, comprehensive or polyvalent institution. The torments of the "eleven plus" or "entrée en sixième" are virtually no more; even in West Germany an observation or "orientation" stage of one or two years' duration determines to which secondary school, in a largely tripartite system, a child should go. Many European countries teach pupils in mixed ability groups, with a common curriculum, up to at least the age of thirteen. Sixteen is now the normal school leaving age, although some politicians are having second thoughts as to whether this is too late - or, in view of youth unemployment - too early. It is true that A Level, the "baccalauréat" or the "Abitur" remain formidable hurdles - even Sweden has such a barrier - before entry to higher education is assured. But access has been broadened and financial support is available - loans in Sweden, grants in Britain, almost a "pre-salary" for the meritorious few in France. Whether such changes are sufficient is what we are about to consider. That they have been achieved in the name of equality or opportunity there can be no doubt. After the Second World War it was an ideal whose time had come.

Its germination had been long. The idea can be traced back at least to the French "philosophes". Condorcet, in his Esquisse d´un tableau historique des progrès de l´esprit humain, discerns a tendency for nations and individuals to move towards an equality of freedom and rights of which popular education would be the instrument. Schooling cannot, he argued, encompass absolute equality, but can help to level out differences. A century later an English philosopher, T.H. Green (an Oxford don and the founder of Oxford High School for Boys), insisted on the right of every child to knowledge.(2) Nor was equality of opportunity a cant phrase of the philosophers. The first public use of the phrase in England goes back to 1895, when Will Thorne, the founder of the Gas Workers' Union, moved at the Trades Union Congress that:

> Our educational system should be completely remodelled on such a basis as to secure the democratic principle of equality of opportunity.(3)

Prussia, however, remained firmly wedded to the principle of élitism. A few years before Green and Thorne, Nietzsche, lecturing on the "future of our educational institutions" had argued that "not the education of the masses can be our goal,

but the education of individually selected people"; to extend
education would destroy "the natural order of rank in the
kingdom of the intellect".(4) The authoritarian principle of
hierarchy took a long while dying both in German education and
German politics. But Germany was not alone in fighting a
rearguard action against the realisation of the egalitarian
ideal.

SOCIOLOGICAL AND POLITICAL VIEWS ABOUT 1960

The evidence of lack of equality of educational opportunity as
Western Europe entered the decade of the 1960s is overwhelming,
as common observation no less than sociological studies showed.
The data regarding Britain, and the work of Halsey, Floud,
Glass and others, are too well known to need reproducing here.
The case of higher education may serve as an example. Despite
unequal chances, Britain in 1961, with some 25 per cent of the
student population drawn from the working classes, did
considerably better than other Western European countries; even
in Sweden the proportion was only 14.3 per cent.(5) Ringer
gives comparative figures for France and West Germany. He shows
that in France in 1959 only 3 per cent of all students came
from the families of industrial workers and that in the
prestigious faculty of medicine - prestigious because of the
lucrative profession with which it was associated - they
comprised only 1.6 per cent of the total,(6) despite the fact
that industrial workers made up more than half the working
population. At the highly prized "grandes écoles" (which
perform for France what Oxbridge has done in the past for
England) in 1962 the social origins of students were as
follows:(7)

Institution	Industrial workers	Liberal professions, academics and top civil servants
	Per cent of total.	
Ecole Normale Supérieure	3	47
Institut d'Etudes politiques	2	29
Ecole Polytechnique	2	43

In Germany, a similar situation prevailed, according to Ringer:
despite making up 55 per cent of the working population, the
children of industrial workers represented only 5.9 per cent of
the total of university students, and only 2.9 per cent of the
medical students.(8) At the same level Ralf Dehrendorf, the
title of whose book, Bildung ist Bürgerrecht ("Education is the
Citizen's Right": 1965) became a slogan in the 1969 Federal

elections for the Social Democrats, cited figures for 1962-3
which showed up the distorted image that higher education held
up to the nation. Those who had already been through higher
education - circa 1-2 per cent of the population - provided
children who formed 35.5 per cent of the student population.
The table below sets out the position in greater detail.(9)

Category	Per cent in Population	Per cent students
Ind. and Agric. workers	49.8	5.2
White collar workers	22.7	29.3
Tradesmen and artisans	10.6	14.5
Self-employed agric. workers	8.7	3.5
Civil servants	6.7	33.7
Liberal professions	1.5	1.5

Side by side with the sociological studies, which in any
case were sometimes politically motivated, developments were
occurring in the political field. In Britain the Labour Party
conference had officially committed itself for the first time
to comprehensive schooling. In the early 1960s a Conservative
education minister such as Lord Boyle (as he became) was not
unsympathetic and wanted experiments with comprehensive
schools. In 1959 de Gaulle, who had returned to power in France
the previous year, initiated the most far-reaching educational
reforms since the Ferry reforms of the 1880s. During the short
interregnum in which he ruled by decree the general began by
raising the leaving age for those entering school in 1959 to
sixteen, and started the virtual generalization of secondary
education. However, about 20 per cent of children would not
qualify for secondary education as such but the rest would
enter a guidance phase at the end of which, at thirteen, they
would be steered to the kind of education most appropriate for
them. In Sweden, of course, things had moved much faster. In
1950 already experiments in unitary comprehensive schools from
7-16 had been authorised, and in 1959 these were being extended
to the whole of the country.(10) By contrast, in 1959 West
Germany remained firmly traditionalist. There was published an
"Outline Plan" for education which effectively came out in
favour of maintaining tripartism, on the grounds that it had
"proved itself" (the "economic miracle" may be some
demonstration of this assertion), that the three types of
school corresponded to psychological views on the three types
of ability - theoretical, practical, and a blend of both; also
to the three main social classes, as well as the three main
kinds of employment.(11) On the other hand, change was
stirring: the Socialist party formally abandoned its Marxist
principle and became a social democratic party, although it had

120

A Comparative Political and Sociological Analysis

to wait a decade before it achieved full power and the
opportunity to effect some educational reforms.
    These political attitudes reflected differing ideologies.
The British, empirical as ever, believed that reform was
justified on social grounds and also as a means to increasing
national prosperity. Sweden was perhaps more greatly imbued
with a "social engineering" philosophy of education, but the
social democrats, in power since 1932, had been careful to
leave education until last in their measures of social reform.
Before schooling could be changed "welfarism" had to be
achieved in other areas of the social field. On the other hand,
French Cartesianism had now been blended with Gaullist
pragmatism: if the Langevin-Wallon Plan of 1947, which de
Gaulle now claimed to be implementing, had adumbrated justice,
his new technocratic approach to governing France meant that
education had to expand in order to provide technicians and
higher cadres on an unprecedented scale. West Germany was more
circumspect. Adenauer´s Christian Democrats saw little reason
for change: their educational philosophy was based upon the
family. German economic recovery, then in full swing, demanded
a disciplined labour force which, with virtually compulsory
apprenticeship for those who had left formal education, was
obtainable through the part-time education system. The
education system was modelled on that which had existed before
the Nazis had come to power; drastic changes in it might rock
the economic boat. As late as 1968 Dahrendorf could claim that
"the rhetoric of equal educational opportunity was, and still
is, missing in German politics of all parties".(12) What
national attitudes had in common was that national wellbeing
depended upon education, even if, as in Germany, it depended on
nothing being changed. The other nations in Western Europe
shared a common belief that educational reform could bring
about peaceful social change: for the first time the right of
the individual to a good start in life coincided with the
national interest, both socially and economically. Events were
to prove that these theories regarding the power of education
in the social apparatus were false.

THE 1960s AND EDUCATIONAL REALITY

If equality of opportunity had become something of a catchword
in the 1960s, how was it reflected in reality? In Britain the
most radical educational reform of the century, the
legitimisation of comprehensive education, was ushered in, not
by a law, but by a circular eleven pages long,(13) which
advanced a series of stopgap measures as to how local
educational authorities might proceed, and ended up by saying
that there was no money to do better. ("Government by circular"
was also attempted, unsuccessfully, by education ministers in
France). For some, comprehensive education brought no
improvement: it meant remedial classes sited in temporary huts

for the less bright pupils; "split sites"; even when new
schools were built, extra teaching rooms had to be added on
almost immediately. In France, where the building programme was
more systematic after lower comprehensive education had been
introduced for all in 1963, it was said that some children had
spent their entire school career on a building site. Baudelot
and Establet have painted a graphic picture of how the bottom
20 per cent of the secondary intake were sometimes treated.(14)
Relegated to an annexe, they lived in a sort of apartheid from
their schoolmates. The more qualified teachers - "<u>professeurs</u>"
→ practised a sort of ostracism of their colleague, a mere
"<u>instituteur</u>" (ex-primary teacher), who looked after the
"disinherited". His charges worked away at arithmetic,
dictation and vocabulary, whilst the brighter children studied
mathematics and literature. They ate lunch in a separate
building, or after all the others had been fed. They learnt, as
one official text put it, "le petit trésor d'idées dont ils ont
strictement besoin" in order to become the unskilled labourers
of industrial society. Even in egalitarian Sweden, where mixed
ability classes were almost invariably the rule, and all pupils
followed a large "common core" of subjects, classes which were
remedial in all but name had to be started. In all countries
teachers were initially not trained to deal with comprehensive
schooling. It was a Swede, Sixten Marklund, who said that the
greatest obstacle to reform in his country had been the
teachers. The French criticized the British for the burgeoning
of new curricula, often thought out by a few enthusiastic but
inexperienced teachers, necessary to deal with the new type of
secondary pupil. The British criticized the French for
attempting to apply what was essentially a grammar school
curriculum to all pupils, conveniently forgetting that this was
what Harold Wilson, and a large proportion of the electorate
who had been roused by the comprehensive issue and had voted
Labour in 1963, thought comprehensive education was all about.
Rebellious pupils aped their seniors, the rebellious students,
in many countries after the events of 1968. "Sin bins" for
disruptive pupils soon became institutionalised in a number of
British schools. In Sweden and France truancy was a problem -
in France the police had orders to conduct to school any
youngster found wandering on the streets alone during school
hours. Vandalism, hooliganism and delinquency increased: this
form of "equality of opportunity" did not bring "sweetness and
light" to schools.

The "democratisation" of higher education was just as
difficult to accomplish. In England and France one side-effect
of comprehensive education was the boom in private education,
whether in the so-called "public school" or the Catholic
"college", which were more effective in getting pupils into the
prestigious areas of higher education. The student riots of
1968-70, whether in London, Berlin or Paris, were symptomatic
of an educational malaise, as well as of many other ills in

society. Yet the universities had remained stubbornly resistant to change. Everywhere governments set up new institutions to open up higher education to "first generation" students. Crosland's impatience with the universities led to the creation of the polytechnics and the so-called "binary" system. In France, University Institutes of Technology had been set up in 1964 not only to produce more technical personnel but also to alleviate the chronic overcrowding in the universities. In West Germany, the "Fachhochschulen" were created to produce lower-level engineers and more intermediate cadres. In reality nobody was taken in. In Britain, the universities retained their paramountcy - and their largely middle-class clientèle - as did the "grandes écoles" in France, and established institutions like the Technische Hochschule in Aachen. In Sweden, higher education was eventually "zoned", so that great universities like Upsala were grouped with less prestigious institutions. It is doubtful if all these measures to widen the scope and access to higher education will have produced much change; élites who will by the turn of the century occupy the top positions in society will only be slightly less middle-class than before. By this and similar yardsticks of success equality of opportunity will have been unattainable.

THE ANATOMY OF FAILURE

In view of the vast sums of money expended - during the 1960s the proportion of the GNP spent on education in the leading European countries increased by a minimum of 2 per cent - the enthusiasm for education of ordinary people, the devotion of the teachers, and at least the complaisance of governments, why did the "great leap forward" fail? Here there is space to deal with only four arguments that might be advanced in explanation: one technical, one psychological, one economic, and one - the most disputable - political.

The technical argument concerns regional disparities within countries and between countries.(15) The inter-country differences are not our concern here, although we may note that they are broadly speaking a function of poverty and wealth. The "disinherited South" - Mediterranean countries such as Spain and Greece - enjoy less educational facilities than does the more prosperous North, such as the Scandinavian countries. It might be argued that in more agricultural economies education is not such a social necessity as in industrial ones. Within countries one might expect opportunity to be more equalised where population is dense, distances are small, and communications are good. Belgium,(16) territorially small and with one of the highest population densities in Western Europe, would - and does - experience less difficulties than does Sweden, with a territory over 1,000 miles in length, and extending to the difficult climatic conditions beyond the Arctic Circle. Thus, although Sweden, in post-compulsory education, offers 23 "lines" or options, many of these are only generally available in the areas around Stockholm, Goteborg and Malmo. In France a large number of options are available in upper technical education, but in order to take advantage of the less common ones, it is often necessary to go as a weekly boarder - as do, in fact, some 10-15 per cent of French children in this age range. In such circumstances the technical argument spills over into the psychological: parents and pupils alike are often not willing to take advantage of facilities offered when to do so entails leaving home.

The technical argument also overlaps with the cultural. Even in countries where arguments of distance do not apply, regional disparities - not necessarily related to financial provision - persist. In Britain latest statistics show a higher than average Age Participation Rates in higher education for Southern and North-West England and lower than average ones for the Midlands, East Anglia, the North, Yorkshire and Humberside.(17) In all these areas difficulties relating to distance do not apply. Since youth unemployment can no longer be a factor because it is now so widespread and general, the disparity would seem to be cultural. This is confirmed by the figures for Wales and Scotland, where the A.P.R. is higher than average and yet accessibility can present problems. Commonly the Welsh and the Scots are alleged always to have held education in greater esteem than the English. Likewise Northern England has traditionally not prized it as much as the South: the latest UCCA figures show that in 1982 London and the South-East provided 39 per cent of first-year undergraduates, and for Oxford the figure, at 48 per cent, was even higher.(18)

At school level also, cultural differences would seem to play a part. In 1961 in West Germany there were considerable fluctuations in the percentage of 16-19 year-olds participating in full-time education: in Saarland, the proportion was 12 per cent; in West Berlin, 21 per cent. Furthermore, out of the 24,500 municipalities that make up the Federal Republic, some 8,000 at the time did not have one single pupil in the age group in full-time education.(19)

Nor would this appear to be a phenomenon confined to largely decentralised or semi-centralised systems such as Britain and West Germany. In Southern France, attendance beyond the school leaving age is much higher than in the North, although in the Midi access to educational institutions is much less easy than in the more densely populated areas of the industrial North.(20) So clear-cut is the distinction that the dividing line almost follows the old linguistic separation between the "langue d´oc" and the "langue d´oil", as if the areas where Roman influence were strongest have been bequeathed a stronger · cultural legacy. Until recently, of course, employment was much easier in the North, and this undoubtedly played a part. The explanation may also lie in the youth culture, more sophisticated in urbanized areas, more anxious to turn its back upon education. The French are perhaps more aware than others of regional disparities and have attempted to deal with the problem. The centralised administration has been able to devise a "school map" for the whole of the country, which is periodically updated to take account of population shifts and local economic needs, and ensures a more rational - and hence fairer - distribution of educational institutions. The territory is divided up into "rural", "mixed" and "urban" sectors, and planning takes place on the assumption that 25 per cent of children will leave school at 16, 40 per cent will follow some form of technical education beyond that age, and a further 35 per cent will stay in academic education until 18. The system of methodical divisions has, however, been criticized as not being helpful to equality of opportunity: "Zoning simply confirms segregation according to housing".(21) A lower comprehensive secondary school in the Paris "Red Belt", or for that matter in the Gorbals district of Glasgow or downtown Cleveland, is not the same as one in Passy, the Cathcart area, or Shaker Heights. Unless housing types are suitably mixed, "ghetto" schools will most certainly arise in the slums. Moreover, there are practical difficulties in equalising the location of institutions. Local employment needs change rapidly. The pace at which depopulation of rural areas has gone on, which has been such a feature of areas such as Brittany or Baden-Württemberg, is unpredictable, as is the rate at which settlements in large towns of immigrant colonies have occurred - North Africans in Lille, Pakistanis in Bradford, or Turks in Frankfurt. On the whole, however, a central authority is better able to cope with such changes. But to ensure that regional disparities are entirely levelled out requires a degree of direction from the centre that few democracies would be willing to accept, even in the cause of educational equality.

Another cause of failure in the 1960s, far less apparent, if at all, in Britain, but most striking in France and West Germany, was the somewhat unexpected phenomenon of the reluctance of a section of the industrial and agricultural workers to seize the opportunities that were offered their children. In France, peasants not only feared the loss of labour and income that would occur if their children were not on hand to help them, and instead went off to study at the university, but they also harboured the feeling that their more educated children would grow away from them; the boy would become "un petit monsieur" - "a little gentleman" - who would be ashamed of his social origins and want nothing more to do with his parents. In West Germany, Grimm(22) came up with a similar conclusion regarding industrial workers, who, he noted, were wary of secondary (grammar) education for their children. This "social distance" on their part took two forms: the first was a sheer lack of information; the second, Grimm termed "affective distance", where fathers wanted their children to follow the same occupation as themselves. Another sociologist, Hitpass, documented this still further. Secondary education was only for the rich. The German "Gymnasium" appeared to the industrial worker to be "strange, threatening, unpleasant, rigid, demanding"; as for the university, this was even worse, being "located in space, sinister, incomprehensible like Picasso". Today these attitudes are not very prevalent. In England, however, there is some evidence that the loss of unemployment benefit if a child stays on at school is unacceptable to the family, where the adults are unemployed. By contrast, the middle class, when faced with the possible unemployment of their child, tend to insist upon his continuing his schooling. Not only, therefore, is there a psychological handicap to be overcome, but equality of opportunity would seem to postulate a minimum of economic wellbeing.

The economic argument has also influenced the doctrine of equality of opportunity in another way. The postulate that prosperity was dependent upon educational expansion was launched by Schultz with his celebrated paper on "human capital" in 1960. At an OECD conference in Washington this view received the approval of the Western nations, although at another OECD conference before the decade was out misgivings as to the accuracy of the postulate were already being voiced. Does more education produce more economic growth, or does more economic growth produce more education? It has been argued that it all depends upon the circumstances. Looking back on a decade and a half of almost continuous educational growth, we can see that economic prosperity has not proceeded pari passu with educational development. Since education is a long-term enterprise it was argued that we should not expect an immediate economic return. It is about now, if the theorists are correct, that we should be reaping the economic benefits of the educational seed sown in the 1960s. We are, of course plunged into the worst economic blizzard since the 1930s.

As economic prosperity eludes us, public disillusionment with education has become widespread. Teachers have been vilified, and educational cuts produce nothing but muted reproaches all over Western Europe. In Britain, the Ruskin College speech and the "great debate" that followed became the occasion for condemnation of the education system by politicians and the general public alike. In France, the economic planners no longer give overriding attention to education in the National Plan. Nor has the recent alternance of power in Britain (1979), France (1981), Sweden (1982) and West Germany (1982) meant any change of heart on the part of the political authorities. It would seem that, at least for the time being, the expansion of educational opportunity, which came to an abrupt halt with the "oil crisis" of 1974/5, cannot win justification on economic grounds.

The functionalist sociology that seemed to legitimize equality of opportunity has also been challenged by neo-

Marxists who do not believe that it is an attainable goal in a
capitalist society. The "new" sociologists are a European
phenomenon. Already in 1966 Bourdieu could declare: "What the
education system both transmits and requires is an aristocratic
culture and, above all, an aristocratic relationship with
it".(23) By 1970 this had blossomed out into a full-blown
theory of the educational system acting as the agent of
cultural "reproduction",(24) where the culture was that of the
dominant class. Schooling under capitalism could do no more
than reproduce already existing inequalities, legitimising them
in order to provide a docile work force. By 1973 such theories
had found currency in Britain and West Germany. Bourdieu
elaborated a theory of cultural capital, which children inherit
(or, in the majority of cases, fail to inherit) from their
parents:

> The educational system reproduces all the more
> perfectly the structure of the distribution of
> cultural capital among classes (and sections of a
> class) in that the culture which it transmits is
> closer to the dominant culture and that the mode of
> inculcation to which it has recourse is less removed
> from the mode of inculcation practised by the
> family.(25)

Bourdieu's associate, Monique de Saint Martin, was even able to
quantify: in the extended family, among industrial workers 0.80
adults had been in some form of higher education, as compared
with 4.04 adults in a family of top-level scientists.(26) An
even more overtly political analysis had been made in 1971 by
Baudelot and Establet, who claimed that certain school subjects
had been reserved by the ruling classes for themselves (Latin,
French classical literature and modern languages) because:

> In reality the dominant class requires this body of
> literary knowledge to reinforce its ideological
> identity, to be aware of one another, to distinguish
> itself from the dominated classes and to impose its
> domination upon them.(27)

Thus the less privileged are, for example, fobbed off with
history textbooks which "tend to form proletarians passively
subject to the dominant ideology, whilst the élites are
learning through history how to become the interpreters of
bourgeois ideology".(28) Massive reinforcement of these views
had already come to Britain - and to a lesser extent, to Sweden
and West Germany - from across the Atlantic. Jencks'
Inequality (1972) concluded that in the search for a more equal
society schools were "marginal" and that real equality in
society could only come about through a redistribution of
income. Sam Bowles also echoed Bourdieu's thesis.(29)

Particular attention was paid to language. In the early 1960s Bernstein partly explained the inferior attainment in school of working class children in terms of a middle class language code which was unknown to them and yet the one in common use in school. In West Germany research based on Bernstein's work, carried out in 1965, by H.Oevermann(30) showed that "codes" existed also in German schools. In France Bourdieu and Passeron confirmed that "the unequal distribution between the different social classes of a profitable linguistic capital" inhibited school attainment. Monique de Saint Martin again substantiated this concretely: among university students those who said they did best in French at school came from the top social groups, those who said they did worst from the ranks of the industrial workers.(31) This was because the "pedagogical language" of the school accorded well with "bourgeois" language.

Bourdieu summed up the position generally as follows:

> The culture of the élite is so near to that of the school that children from the lower middle class..... can acquire only with great effort something which is given to the children of the cultured classes - style, taste, wit - in short, those attitudes and aptitudes which seem natural to members of the cultivated classes.(32)

Little of this was, of course, new. As early as 1964 Wiseman had demonstrated the predominant influence of the home on a child's performance in school. The findings of the Plowden Report (1967) gave added force to this view. What was new were the political implications, and the belief that no interventionist policies to compensate for educational disadvantage were likely to prove successful.

The political mood of disillusion that followed the initiation of the drastic educational reforms of the 1960s set in gradually. In France, the events of May 1968 were the catalyst. In the end, although not immediately, they contributed to the downfall of de Gaulle. In his memoirs this ex-son of a schoolmaster turns his invective against the teachers who, he claims, sabotaged the reasonable reforms that his ministers of education had tried to introduce. In Britain, when the Conservatives returned to power in 1970, the great debate of the decade regarding the nature of secondary education was placed in the background. The 1972 White Paper dealt with it hardly at all. In West Germany, although the Social Democrats were at last in a position to effect large-scale educational reforms, they were curiously loath to do so. It was as if the example of other countries had deterred them. In Sweden, the Social Democrats introduced an educational system that was in many ways enlightened, but they finally lost the power they had clung to for thirty years because of allegations that educational opportunities were not equal and because of the way in which young people were beset by problems of sex, alcohol and drugs. As a result, the right wing coalition that succeeded them backpedalled on education. In Britain, the Labour government, whose pioneers such as R.H. Tawney had been the great protagonists of equality, indulged in fierce criticism of the educational system as it had developed. Everywhere in Western Europe the educational party was over. It was plain that from the mid-1970s education, whether for equal opportunity or for economic prosperity, was no longer the "priority of priorities" that it had once been for politicians and public alike.

INEQUALITY IN THE 1980s

It is apparent that the equalisation of opportunities through the methods employed to date have not been a success. Even in the U.S.S.R. there is evidence that shows that in the mid-1970s a child's social status "determines to a considerable extent" his chances of entering higher education.(33) The evidence of failure in Britain - which can be mirrored by similar evidence from other European countries - is overwhelming. In Britain the social composition of the university population has not changed significantly for a quarter of a century. Indeed there is evidence that chances may have grown more unequal. In 1956 there were proportionally more working class men and women accepted for entrance to university (26.8 per cent men, 19.1 per cent women) than in 1980 (20.1 per cent men, 18.5 per cent women).(34) This may indicate that a larger proportion of the working class have opted for the polytechnics, which of course did not exist as such in 1956. In medicine, always a key indicator of democratisation, working-class men continued to be under-represented, although the proportion had remained at 17 per cent between 1956 and 1980, and the proportion of working-class women had increased substantially. Basing themselves upon research on the period of the early 1970s Halsey et al.(35) have recently shown how the father's social class determines the successive stages of educational selection:

Father's social class	Whole Sample	O Levels	A Levels	University
Service class	13.7	35.5	49.1	52.4
Intermediate class	31.4	34.2	29.4	27.9
Working class	54.9	30.2	21.5	19.7
Total	+/-100	+/-100	+/-100	+/-100

Despite the predictions made in the late 1960s and early 1970s
Martin Trow states categorically that "Western European nations
are not moving steadily towards a diversified system of mass
higher education".(36) Selectivity, and hence elitism, remains
as before, based strongly upon social class.

Smaller European countries have fared no better. Evidence
from a very democratic country, Norway,(37) shows that in 1975
in its higher education system, which offers forty possible
specialisms, only in two cases does the lowest socio-economic
group provide more than ten per cent of the total number of
students. By contrast, for the top group (socio-economic group
I) only in three cases out of forty does the proportion drop
below thirty per cent of the total. For medicine and
architecture, the more prestigious fields of study, Group I
provides over 57 per cent of all students. The report
concludes:

> ...there is a clear tendency that long-term studies
> (e.g. medicine, architecture, law) are dominated by
> the upper social classes .

These choose the university in preference to a lower-status
institution. All efforts have resulted in little real change.

CONCLUSIONS

Whether the neo-Marxist is right or wrong, he offers no
alternative to the present system and must consequently be
rejected. Yet we can but accept the verdict of a high OECD
official who stated in 1975 that as regards equalising access
opportunities there had been a "disappointingly limited
impact". Anweiler et al., citing Sweden, declares that:

> the school system can only to a very limited extent
> act as a valid instrument for the dismantlement of
> inequality; the "inherited environment" of the family
> and social class remains the most important factor
> for deciding one´s school career and occupation.(38)

There is indeed some evidence that goes to show that attempts
to equalise educational opportunity may be counter-productive
and result in the even greater promotion of the already
privileged. We may accept the Swedish view - although the
Swedish experience does not necessarily bear this out - that
equalising educational opportunities must go hand in hand, or
even precede, other social reforms. We can also but continue to
accept the functionalist view that a more just, more equal
society may arise from a more rational distribution of
educational chances. What the experience of the last two
decades has taught us is that the methods we have employed up
to now have failed. In Horace Mann´s terms, education may yet

A Comparative Political and Sociological Analysis

prove to be the "great equalizer". <u>Eppur si muove</u>.(39)

NOTES AND REFERENCES

1.Shell,K.L. (1970): "Demokratie", in: Görlitz,A. (ed): <u>Handlexikon zur Politik-Wissenschaft</u>, Munich, p.56.

2.In: <u>Lectures on the Principles of Political Obligation</u>, delivered at Oxford, 1879-80.

3.For this reference I am much indebted to my pupil, Dr. Hee-Chun Kang, <u>Educational Policy and the Concept of Equality of Opportunity in England, 1900-70</u>, Unpublished Oxford D.Phil. thesis, 1982.

4.Nietzsche,F., in a lecture delivered at Basle in 1872 entitled, "On the Future of our Educational Institutions", quoted in: Craig,C. (1978): <u>Germany, 1866-1945</u>, Oxford, pp.187-8.

5.Peisert,H. (1967): <u>Soziale Lage und Bildungschancen in Deutschland</u>, Frankfurt.

6.Ringer,F. (1979): <u>Education and Society in Modern Europe</u>, Bloomington, Indiana, p.344, Table XIII.

7.Ringer,F., op.cit., pp.347-8, Table XIV.

8.Ibid, p.311, Table VII.

9.Dahrendorf,R. (1965): <u>Bildung ist Bürgerrecht</u>, Osnabrück, p.51.

10.The most comprehensive review of Swedish Education to date is by Boucher,L. (1982): <u>Tradition and Change in Swedish Education</u>, Oxford.

11.For a brief summary of the period, cf. Halls,W.D. (1980): "Education in the Third Reich and in the Federal Republic of Germany, 1939-64", in <u>Aspects of Education</u>, No.22, Hull, pp.122-35.

12.Dahrendorf,R. (1968): <u>Society and Democracy in Germany</u>, London, p.74.

13.Department of Education and Science. Circular 10/65.

14.Baudelot,C. and Establet,R. (1977): <u>L'école capitaliste en France</u>, Paris, p.127.

15.An interesting discussion of this phenomenon on a

A Comparative Political and Sociological Analysis

European scale is given in Ryba,R. (1979): "Territorial Patterns of Diversity in Education", Comparative Education, (Oxford), 15:3, October 1979, pp.251-6.

16.Cf. Halls,W.D., "Belgium: A Case Study in Educational Regionalism", Comparative Education, (Oxford), Vol. 19, 2, 1983.

17.Farrant,J.K. (1982): "Trends in Admissions", in Fulton,O. (ed): Access to Higher Education, Society for Research into Higher Education, London, p.63.

18.Oxford University Gazette, Supplement (2) to No. 3892 of 23 September 1982, Table II, p.20.

19.Peisert, op.cit.

20.Beattie,N., "The French Schools Map in Context", Comparative Education, (Oxford), 17:3, 1981, pp.263-9. For an earlier discussion of the French rural-urban phenomenon, cf. Halls,W.D. (1967): "Les effets de l'Urbanisation sur l'éducation française", International Review of Education, 13:4.

21.Beattie, op.cit., p.268.

22.Quoted in: Hitpass,J. (1965): Einstellungen der Industrie-Arbeiterschaft zur höherer Bildung, Ratingen, pp.7-8.

23.Bourdieu,P. (1966): "L'école conservatrice: les inégalités devant l'ecole et devant la culture", Revue française de sosiologie, 7:3, July-September 1966, pp.325-47.

24.Bourdieu,P. and Passeron,J-C. (1970): La Reproduction. Eléments pour une théorie du système d'enseignement, Paris.

25.Bourdieu,P. (1973): "Cultural Reproduction and Social Reproduction", in Brown,R. (ed): Knowledge, Education and Cultural Change, London, p.80.

26.Saint Martin, Monique de (1971): Les fonctions sociales de l'ensiegnement scientifique, Paris, p.60.

27.Baudelot and Establet, op.cit., p.149.

28.Ibid, p.160.

29.Bowles,S. and Gintis,H. (1976): Schooling in Capitalist America, London.

30.Oevermann,U. (1970): Sprache und soziale Herkunft,

132

Berlin (West).

31.Saint Martin, Monique de, op.cit., p.198.

32.Bourdieu, 1966, op.cit., quoted in translation in: Hargreaves,D. (1982): The Challenge to the Comprehensive School, London, p.72.

33.Dobson,R.E. (1977): "Social Status and Inequality of Access to Higher Education in the U.S.S.R.", in Karabel,J. and Halsey,A.H. (1977): Power and Ideology in Education, London, p.269.

34.Farrant, in: Fulton, op.cit., p.60 and p.87.

35.Halsey,A.H. et al. (1980): Origins and Destinations: Family, Class and Education in Modern Britain, London, Tables 2.1 and 10.6.

36.Trow,M. (1982): "Comparative Perspectives on Access", in Fulton, op.cit., p.95.

37.Aamodt,P.O. (1982): Utdanning og Sosial Bakgrunn (Education and Social Background), Statistik Sentralbyra, Oslo, p.166 and Table IV, p.202.

38.Liegle,L. and Sussmuth,R., (1980): "Einführung" to: Anweiler,O. et al., Bildungssysteme in Europa, 3rd Edition, Weinheim, p.29.

39.Husén,T. (1979): The School in Question, Oxford, passim, with great experience of international trends, appears to draw an even more pessimistic conclusion.

Chapter Nine

HIGHER EDUCATION IN THE UNITED STATES: SOME POSSIBLE LESSONS
FOR THE UNITED KINGDOM

Nigel Grant

INTRODUCTION

Comparative educationists, quite understandably, have become
wary of the notion that other systems can readily be used as a
quarry for educational ideas. Uncritical importation, without
regard for context, has been tried often enough in the past.
Sometimes it has worked well enough; more often, however, the
results have been as incongruous as the reassembly of Cotswold
forges or Norman castles in America or, worse, as damaging as
the liberation of rabbits in Australia, where they multiplied
to plague proportions in a quite different environment. Former
British and French colonial territories (and, for that matter,
Scotland and Ireland) can offer plenty of examples of both
types of educational borrowing. It is not surprising that
comparativists have tended to shy away from being cast in the
role of educational import brokers.
    Needless to say, this does not mean turning our backs on
our own systems. As Vernon Mallinson put it:

> By the expression "comparative study of education" we
> mean a systematic examination of other cultures and
> other educational systems deriving from these
> cultures in order to discover resemblances and
> differences, and why variant solutions have been
> attempted (and with what result) to problems that are
> often common to all. To identify the problems of
> education thus becomes the most important preliminary
> task of the research worker in the subject. <u>To
> become familiar with what is being done in some
> other countries other than their own, and why it is
> done, is a necessary part of the training of all
> serious students of educational issues of the day.
> Only in that way will they be properly fitted to
> study and understand their own systems and to plan
> intelligently for the future which....is going to be</u>
> one where we are thrown into ever closer contact

with other peoples and other cultures.(1)

Insistence on the importance of context __and__ the relevance of perception gained to our own situation could hardly be more clearly stated.

The argument, however, can be pushed a little further. Mallinson refers also to "the basic cultural changes which have taken place with such astonishing rapidity throughout the nineteenth and twentieth centuries", and it is becoming ever clearer that the pace of change is accelerating and likely to go on doing so. This means new responses to new challenges, new institutional structures and learning modes to meet new educational needs. Complete originality, however, is as rare in education as in anything else. We adapt, usually minimally, our own institutions and procedures, sometimes; or we take models from elsewhere, sometimes (but too rarely) adapting them suitably to take account of the "resemblances and differences" between the cultures concerned. As already observed, the results are not always happy, but this can be attributed to inappropriate borrowing and insufficient adaptation rather than to the process itself. There have been occasions in the past when a new need arose for which the indigenous system lacked a suitable model, and when ideas and practices from elsewhere, intelligently modified, were able to fill the gap. The spread of the Folk High Schools throughout Scandinavia is a case in point, as is the use of Scottish models for the development of Civic Universities in England. More recently, the Open University developed its credit system - a central feature of its operations - in the light of models from Scotland and North America, but shaped them differently to fit its own needs.

It must be obvious to anyone working in higher education in the United Kingdom that the system is in deep crisis. The most pressing aspect of this is, of course, the shortage of resources, but this is not the whole of it. Most demographic projections spell out a drastic fall in numbers if the present patterns of admission are adhered to. At the same time, new needs are arising and old needs are being cast into a new clarity. The social class composition of the intake has hardly changed since pre-War days; it is difficult for people in employment, or in geographically remote areas, or in groups which have missed out on the usual sequence through academic schooling to further their studies. The institutional gap between universities, other higher education institutions and further and adult education is still wide, paradoxically producing both gaps and overlaps in provision. In England at least, the specialist nature of the syllabus closes options (in the school and in subsequent careers as well as in the higher courses themselves). Most important of all, perhaps, there is little provision for lifelong and recurrent education in the mainstream of the system. There have been some improvements, here and there, in all of these fields, but on the whole the

existing structures have proved resistant to the changes needed
to meet these challenges. Again, this is partly because of the
shortage of resources, for this tends to inhibit rather than
encourage innovation. But it would be as well to admit that we
are not just short of money; we are also short of workable
ideas. It is worthwhile, therefore, to look around for possible
sources (subject to the safeguards already mentioned, of
course) and ask whether the Americans, among others, have
anything to teach us.

AMERICAN HIGHER EDUCATION - MYTH AND REALITY

For many British academics who are ignorant of comparative
education (the vast majority), the very suggestion that we
might have anything to learn from the USA, of all countries,
and in higher education, of all sectors, is hardly acceptable.
Many, of course, have had enough experience of the American
higher educational scene to avoid the grosser superstitions,
and some universities have gone so far as to establish links
and exchanges with their American counterparts, but myths about
the academic world across the Atlantic are still common enough.
It is not all that long since the "awfulness" of American
education, particularly higher, was being widely offered as an
argument against making much change in the existing state of
things in the United Kingdom. The Panglossian assumption that
all is ordered for the best in our own institutions has been
shaken by governmental hammer blows during the last few years,
but the assumptions that things are worse elsewhere remain.
Crudely, they might be summarised as follows.(2)
    American universities, it is often asserted, are raw,
inexperienced institutions. Some of them may be allowed a
certain vigour, but they lack the stability that only
continuous and long tradition can give. They are massive in
size - 40,000 or even 80,000 students - and therefore bound to
be remote, impersonal degree factories. Academic standards are
generally much lower than they are here; comparisons are often
made between an American first degree and a decent A level or
Higher grade group (not always to the advantage of the former),
and degrees in driver education and cosmetology are instanced
as examples of the kind of thing they will admit to the
curriculum; they even have remedial reading classes. As for the
curricula, these are made up of bits and pieces with no
coherent overall structure and no opportunity for study in
depth. Many of the functions of this mass system of higher
education are really the equivalent of British secondary
schools. Even so, barely half of this huge intake make it to
first degree level, the rest dropping out during the course.
    Myth, by most definitions, is a fanciful account that may
include elements of fact; so it is with these perceptions of
higher education in the United States.
    The question of lack of experience or continuity can be

Higher Education in the United States

easily dealt with. It is true that most American universities
are creations of the present century, but that is true of
Britain as well (and most European countries too, for that
matter). It is also true that many of them are "promoted"
colleges, like Eastern Michigan at Ypsilanti (originally a
Teachers' College) or Western Michigan at Kalamazoo (an
agricultural college) but that is true of the UK as well, as
witness Strathclyde, Heriot-Watt, Aston in Birmingham, Bradford
and a host of other universities "created" in the 1960s. What
this has to do with quality is not clear in any case, unless we
care to endow our older institutions with some mystic quality
connected with antiquity rather than present activity
(overlooking the fact that even the oldest institutions change
functionally over the centuries anyway).(3) Nor is it clear why
antiquity itself should be held to confer an advantage; but if
it does, the Americans should be the last to worry. Harvard was
founded in 1637, William and Mary in 1693, Yale in 1701,
Columbia in 1754, Dartmouth in 1769 and the state universities
of Georgia and North Carolina in 1785 and 1789 respectively.
This still does not exhaust the list of universities in
existence by the end of the eighteenth century, at a time when
England had two universities and Scotland four. On the whole,
it would seem better to recognise the argument about antiquity
as irrelevant to the case.
    Much the same could be said about size.(4) It is quite true
that some American universities are very large. The University
of Illinois has 60,705 students, Michigan State University over
44,000, Pennsylvania State 63,000, and so forth. Many of the
giants, however, are in effect federations of smaller
institutions, like the University of California (135,000) or
the State University of New York (356,000), whose vast numbers
are in fact spread state-wide over nine and eleven component
institutions respectively. It remains true that many
institutions seem enormous by British standards, like Michigan
or Purdue, both with well over 30,000 students on the main
campus as well as some thousands more in their regional
centres. Even institutions that Americans tend to think of as
middle-sized seem big to most British academics, like Kent
State University, Ohio, with some 25,000 students.
    But conspicuous though they are, the giants are not typical
of the system as a whole; the variety of American higher
education extends to size as to other things. Some of the tiny
institutions are special cases. The Rockefeller University in
New York is essentially a research centre, which explains the
apparently startling staff-student ratio (220 teachers for 112
graduate students); likewise with the Webb Institute of Naval
Architecture in New York, with 14 teachers and ten students. In
a rather different way, Don Bosco College, New Jersey, and
Dropsie College, Pennsylvania, with 83 and 50 students
respectively, specialist religious foundations, hold the record
for small size, but there are many others with students

137

numbered in hundreds rather than thousands. Some are specialist institutes, others liberal arts colleges (often single-sex, like Sweet Briar College in Virginia, with 740 women students), and many are religious foundations (two of which, the Holy Names College in California and Kentucky Wesleyan College, have, presumably by coincidence, student enrolments with the diabolical number 666). Some of the small colleges may be little more than finishing schools, and the fact that every example quoted here is a fully accredited institution may not carry too much weight. But it would be rash to try to correlate size with quality, either way. Universities generally accepted as of high standard come in all sizes: Michigan, Texas, UCLA and others on the large side; others in the middle might include the Massachusetts Institute of Technology (9,365), Georgia Tech. (11,500), the University of Chicago (7,977) and Yale (9,000), while Vassar (2,250) and Oberlin (2,700) look distinctly small. Of the accredited higher institutions in the USA, some are certainly large - 240 with over 10,00 students, 30 with over 30,000 - but there are many more small ones: for every one over 10,000 there are two with fewer than 2,000 students, the average being about 4,500. It is the range and variety, not the average, that is significant.

The question of scale may seem of little relevance, but it has been allowed to influence thinking in the UK. One university principal stated some years ago, when expansion was still generally accepted as the order of the day, that the price of mass higher education on anything like the American scale would inevitably be the growth of huge, unwieldy universities and colleges. When one looks at the figures, however, it would seem that the proliferation of small and medium-sized institutions had far more to do with it.

As for standards, it would be impossible for any fair-minded observer to deny that the accusations are frequently true, though reliable measures have yet to be devised. This applies not only to the non-accredited "box-top" campuses or "degree factories" (of which Ian Paisley's _alma mater_, Bob Jones, is the most commonly cited). Britain has its unrecognised "Mickey Mouse" colleges too, though perhaps they are taken less seriously by at least the native population. That _acredited_ institutions, public and private, can also be extremely mediocre is not seriously denied by Americans; the common European mistake is to assume that the notion of a fairly uniform "university standard" also applies across the Atlantic - hence the tendency of some to generalise from the particular examples they happen to have come across. That there are also institutions that can more than hold their own in the international league is generally conceded; what is less widely realised is that these are not a handful of exceptions, nor are they confined to the "Ivy League" of Harvard, Yale, Princeton and the rest, but include a great many state schools as well - Michigan, California, Chicago, Pennsylvania, Wisconsin and

Texas perhaps spring most readily to mind, but there are plenty of others. Where judgments differ is where the line should be drawn.

But, as usual, it is not quite as simple as that. Although American institutions have their ways (as have the accrediting agencies) of rating universities and colleges by a complex set of criteria (including the degree of selectivity, the number of volumes in the library, the proportion of the faculty with Ph.Ds - not a particularly informative criterion when one considers how much they can vary), it is well known that quality can be uneven within institutions themselves. Even the better ones have their dead spots; and some of the generally mediocre have managed to attract "distinguished professors" with high salaries and lavish research grants, in the hope - sometimes realised - of leavening the lump. Ironically, contraction may be playing a part in this process too. There are many bright younger academics from (say) Michigan or Columbia, products of the great doctorate boom of the 1960s, who have accepted, gratefully, posts in Universities (which had better be nameless) that they would not have considered in better times. These factors, too, are taken into account in the constant "grapevining" by which universities (and schools within them) assess each other, especially when student transfer is being considered.

That elementary and remedial classes are sometimes run, even in generally high-quality institutions, is partly a reflection of the unevenness of high school standards, partly an attempt to give a chance to people who would normally have been prevented by the quality of their schooling from profiting from higher education, and partly a means of keeping options open as far as possible. Why this should be a matter for scorn is not clear, since such practices are becoming increasingly common in Europe, East as well as West. In the USSR, for example, "preparatory faculties" help students from rural areas to catch up with their urban counterparts, on the grounds that there is not much point in favouring the disadvantaged over admission if they are then left to sink or swim, without doing anything to counteract the factors that made such discrimination necessary in the first place. Mank UK universities, even in the present time of contraction, run support courses in study skills for mature students, or elementary classes in languages not widely available at school, or bridging courses for overseas students, without being thought to sully their overall academic standards. The realisation is growing (though slowly) that the quality of a university's work can be judged not so much by what the students are like when they enter as what they are like when they leave. This has long been taken for granted in American higher education: it has yet to be appreciated amongst many British academies.

It is quite true, of course, that there is little scope for

specialist study in depth, even at the more prestigious universities, until the graduate stage. But, unless one accepts the view that specialisation is in some way an essential feature of academic respectability, there is much to be said for continuing beyond school a broader range of study and the chance to sample other areas. The specialist ethos is still taken for granted in most English institutions (though less so in Scottish ones), but this is not so in the USA; and, with the growth of interdisciplinary studies and the realisation that the pace of change requires the capacity to learn and re-learn throughout life, it is being increasingly questioned in England too, however quietly and hesitantly.

As for the drop-out rate, this certainly does seem alarming <u>if</u> one reckons only up to the mid-twenties age-group and <u>if</u> one assumes that the completion of a self-contained, discrete programme of degree-level study is the only justification for going into higher education at all. In the first place, many of those who drop out drop back in again later; the system of earning a degree by the accumulation of credits allows this. More fundamentally, perhaps, Americans are less inclined than the British to regard an incomplete course as wasted time. A relatively open policy gives more people the chance, even if some do fall by the wayside, and many would argue that such courses as they have managed to take represent a real educational gain. Arguably, the first approach could be called an expensive way of opening up the system, which is under pressure anyway - one critic has described the freshman year as "holding a shipwreck to see who can swim" - but the second signifies a somewhat different perception of what higher education is for.

Finally, it has to be recognised that the charge of bittiness does have a good deal of force. The common practice of making up a programme, usually over four years, of credit units each corresponding to a semester's work (or even less) in a particular subject, measured by contact hours, makes transfer and dropping in and out much more feasible and does open more options; but it can result in programmes consisting of a mosaic of unconnected fragments with little intellectual coherence and even less carry-over of perceptions from one discipline to another. Complaints about grade-chasing during the course and total oblivion afterwards are commonplace, and it is frequently observed that even conceptually related courses can be pursued in total isolation. (One example that comes to mind concerns a course on "The social foundations of 20th Century education", in which the visiting professor kept bringing in illustrations from the historical, philosophical and comparative fields; this rather bewildered the students, many of whom felt that these were matters relating to quite separate courses which they had "taken" already. In most cases they had forgotten all about them, but still felt that they had "done" the courses and therefore should not be expected to know the material for the course in question. They were not necessarily typical of the entire group, but certainly represented a large body of opinion).

But it is important not to exaggerate this. The conceptual rag-bag so often complained of is not necessarily typical of actual practice. Safeguards are possible, and frequently effective, by means of curricular patterns with major and minor emphases, required and limited option courses, outside subjects and the like. There is, ironically, the concomitant danger that so far from being diffuse, the curricula can become so rigid that intellectual coherence can succumb to bureaucratic formalism; but that is no more an innate feature of the credit system than is fragmentation. Both dangers are there, of course, but can be and often are avoided.

Little of all this should really need saying, and certainly would not need to be said among comparative educationists. But among British academics and, possibly more to the point, the policy-makers, the over-simplifications, the invalid generalisations and the anecdotal perceptions are still widely current. This is not necessarily anyone's fault; American higher education is diffuse and enormously variable and (with all due respect to the efforts of the accrediting agencies) the procedures for making accurate and objective assessments on such matters as academic standards are imprecise at best. Even for specialists evaluation is difficult. But academics hold their posts (one assumes) because of a high level of expertise in their own disciplines, and this does not necessarily extend to knowledge of educational realities in the USA, or in the UK for that matter. In the more benign atmosphere of expansionist times this was perhaps of little importance; but at a time when we are under increasing pressure to re-examine our institutions and their functions, it is important that we see the wider academic world more clearly if we are to derive useful lessons from it. In particular, if we are to learn anything of consequence from American higher education, there remains a major task of demythologising to be done in our own institutions.

LEARNING FROM AMERICA

That being said, it may be useful to consider some of the distinctive features of American higher education, with particular attention to those which can make flexibility and innovation more feasible, a matter of some urgency in our present fluid and threatened position. Without (once again) suggesting that any one of them could or should be adopted as it stands, three in particular may provide some food for thought.

1. The transferable credit system

Higher Education in the United States

This, as already mentioned, has come in for considerable criticism. Apart from the dangers of bittiness, it can be cumbersome to operate; and, in the American context of great disparity between and within institutions, equivalence may be difficult to determine, and may often turn out to be more formal than real. It does, however, open a number of possibilities much more difficult to achieve in the more specialist and holistic curricula of the UK. Students can change the direction of their studies in the light of their experience and the development of their interests, and are thus less constrained by early and possibly ill-informed decisions. Transfer from one institution to another is commonplace, despite the difficulties over equivalence; and this practice, when properly used, can provide a richer range of offering to the student and a broader base for further intellectual development. Also, in a country where grants are hard to come by (and look like becoming harder), this system is well adapted to combining full-time and part-time study, and makes it feasible to leave and enter higher education as personal circumstances permit. It also makes it possible to service remote areas to an extent rare in the United Kingdom. Satellite campuses can offer courses within the limits of their resources and local demand, as well as drawing on the expertise and facilities of the parent body. People living in more sparsely populated areas are thus not limited to the resources of these areas alone, nor have they to be content with qualifications of limited currency only. By the same token, study need not be confined even to one country, as several current exchange schemes demonstrate. Indeed, the University of Maryland extends its facilities to US servicemen abroad, New England College (New Hampshire) maintains a branch campus at Arundel in Sussex, and so on. The credit system has its problems, but it does extend the potential of "outreach" education in a way that makes the principle itself worthy of close consideration.

2. Community and Junior Colleges

These are too well known to require description here, and the immediate point is not to consider how far they meet the needs of school leavers or how far they adequately discharge the function of a "non-advanced" further education system. The essential point for our purposes is that they can operate - again, thanks to transferable credits - as a part of the same continuum as higher education proper. If all that a student wants (or can manage) is a two-year course leading to an associate degree, that is still a viable and marketable qualification. So far, this is not too different, at least in function, from certain kinds of further education provision in the UK, or post-secondary but non-higher colleges in some European countries. But in the US system the options, once again, are much more open. Desire, circumstances and capacity

142

permitting, it is possible to transfer to a full bachelor's programme at a senior college or university without having to start all over again. A similar idea was floated by Lord James for England and Wales in the form of the Diploma in Higher Education.(5) Short-cycle courses have been developed, rather more effectively, in France, Yugoslavia, Scandinavia and elsewhere, while the Province of Quebec puts all higher education students through such a stage. Again, variability of standards in the US can make equivalence problematical at times, but as a means of securing some degree of flexibility the idea, at least, is of some interest.

3. Extension courses and summer schools

Something like the first of these is familiar enough in the UK, in the form of university extra-mural departments with their evening classes and short courses, on and off campus; the second is much rarer (with, as usual, the exception of the Open University). In the USA, the crucial point once again is that the nearest equivalent to courses of this type are credit-earning, and thus can in their own way make higher education more widely accessible, in both the literal and the figurative sense. Naturally, there are dangers, especially in the latter case. Few who have taught a summer school where what would normally be a ten-week course of daily one-hour meetings is squashed into five weeks of double sessions would expect the students to have much time for reading and reflection. Doubtless it is for this reason that most universities set a limit on the amount of credit that can be earned in this way. Against this, it can be argued that not only does this method spread the availability of courses (teachers in particular are in a good position to benefit), but also that it makes more effective use of university premises, plant and staff; it also provides the chance for staff to work in other institutions and thus maintain some cross-fertilisation at a time when the normal flow of career mobility has been slowing down in the general contraction. Summer schools, certainly, have shrunk in the adverse economic climate of the last few years, but the structure is still there to meet needs as they arise. As for extension classes, it may be regretted that they have to be slotted into the qualification system, that interest alone is not enough to sustain them; but in a world where qualification looms so large, where the Danish Folk High Schools and the WEA are in a small minority in setting their faces against the whole idea (and are having some difficulty in sustaining this position), this form of "outreach" too has its obvious attractions.

At the risk of repetition, it has to be stressed that these are specifically American ways of meeting American needs, and that their particular form (and some of the problems too) are specific to the American context. The position in the UK is different in certain vital respects, notably a much more effective system of student support, a much narrower range of quality (Oxbridge assumptions notwithstanding), and a reasonably effective machinery for checking the comparability of standards in the form, principally, of the system of external examiners. These could be turned to advantage, however, in adapting some of these models. But we are not looking for models only. More important, we are looking for some indications of what can be done (and for indications of some of the dangers too) at a time when new demands are making themselves felt, and when it is becoming increasingly clear that our own institutions cannot deal with them adequately without some major alteration of their structures and procedures.

In the United Kingdom system of higher education the most obvious problems, the shortage of resources, have already been touched upon. In this, the Americans have their problems too, and in neither country can much hope be held out of a return to more spacious days. In the slightly longer term, we also share with the Americans the problem of contraction as a consequence of a decline in the birth-rate, quite apart from the economic climate. At the moment, higher education in the USA is working at about 90 per cent of its capacity (compared with some 70 per cent in industry), but with a drop of about 15 per cent projected for 1990, major shrinkage or major restructuring (or both) can hardly be far off. In our own case, the coincidence of larger numbers of qualified school-leavers with government-imposed cuts in the number of places, has created a surplus of applicants, but in the longer term, as has already been noted, a substantial drop in the age-cohort is expected here too. This means that if the present patterns of course-entry are adhered to - i.e. overwhelmingly, full-time degree courses pursued by qualified school-leavers - further shrinkage can be expected here too. At the same time, public policy has made life much more difficult for the part-time or self-financed student by raising the fees out of the reach of many, to a rather higher level than that in the United States, for example. Thus, extending higher educational services to other types of student becomes not only a matter of meeting wider social needs - which our own institutions have not always been quick to recognise - but also a matter of survival, which may turn out to be a more persuasive argument. For whatever reason, our institutions need to extend their functions and their reach; and, so far, seem less well structured than the American system to do this.

FUTURE NEEDS

In the following suggested areas of need, none is completely barren territory, as it will usually be found that someone, somewhere, has been innovating, often successfully. But they are not widely developed, and lack both the structure and the overall policy to make them widely available.

1. Extension courses, geographical outreach

Adult education is one of the Cinderellas of educational provision in the UK, receiving about one per cent of the total education budget. Some university extra-mural departments are doing lively and imaginative work, but by and large their activities are quite separate from the mainstream university courses; their offerings are not normally part of the degree system at all. As for physical extension, extra-mural classes and the Open University apart, there is hardly any, and in the areas of greatest need (such as the Scottish Highlands and Islands) there is as yet nothing at all. There is some further education provision but, unlike its American counterpart, this does not slot into the higher system either.

2. Effective use of scarce expertise

As our institutions shrink, certain minority specialisms are coming under particularly strong pressure, and justification for maintaining them becomes more difficult in terms of staff-student ratios and the notions of cost-effectiveness under which we are compelled to operate. No one argues that every university can offer (say) Sanskrit, Chinese or Tamil, given the scarcity of experts and the paucity of students taking these subjects; but the desirability of having them available somewhere must be obvious enough. This is why the Scottish Committee of Principals has taken the view that each discipline should be represented somewhere in Scotland at least. (Availability elsewhere in the UK will not do, given the differences between the Scottish and Anglo-Welsh degree structures). Thus, a strong case is made for retaining Polish and Czech in Glasgow and for retaining Turkish and Persian in Edinburgh. As things stand at the moment, however, the value of such resources is virtually limited to the institutions in which they happen to be located; but the presence of Slavonic languages in Glasgow and Oriental languages in Edinburgh is not much help to a student in Dundee or Stirling (or, for that matter, in Strathclyde or Heriot-Watt, though these are located in Glasgow and Edinburgh respectively). Transfer is possible in some cases, but is far from straightforward, and in any event does not apply across the "binary" divide to the rest of the higher educational system. Not only does this impoverish students' choice; it also threatens certain departments. If minority subjects have to stand or fall by the demand for them within one institution alone, they could vanish altogether, to the further loss of the whole higher educational system.

3. Part-time courses

Some universities do offer part-time courses, and some do make it possible to combine full-time and part-time study in various ways. These initiatives tend to be piecemeal, however, and the adaptation for traditional course patterns has usually been minimal. There has been little sign of attempts at a major effort to address, or even to define, the needs of those who have to combine work and study or to vary the pace of study to fit in with work and personal commitments. Nor is there much sign of a coherent policy of meeting the demands of continuing education as new learning needs arise, from the elementary to the advanced. Such initiatives as have taken place tend, once again, to be ad hoc, even exceptional measures. But this, surely, is an area which needs to be developed for the future, in the interests of the wider society as well as of the institutions themselves. The needs are more widely realised than they used to be (which is not saying much), but the structures prove more difficult to adjust.

4. Short-cycle courses

The various British educational systems do not lack middle-tier or short-cycle provision; what they do lack is a credible link between such provision and the higher system. As a result of the fragmentation of post-secondary education (of which the "binary" division is only one approach), directions chosen at the point of entry can be difficult, often impossible to alter. Admittedly, some links and bridges do exist, but again in a piecemeal and ad hoc fashion. There is no systematic machinery for transferring from one line of post-secondary education to another. At a time when the pace of change puts a premium on flexibility, this is surely more rigid than we can justify.

CONCLUSIONS

These are only a few areas where action is called for; the actual attempts here and there to tackle some of these problems point both to a growing realisation of the need and the lack of suitable models. There is a distinct impression that we are groping in the dark. In each case, there is an American parallel, and one of its essential features is the transferable credit system in its various applications. The advantages and dangers of the American method have already been touched on, but we are not here considering the viability of that specific model; like the variability of standards, the huge variety of institutional size, the public-private divide and other features, which are specific to the American system and the conditions under which it has developed. We are not, surely, still at the stage of looking at an American model and asking whether it would work here. We have to look at its essential feature, which seems to be this: by structuring teaching and learning in a series of discrete units - we can call them

modules or some such term if we need to get away from the
specifics of the American case - units that can be varied in
sequence if feasible, and varied in location and mode of study,
it has proved possible to deal rather more effectively than in
the UK with problems such as those outlined above; and this has
worked tolerably well in spite of the great disparity of
standards and the lack of any overall co-ordinating mechanism.
Without making the point any stronger, we can see that a
particular approach to curricular structure opens up many
possibilities in what are to us problem areas. The American
system is not ours, nor are the problems; but the challenges
are similar. If all that American practice does is to give some
idea of what is possible, and can provide the stimulus to
working out our own ways of dealing with these challenges, then
it will have provided something far more valuable than a model
for emulation, namely a lesson in the true sense.

NOTES AND REFERENCES

1.The quotation is from Mallinson,V.: An Introduction to
the Study of Comparative Education, pp.10-11, emphasis
supplied.

2.The strictures on American higher education are mostly
oral, gleaned from a wide range of academic colleagues
throughout the United Kingdom.

3.See for example, Bell,R. and Grant,N. (1974): A
Mythology of British Education, St. Albans, Panther.

4.The enrolment figures are calculated from The World of
Learning 1982-1983, from which some other data, such as
location and affiliation, have also been gathered, though
personal experience of certain US higher institutions (covering
a fairly wide spectrum of standard) has also been used.
Estimates on the use of higher educational capacity and future
projections has been received from the Department of Higher
Education, State of New Jersey.

5.Department of Education and Science (1972): Teacher
Education and Training, (The James Report), London, HMSO.

Chapter Ten

COMPARATIVE EDUCATION AND THE GEOGRAPHICAL FACTOR

Colin Brock

Vernon Mallinson's major contribution to the standard literature of Comparative Education was first published in 1957.(1) After several new editions it is still a popular text, widely used in the colleges and universities of many countries. Like many of Vernon Mallinson's former students I am considerably in his debt, not only for this most readable of texts, but also for his provocative and challenging tutorials. Nonetheless, as a geographer I am bound to record a sense of disappointment at the treatment of the "geographical factor" in that text. Ryba(2) has described Bereday's approach to the same issue as being "unsophisticated" - a clear case of comparability, one feels.

And yet one must also record that Mallinson always encouraged an indulgence in one's formative discipline, seeing comparative studies in education as a collaborative rather than a polymathic exercise. Thus I was encouraged to make some modest contributions to what is coming to be known as "the geography of education",(3) which combine to provide the basis of this paper. So lest my initial criticism be thought somewhat churlish in the context of a Festschrift, I am confident that my mentor will accept it as the identification of a point of departure for an attempt to repay the debt in a spirit of mutual interest.

A GEOGRAPHY OF EDUCATION

It is not only Mallinson and Bereday who have treated the "geographical factor" in a limited, deterministic and usually physical way. Indeed, all other major contributors to the standard literature of this field either adopt a very similar approach, or even fail to mention it at all. Again, there are mitigating circumstances. As I have argued elsewhere:

> That the image of the geographical factor is outdated
> is at least as much the fault of geographers as it is
> of comparativists. Despite the widespread and

developing utilisation of land for educational
purposes, very few geographers have been stimulated
to apply modern techniques of spatial and locational
analysis to these phenomena. It is not surprising
therefore, that geography is viewed by many
educationalists almost exclusively in physical terms,
and even then altitudinal and scenic images
predominate. Consequently, the geographical factor is
seen as a constant, whereas in reality it is
continually changing in temporal as well as in
spatial terms.(4)

Such an image represents a very positive and ingrained type of
misconception. Nothing short of an immersion in modern
geographical practices is likely to have very much effect on
the perceptions of those accustomed to seeing geography as the
backcloth rather than the stage. There is, potentially at
least, a "geography of education". Ryba was calling for it as
long ago as 1968,(5) as well as for a generic compatibility
between geography and comparative education in particular.
    While it is easy to see how the image of geography has
fossilised, given the politics and evolution of the school
curriculum, the relative neglect of educational themes by
professional geographers is nothing short of extraordinary.
According to one university geographer who has grasped this
nettle, the reason lies in an equally bland misconception:

The main reason for the relative lack of interest in
the past, and, despite the important reassessments in
the scope and methodology of geography in recent
years, the present, is probably the assumption by
geographers and others that educational opportunity
and provision are evenly distributed throughout the
population.(6)

    To an educationist, acutely aware of the incidence of
disparities of provision and performance, such naivety may be
beyond belief, but unless and until the spatial skills of
modern analytical geography are taken on board, the quality of
that awareness is likely to be less than objective.
    Modern geography takes a dynamic view of spatial phenomena,
however transitory, and shares with related social sciences
such characteristics as: the establishment of a quantified data
base; the employment of nomothetic models; the "issue-based
approach" as a mode of entry; an awareness of the significance
of the behavioural dimension. It is distinctive in applying
such techniques spatially, and so long as education as a human
activity remains a user of space it will have a geographical
dimension to be analysed, and possibly thereby exploited to
greater advantage in terms of economy and performance. Merely
by relating the four techniques mentioned above to educational

themes, the potential of a new geographical factor in comparative education becomes apparent.

Fig.1 <u>BASIC GEOGRAPHICAL SKILLS APPLIED TO EDUCATIONAL THEMES</u>

SKILL	APPLICATION EXAMPLE
Quantified data base	School mapping
Nomothetic models	Identification of generalised educational surfaces
Issue approach	Spatial implications of alternative policies of educational contraction
Behavioural dimension	Mental maps

From this basic application of everyday techniques of modern geography to educational themes, one may attempt to apply the structural components of geography, as perceived by contemporary exponents, to such themes. For this purpose, models by Haggett(7) and Walford(8) have been selected, and together with suggested applications, comprise Fig.2 and Fig.3.

Fig.2 AN INTERNAL STRUCTURE FOR MODERN GEOGRAPHY WITH EXAMPLES OF POTENTIAL APPLICATION TO EDUCATIONAL PHENOMENA

A. MODERN GEOGRAPHY (Comprises)		
1. Spatial Analysis	a.Theoretical	Spatial interaction theory Expansion Diffusion theory Relocation Others
	b.Applied	Watershed development Urban Problems Others
2. Ecological Analysis	a.Theoretical	Environmental Structures Ecosystems Others
	b.Applied	Natural resource geog. Hazard appraisel Others
3. Regional Complex Analysis	a.Theoretical	Regional growth theory Interregional flow theory Others
	b.Applied	Regional forecasting Regional planning Others

Source: Haggett,P.: Geography: A Modern Synthesis, Harper and Row, 1972, p.583.

Fig.2 AN INTERNAL STRUCTURE FOR MODERN GEOGRAPHY WITH EXAMPLES OF POTENTIAL APPLICATION TO EDUCATIONAL PHENOMENA

B. APPLICATION

(Examples)

Examination of patterns of location of educational provision and activities. The possible effect of policy decisions thereon; secondary reorganisation schemes, abolition of direct grant status. Diffusion of education items, development of education networks, projects and ideas.

Catchment analysis.

Models of educational activity in spatial terms in different urban structures. Educational zonation in cities. Flow of information, materials, students (ref. dual sites, feeder system). Education and town planning, activity grids (e.g. Milton Keynes).

Possible application to the location and work of agricultural colleges and other environmental institutions, e.g. field study centres, whose work may involve modifications to or conservation of the landscape; education/tourism overlap, e.g. National Park education schemes.

Educational institutions as economic growth points in a regional context. The multiplier effect and its geographic consequences. The implications of reorganisation of higher education in spatial terms e.g. College of education rationalisation, development of polytechnics. Journeys to school in regional context, e.g. week boarding comprehensives. Long term effects of interaction between education and other systems, e.g. land use conflicts, priorities and co-operation. Educational zones.

After: Brock,C.: A Role for Geography in the: Service of Comparative Education, Compare, Vol.5, No.3, 1976, p.36.

Fig.3 <u>WALFORD'S MODEL OF DYNAMIC THEMES IN GEOGRAPHY AND ITS</u>
<u>APPLICATION TO EXAMPLES FROM EDUCATION IN A SPATIAL</u>
<u>PERSPECTIVE</u>

Model:

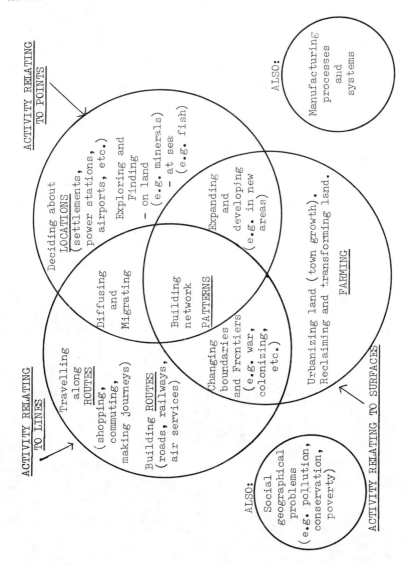

Source: Walford,R.(Ed): <u>New Directions in Geography Teaching</u>,
Longman, 1973, P.105.

Fig.3 <u>WALFORD´S MODEL OF DYNAMIC THEMES IN GEOGRAPHY AND ITS APPLICATION TO EXAMPLES FROM EDUCATION IN A SPATIAL PERSPECTIVE</u>

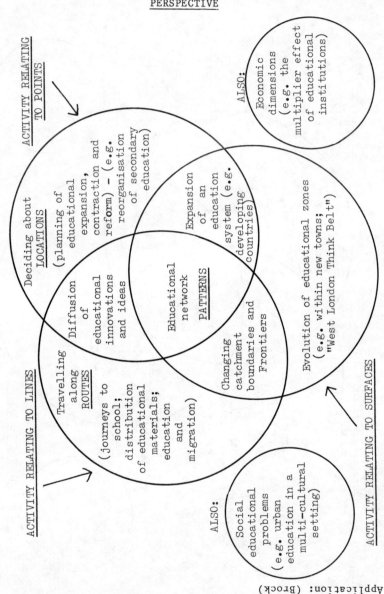

Source: Walford,R.(Ed): <u>New Directions in Geography Teaching</u>, Longman, 1973, P.105.

It is clear from these initial applications of the style and nature of modern geography that almost any facet could be applied to some aspect of education. So one would certainly agree with Rawstron(9) that:

> There is an enormous field of research awaiting enquiry throughout the world.

Two simple examples will suffice at this stage to illustrate geographical dimensions and implications of educational provision, one urban and one basically, though not entirely, rural.

First, sector analysis in urban geography. The massive growth of towns and cities in developed and developing nations alike is a major geographical feature. Given the diffuse relationship between formal education and urbanity, it is not difficult to predict that not only would one find a concentration of educational provision in towns and cities, but also that in terms of status and quality there will be a gradient from urban to rural.(10) Models have been devised to assist studies in urban growth, structure, decay and other characteristics of towns and cities. The general idea behind sector analysis is that certain, sometimes related, activities tend to cluster in distinctive areas of towns, and that there is a dynamic element in the growth and maintenance of such sectors which has to do with differential mobility and structural inertia. Most of this analysis has concentrated on clustering of industrial, commercial and residential features. Why not apply this concept, however crudely in the first instance, to education? Applied to the City of Leeds, for example, we find a clear concentration of "high status" educational land use extending north-west from the centre, indeed confined almost entirely to the narrow sector diverging between the A660 and the A65. Within this zone are located the vast majority of further and higher education institutions, including two of the largest universities and polytechnics in Britain, the most prestigious secondary schools, the teachers' centre and even the offices of the education authority. Fig.4 comprises a simple diagram of this, alongside the outcome of a similar analysis for the City of Kingston-Upon-Hull. There is at least sufficient comparability to encourage further and more sophisticated researches along these lines.

A simple application of distance decay function to primary school enrolment in rural East Africa is illustrated in Fig.5. As applied in this case, the analysis is concerned to find the "break-point" distance between home and school, beyond which a child would be deterred from enrolling or attending. The distance discovered as being crucial will almost certainly not be the same in respect of different routes, and reasons for this may or may not have to do with the incidence of additional spatial phenomena.

Fig.4 <u>EDUCATIONAL SECTORS IN THE CITIES OF LEEDS</u>
<u>AND</u>
<u>KINGSTON-UPON-HULL</u>

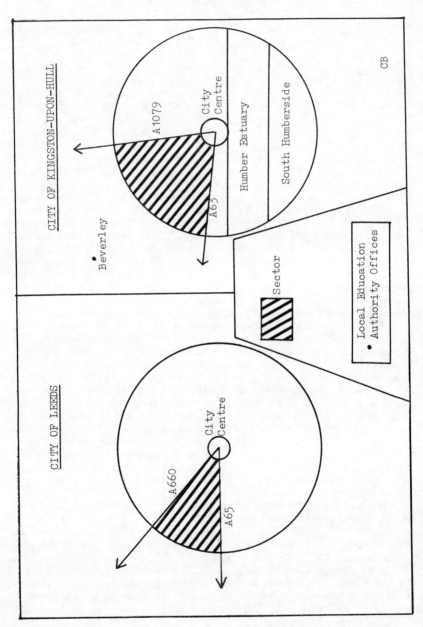

Fig.5 <u>DIAGRAM ILLUSTRATING DISTANCE DECAY FUNCTION IN RESPECT</u>
<u>OF EAST AFRICAN PRIMARY SCHOOLS</u>

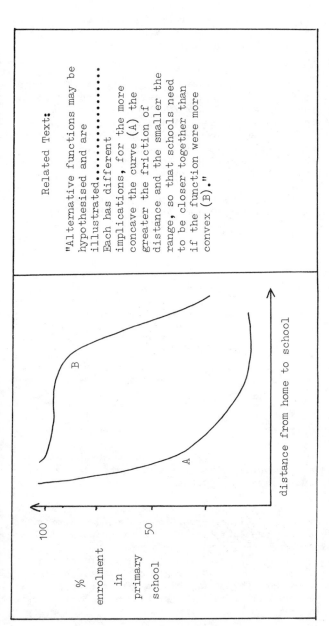

Related Text:

"Alternative functions may be hypothesised and are illustrated............. Each has different implications, for the more concave the curve (A) the greater the friction of distance and the smaller the range, so that schools need to be closer together than if the function were more convex (B)."

Source: Gould,W.: "Geography and Educational Opportunity in Tropical Africa"
<u>Tijdschrift Voor Economische en Sociale Geografie, No.62, 1971, p.88.</u>

> The direct effect of distance may be increased where sending a child to school is considered with the alternative of having the child at home to work on the farm or help with domestic chores, fetching water in particular. The further the child is from school, the more likely it is that keeping the child away from school is considered the more reasonable alternative.(11)

This apparently simplistic observation is in reality a matter of major concern for providers and receivers of education in "third World" rural areas, for its resolution depends on more detailed research into further dimensions of spatial constraint, including the behavioural.(12) The plotting of the results of such a function is at least a first step towards a more accurate understanding of the actual use of what may have been intended as a universal provision of educational opportunity.

Space does not permit of an example of each of the many applications selected for inclusion in Figs.2 and 3, but from the two very basic illustrations given, the potential is clear, and one must wonder again at the neglect of educational phenomena at the hands of the geographers. Even writers in the new and relevant field of "welfare geography" such as Massam(13) and Knox(14) pay scant attention to educational issues. Furthermore, it is clear that not only is there a "geography of education", but that educational activity with its dynamic spatial dimension is itself a geographical factor. That is to say, educational phenomena may act, _inter alia_, as casual factors in the ever changing matrix of human activities on the surface of the earth. As one of a number of geographical factors, does education have a particularly distinctive role? Spencer and Thomas(15) see education systems as being "space adjusting techniques", because:

> they seek to create cultural uniformity and continuity over all the territory occupied by the society operating the educational system.

and Abler, Adams and Gould(16) recognise this factor as crucial to the spatial integrity of any country when they say:

> Part of the information sector of a nation´s space economy is neither product oriented (like most industrial corporations) or service orientated (like most governments). Instead its job is to produce new knowledge, new application of ideas, or to transmit formalised bodies of knowledge and to train people in the knowledge business. Thus a nation´s educational system together with its research and development effort forms a cornerstone for the entire society.

Such perceptions relate to the fields of cultural and political geography, but it is evident also that education, in the widest sense, is a massive economic exercise, a growth point in the modernisation of nations at all levels of development. Much of this expansion in advanced societies is not necessarily taking the traditional form of the establishment of centres of learning at fixed locations. With the provision of new media - the cybernetic revolution - and the massive availability of information for self-selection, the spatial implications of educational activity become more diffuse. Alongside the non-place realm concept of the geographer runs what Price(17) describes as "multi-disciplined self-paced learning", creating new educational complexes and rendering an increasing proportion of plant obsolete. So the economic ramifications of different forms of educational contraction and expansion have significant effects well beyond the circle of those directly involved. For example, the multiplier effect of the establishment and operation of an institution of higher education can be considerable, with geographical consequences outside areas of specifically educational land use. This community and occupational enmeshment of educational space with other forms of space makes a clear case for the development of a "geography of education" replacing the determinism of the geographical factor and capitalising on the generic relationship with comparative education in particular.

Before considering this relationship, especially with respect to the question of scale, a survey of selected literature will serve to illustrate the fact that there does exist a small but significant body of work that can be assigned to various components of this emergent sub-discipline illustrated in Figs.2 and 3 above. For the most part, the pieces of work in question have arisen independently and not as part of any awareness of the building of a sub-discipline as such on the part of the respective authors. It is hoped that the following sequence of surveys will serve to enhance the perception of their kinship and of the distinctive contribution of a geographical approach. They were selected for inclusion in aforementioned conference papers of the writer,(18) without the object of providing an exhaustive list, and broader surveys of the field have been carried out by both Meusberger(19) and Ryba.(20) Reference may also be made to an occasional bulletin of The International Geographical Union.(21)

LITERATURE SURVEY

The following selection of writings, illustrating the geographical dimension of educational provision, is in chronological order of publication.

Cox(22): A Geographical Assessment of Regional Educational Education Patterns: Turrialba Canton, Costa Rica.

Comparative Education and the Geographical Factor

In common with many developing countries, regional education data in Costa Rica is difficult to obtain or inadequate in nature for studies leading to possibilities of rural and community development. Techniques are therefore considered by Cox for using the school, and the school-based community, as the spatial context for the receipt and application of socio-economic information. In reality, this means the catchment area, both in theoretical and effective terms, for each school. In this way, some of the generalisations of data based on political areas not coincident with local community watersheds are avoided. Cox concludes that this technique can be rapid, inexpensive and reliable in obtaining: "a closer approximation to the regional reality". It also has that necessary contact with local attitudes and practices so vital to the grafting of any developmental scheme that may follow.

Gould(23): Geography and Educational Opportunity in Tropical Africa.

In this article consideration is given to the general applicability of geographical approaches to the study of educational phenomena, and within this there is a concentration on: regional differences in educational opportunity; the location of schools; the spacing of schools. Stress is laid on the problems of researching such apparently quantifiable themes, by examining also the degree of colonial penetration; parental aspiration; religious differences and other social disparities. These qualifying factors are related to the quantified patterns of educational provision to form an integrated picture of local and regional infrastructure. The crucial significance of roads, and the application of the idea of distance decay function are also features of this widely ranging article. In the final resort, Gould acknowledges that: "the final decision is a political one", and concludes that a wider perspective would be given to planning teams by the inclusion of a geographer.

Hones(24): Some Problems in the Application of Central Place Theory to Educational Planning, with Special Reference to the Bath Area of U.K.

Hones sees the role of the geographer in the spatial planning of educational systems as being concerned with "the location of individual establishments, their pattern of distribution, and the interacting relationships which comprise the network - as well as relating this to the surface, physical and human, on which the system operates". The modern geographical concept of surfaces is illustrated in Fig.3 above. Hones in effect finds that the application of geographical techniques to educational patterns and practices reveals so great a level of environmental influence that "the use of a theoretical model

160

can be questioned". Local attitudes are also seen to be variable, and crucial to the understanding of the pattern. So this is not really a repudiation of the geographical factor, but a call for greater sophistication and qualification in the spatial analysis of education, and for more detailed case studies to range alongside the theory.

Maxfield(25): Spatial Planning of School Districts.

Maxfield illustrates the capacity of techniques of spatial study and linear programming to enable administrators to reach better decisions concerning the micro and macro planning of school districts. Application is made to the specific problems of overcrowding, desegregation and the assessment of future needs. A dynamic spatial approach is obvious in such statements as: "Within the framework of a multi-locational supply and multi-locational demand problem, the transportation routine solves problems where the end result is to minimise a function of distance (i.e. cost, time, or miles) when many alternative choices of routing are available". A case study of the application of such techniques to a school district in Georgia illustrates clearly the need for a local dimension in the co-ordination of short and long term needs and objectives in the spatial planning of educational provision.

Rawstron(26): Location as a Factor in Educational Opportunity: Some Examples from England and Wales.

In this study, explanation is sought through geographical means, for the immense variations in different aspects of education between the various Local Education Authorities of England and Wales. Rawstron indicates that these cannot be explained merely as inevitable concomitants of a form of decentralisation. If they represent complicated local differences in patterns of facility and attitude, then geographical techniques should help in bringing these to light. He shows how spatial approaches can be made to selected sectors of provision, e.g. "opting out of the maintained sector", and "staying on into further education". Problems of data are raised in a somewhat similar fashion to Geipel (below), but he comments: "It should be emphasised in conclusion that the scope for research extends from the micro study of data for individual school catchment areas to macro analysis leading to the discernment of broad spatial trends". This is a challenge to comparativists to be willing to operate at various levels of scale, and one which informs the next section of the present paper.

Ryba(27): The Geography of Education and Educational Planning.

This is a most valuable study, and one that will become to be

seen as an important formative agent in the establishment of
the sub-discipline "geography of education". Ryba refers to the
dearth of research in this field as being: "paradoxical in view
of the very high proportion of geographers in most countries
who devote themselves on graduation either to education or to
planning". This may be symptomatic of our obsession with
specialisation, leaving a general inability to grasp
interdisciplinary links and carry forward expertise gained at
one stage of one´s educational career to another. Ryba
considers three approaches to be especially worthy of further
consideration: the geographical examination of factors
underlying education; the examination of the spatial patterns
of educational phenomena; the role of education as a factor
influencing the geographical patterns of other social and
cultural phenomena. He goes further than Gould in relating
spatial aspects of education to other space users, and in
predicting in a similar way to Price that educational activity
has a profound and probably increasing influence on patterns of
settlement and networks of activity.

Geipel(28): Regional Research on Education.

In this paper, a résumé is given of the application of spatial
planning to eliminate disparities as between the Bundes
länder of West Germany in respect of educational provision. He
highlights a very real problem for any researcher into the
potentially embarrassing issue of educational disparities,
namely dependence on the co-operation of the authorities
presiding over such irregularities. In this case the
authorities, once alerted to the object of the exercise, in
effect took over the studies and cut out the original workers.
Consequently, Geipel advocates individual research at a very
detailed local level on a case-study basis, in the hope that:
"new aspects of geographic theory will be developed ensuring
the continued importance of the Geography of Education.

Gilbert(29): Spatial Variations in Educational Provision in Colombia.

This is a comment on significant educational disparities
between urban and rural areas; within and between urban areas;
between different administrative areas. The influence of a
strong private sector on public provision is noted in spatial
terms, and the fundamental significance of regional disparities
arising from the decentralisation of funding is regarded as
crucial, together with differential local capacities of teacher
education. Gilbert indicates the particular ability of
educational development to stimulate rural based growth, social
mobility and economic development.

Lowry(30): Schools in Transition.

Lowry's paper is concerned with the evolution of the geography of schools in Mississippi in the mid-twentieth century. In particular, an assessment is made of "residential segregation" as being "a most fundamental facet of the spatial structure of the society", and consideration is given to various informal as well as official movements acting in opposition to the location and racial composition of schools in the State of Mississippi. This article is a valuable insight for outsiders of the dynamics of educational manipulation in social and spatial terms as operable within the socio-political framework of the U.S.A. Lowry concludes: "Integrated education might be fundamental to an integrated society, but in the contemporary United States residential desegregation probably is more so". This is so, especially in view of local funding of educational provision in the U.S.A.

Gould(31): Secondary School Admissions Policies in Eastern Africa: Some Regional Issues.

Secondary schools admissions policies are contrasted between Kenya, Uganda, Zambia and Tanzania. The author outlines regional issues in each of these areas that affect the disparate patterns of enrolment. Differential access in terms of tribal concentrations and variations in colonisation and missionary activity in the past are considered. In effect the establishment of a network of secondary opportunity as a crucial factor in overcoming local and regional bias in social opportunity, and in the building of unified nations, is the burden of the study. It is of interest too in comparing the international differences, especially in view of the common experience of British Colonial administration. The role of an anthropological perspective also comes through. It is concluded that the integrating role will be better achieved through day, rather than boarding secondary schools, though this could also create further rural disadvantage.

Thomas-Hope(32): An Approach to the Delimitation of School Districts: the Example of Primary Schools in the Parish of St. Ann, Jamaica.

The object here is to emulate the care and calculation over location so evident in the economic sphere. The central issue is the minimising of journeys to school in time and distance, so as to reduce the influence of distance decay. The problem arises from disparities in provision, and these are illustrated in relation to population clusters in the parish, by the application of a spatial equilibrium model under linear programme. The selection of additional locations is achieved through the application of the Weberian triangle to each area of deficit. The combination of these techniques deals with the problem of the duality of spatial form and social process. The

value of the study to educational planning lies in the
quantitatively measured cost of alternative policies, and also
in the social implications of spatial considerations - an
efficient yet humane input into resource allocation; in this
case, of accessible primary schools in a developing country.

Ryba(33): Aspects of Territorial Inequality in Education.

Having commented on the curious neglect of territorial notions
in comparative education, this paper sets out to illustrate
territorial inequalities in education at different scales, from
intercontinental to local. The enormity of disparities in
literacy levels as between the various continents precedes a
more detailed discussion on less extreme, but nonetheless
startling, disparities at international levels within Europe,
and arising from a more secure statistical base. For
intranational disparities Ryba takes the case of England and
Wales, and with special reference to enrolment in the post-
compulsory sector he comments on the general correlation
between educational deprivation and other forms of social
disadvantage. This is further developed with reference to brief
observations from developed and developing countries,
introducing the notion of an educational gradient. For the
local dimension he selects intra-urban disparities, showing
that this issue goes far beyond the classically simplistic
"slums and suburbs" dichotomy. In questioning the neglect of
the character of education in many comparative studies, Ryba
succeeds in illustrating the practical potential of a more
sophisticated territorial approach.

Marsden(34): Education and the Social Geography of Nineteenth Century Towns and Cities.

An attempt is made here to focus on the incidence of
disparities in educational provision within urban areas by
examining selected cases, especially London and Bootle, during
the last century. By concentrating on a period of both rapid
urban and suburban development and also of the emergence of a
universal provision of elementary education, Marsden succeeds
in illustrating the interconnections between education and
other strands of the urban fabric and society. In particular,
he examines education in terms of the evolution of "secluded
social areas" within towns, that is to say, residential zones
correlated with social class. Even within such zones he is able
to show very localised nuances in respect of both private and
state schooling. Catchments, journeys to school, sexism, fee
disparities and hierarchies are utilised in order to illustrate
spatial patterns. In conclusion he clearly demonstrates the
dominance of general patterns of social disparity and
deprivation over the potentially ameliorative or even
compensatory qualities of educational provision.

Preston(35): Education and Migration and their Relationship
          to the Occupational Opportunities of Rural
          People in Highland Ecuador.

The main object of this paper is to consider the effects of
national manpower and education policies on remote rural
communities, with particular reference to the role of
migration. The research is based on both documentary and
empirical methods, and looks at five communities especially in
terms of attitudes to education. The relationship between
educational planning and provision is examined, clearly
illustrating rural disadvantage as well as the contrast between
the attitudes and perceptions of urban planners and those of
peasant communities. The section on education and migration
examines rural returnees as well as emigrés, and shows a
generally higher educational level among both groups of
migrants as opposed to the "sedentary" rural populations. It is
made clear that migration does not seem to have damaged the
rural community, rather the reverse, and that the main force to
be confronted is the inertia of spatial disparity in
educational provision - the resistance of the rural/urban
dichotomy.

McPartland(36): The Emergence of an Educational System: a
              Geographical Perspective.

From a brief initial comment on the capacity of a geography of
education to include traditional geographical factors; spatial
variations; education as a geographical factor, the author
applies such perspectives to an analysis of the character of
educational development in colonial Massachusetts. He looks in
turn at the origin, support and control of educational
institutions in that colony in comparison with the position
obtaining in England at the time of colonization. He explains
significant departures from the then metropolitan pattern,
through the themes of distance and movement, migration and
diffusion, and core-periphery forces - all, of course, spatial
concepts. He also introduces the behavioural dimension in
respect of the reaction of settlers and pioneer communities to
their perception of the American wilderness. McPartland
concludes that the adoption of a geographical/ecological
perspective on the formative influences of American education
that persist so strongly, albeit differentially, at the present
day, helps to challenge the conventional view of ideological
dominance in the formulation of an education system.

APPLICATION

The selection of fifteen examples comprising the previous
section of this paper will, it is hoped, make clear the range
and nature of a modern geographical approach to the study of

educational phenomena. Nonetheless, if located on the
application of the Haggett or Walford models, (Figs.2 and 3),
there would be a clustering in the areas relating to applied
geography - planning. While this demonstrates the practical and
dynamic possibilities of the emergent geography of education,
it also indicates the scope for many other applications. One,
for example, is represented in the above selection, namely the
historical geography of education (Lowry, McPartland and
Marsden), and the last-named has in fact made a number of other
significant contributions to this dimension.(37) Other facets
likely to reward further geographical analysis would clearly be
migration and education(38); diffusion of knowledge(39); school
mapping(40); intra-urban disparities and patterns(41).

In many detailed ways, the researches and techniques of
modern geography can, and are beginning to, add their
particular contribution to the armoury of educational studies
in general, but why the particular relevance and potential for
comparative education? For this we must return to the
aforementioned generic relationship between comparative
education and geography, so well endorsed by Spolton(42) and
Fletcher(43), though one must have reservations about
Fletcher's apparent contention that geography subsumes
comparative education. For a more realistic view of their
kinship one may turn to one of Vernon Mallinson's
contemporaries and fellow developer of comparative studies of
education in the colleges and universities, George Bereday.(44)
That Bereday's perception of geography extends beyond the
physical dimension is shown by the fact that among the three
candidates shortlisted by him as suitable foster-parents for
the fledgling "comparative education" is political geography.
Certainly it is at the geopolitical scale of the nation state
that the balance of comparative educational study has been
undertaken. This is not surprising, since the formative phase
of the discipline was a response to the development of official
education systems in the emergent, competitive and imitative
national units of the nineteenth century. Indeed, a modest
geographical scale and a unitary education system are implied
in the amalgam of the five factors reckoned by Hans to be
necessary attributes of the ideal nation.(45)

While in their detailed application the various facets of
modern geography can serve comparative studies in education, it
is in that most fundamental element of geographical perception,
the question of scale, that it can most profitably inform. A
glance at the fifteen studies summarised above is sufficient to
show that their scale of reference ranges from the individual
school and catchment, through local, national, regional and
international levels, according to their particular concerns.
It is true that some leading comparativists are keen to consult
the entrails as well as the carcase. As Holmes has observed:
"The main thrust of comparative education research can be
accommodated within an ecological approach".(46)

Undoubtedly a more sophisticated and updated application of the "geographical factor" will assist.

Both ecological and political parameters can range from the individual to the global, in respect of educational systems. On the political side, it is easier to operate an analysis at various scales because of the discretion of political hierarchies which in many nations carry attendant and distinctive functions in respect of educational administration and provision. Hence the data behind such revealing studies of educational disparities within England as those of Taylor and Ayres(47), and Coates, Johnston and Knox.(48) Also into this category of scale fall the excellent studies of regional disparities in educational development carried out by the International Institute for Educational Planning.(49) There would seem to be considerable scope for comparative study here, the politico-spatial picture having been provided.

Thus far, the term "regional" has been used to refer to divisions within nations - perhaps "provincial" would be better, for regional can also mean a part of the world comprising a number of nations. In some cases, clusters of nations have degrees of interdependence in respect of education. This is especially the case with groups of small countries such as exist in the tropical island zones. In addition to obvious problems of political geography and status, there are other spatial issues to be confronted in terms of the logistics of co-operation, and of both I have written elsewhere.(50) Federations provide good opportunities for comparison between components in respect of education; and as Grant(51) has pointed out in respect of Britain, much ground could be made up here. Indeed, it may well be that, given the relative ease of the data issue within a federal state, some of the methodological issues of comparative study could be worked through. At any rate, there is considerable scope for sub-national and intra-federal research, supported by standard techniques of spatial and locational analysis.

While the ecological aproach must be mindful of the political strand, it also offers the possibility of a greater range of variables becoming available for comparative work, and a change to investigate the dynamics of educational systems at various scales, again from individual to international. Several of the papers reviewed above illustrate the importance of the behavioural dimension in terms of attitudes to education, which should be susceptible of spatial analysis. This would of course need collaboration with anthropological techniques, since a persistence is evident in patterns of educational disparity operating both within and across political and administrative boundaries, that would seem to qualify as a cultural feature. As put by Ryba there is often:

> a complex territorially differentiated factor in educational achievement which may be best summed up

167

> as the cultural traditions in the territorial
> context .(52)

Though such patterns are, at most, provincial in scale, they
would seem to go some way towards the concept of national
character in education, much favoured and promoted by Vernon
Mallinson. Whatever one's assessment of that concept,
discussion of which falls to another paper in this volume,
geographical analysis reveals educational disparity, actual and
attitudinal even in the most centralised of systems.

At a similar dimension of scale, and certainly more
susceptible of comparative analysis, would be attempts to
unravel the dynamic involvement of the educational component of
what geographers term a "regional complex" (see Fig.2). That is
to say a geographical area with a dynamic identity, as opposed
to a politically delimited zone. A regional complex is normally
the sphere of influence of a very large urban area, normally a
city, and it is unlikely that the continually changing area
involved will correspond with any one zone of educational
administration. High status in the urban hierarchy is gained by
the incidence of very special services, examples of which in
the educational field would be a polytechnic or a university,
and these would normally be a component of a regional complex.
As has been mentioned above, such institutions have important
multiplier effects in economic terms, and their case against
Government directed cuts in 1981/2 in Britain has normally
included an illustration of the local and regional effects of
such reductions on non-academic employment. Comparison of a
British case with that of the establishment of the Louvain
Catholic University(53), for example, would certainly be
informative in terms of regional complex analysis.

Universities, given their status internationally, provide
in their networks of operation, a degree of convergence between
the political and ecological dimensions of spatial comparative
analysis. Such convergence is crucial in the operation of
regional universities, such as the University of the West
Indies and the University of the South Pacific, which are
shared, albeit unequally, by a number of nations.(54) So, in
addition to having important community functions at a local
scale,(55) universities:

> are disseminators and producers of knowledge in
> their own nations, playing increasingly important
> roles in technological societies. They are part of an
> international knowledge system as well, interacting
> with institutions abroad .(56)

In the same way as spatial systems analysis could be
employed in comparative studies of university operations at
various scales of reference, so it could be employed in respect
of other sectors of educational activity.

Comparative Education and the Geographical Factor

Whether it be politically or ecologically based, the capacity of the analytical tools of modern geography to accommodate the multi-scale context is at the disposal of any comparative educationist aware of the potential and conversant with the techniques.

CONCLUDING REMARKS

This paper opened with somewhat disparaging comments on the limited perception of the "geographical factor" in standard works of comparative educational study. Such perceptions were limited to physical constraints of the environment. It is not that these do not exist, though recognition should not imply determinism, but rather that geography consists of so much more that is influential upon and influenced by educational activity. The object here has been, through some theoretical discussion, a literature survey, and some application to illustrate that geography is not merely a factor or "a determinant"(57) in respect of comparative education, but a relative with much to invest in mutually beneficial and socially significant study.

NOTES AND REFERENCES

1.Mallinson,V. (1957): <u>An Introduction to the Study of Comparative Education</u>, Heinemann.

2.Ryba,R. (1972): "The Geography of Education and Educational Planning", in Adams,W.P. and Helleiner,F.M. (eds): <u>International Geography</u>, University of Toronto Press, pp.1060-1062.

3.Brock,C. (1976): (a) "La Géographie de l´Education: Aspects de l´Apparition d´une Nouvelle Sous-Discipline", <u>Education Comparée</u>, No.8, pp.11-15. Summary of a paper presented to the 1975 Conference of the Comparative Education Society in Europe, Sèvres.

(b) "A Role for Geography in the Service of Comparative Education", <u>Compare</u>, Vol.5, No.3, pp.35-36.

(c) "The Geography of Education: its Further Development", paper presented to the 1981 Conference of the Comparative Education Society in Europe, Geneva.

(d) "An Examination of the Question of Scale in Comparative Education", paper presented to the 1982 Conference of the British Educational Research Association, St. Andrews.

4.Ibid (b), p.35.

5.Ryba,R. (1968): "The Geography of Education - A Neglected Field"? Manchester University School of Education Gazette, December 1968.

6.Gould,W. (1971): "Geography and Educational Opportunity in Tropical Africa", Tijdschrift Voor Economische en Sociale Geografie, No.62, pp.82-89.

7.Haggett,P. (1972): Geography: A Modern Synthesis, Harper Row, p.453.

8.Walford,W. (1973): "Models, Simulations and Games", in Walford,R. (ed): New Directions in Geography Teaching, Longman, p.105.

9.Rawstron,E.: "Location as a Factor in Educational Opportunity: Some Examples from England and Wales", in Adams,W.P. and Helleiner,F.M., op.cit., pp.1058-1060.

10.Goldblatt,P. (1972): "The Geography of Youth Employment and School Enrolment Rates in Mexico", in La Belle,T. (ed): Education and Development: Latin America and the Caribbean, University of California, pp.283-296.

11.Gould,W., op.cit., p.88.

12.Lee,T. (1957): "On the Relations between the School Journey and the Social and Emotional Adjustment in Rural Infant Children", British Journal of Educational Psychology, XXVII, pp.101-114.

13.Massam,B. (1975): Location and Space in Social Administration, Edward Arnold.

14.Knox,P.L. (1975): Social Well-Being: A Spatial Perspective, O.U.P.

15.Spencer,J. and Thomas,W. (1969): Cultural Geography, John Wiley.

16.Abler,R., Adams,J. and Gould,P. (1972): Spatial Organisation: The Geographer's View of the World, Prentice-Hall International, p.200.

17.Price,C. (1970): "Learning", in Cowan,P. (ed): Developing Patterns of Urbanisation, Oliver and Boyd, pp.186-200.

18.Brock,C., op.cit., (1975 and 1981).

19.Meusberger,P.: The Geography of Education: An Interim Account of its Development, Position within Geography and Future Tasks, (translated by Beattie,N.), University of Liverpool, mimeo, undated.

20.Ryba,R.: On Progress in the Geography of Education, paper presented to the 1979 Conference of the Geographical Association, London, mimeo.

21.Following the 1972 Congress of the International Geographical Union within which a symposium on the Geography of Education was held, a Working Party was set up, and has produced a number of bulletins in the interim(5). These have been compiled and edited by Hones,G. and Ryba,R.

22.Cox,P. (1973): "A Geographical Assessment of Regional Educational Patterns: Turrialba Canton, Costa Rica, in Hill,A.D. (ed): Latin American Development Issues, CLAG, pp.146-157.

23.Gould,W., op.cit.

24.Hones,G.: "Problems in the Application of Central Place Theory to Educational Planning with special reference to the Bath Area of the U.K.", in Adams,W.P. and Helleiner,F.M., op.cit., pp.1053-1054.

25.Maxfield,D. (1972): "Spatial Patterns of School Distribution", Annals of the Association of American Geographers, No.62, pp.582-590.

26.Rawstron,E., op.cit.

27.Ryba,R., op.cit., (1972).

28.Geipel,R. (1973): "Regional Research on Education", in Hones,G. and Ryba,R. (eds): Bulletin No.2, I.G.U. Working Party on the Geography of Education, pp.3-5.

29.Gilbert,A.: "Spatial Variation in Education Provision in Colombia", in ibid., pp.8-12.

30.Lowry,M. (1973): "Schools in Transition", Annals of the Association of American Geographers, No.63, pp.167-180.

31.Gould,W. (1974): "Secondary School Admissions Policies in Eastern Africa: Some Regional Issues", Comparative Education Review, Vol.18, No.3, pp.374-387.

32.Thomas-Hope,E. (1975): "An Approach to the Delimitation of School Districts: the Example of Primary Schools in the Parish of St. Ann, Jamaica", Social and Economic Studies, Vol.24, pp.320-339.

33.Ryba,R. (1976): "Aspects of Territorial Inequality in Education", Comparative Education, Vol.12, No.3, pp.183-197.

34.Marsden,W.E. (1977): "Education and the Social Geography of Nineteenth-Century Towns and Cities", in Reeder,D.A. (ed): Urban Education in the Nineteenth Century, Taylor and Francis, pp.49-73.

35.Preston,R.A. (1978): Education and Migration and their Relationship to the Occupational Opportunities of Rural People in Highland Ecuador, Working Paper 237, School of Geography, University of Leeds.

36.McPartland,M.F. (1979): "The Emergence of an Educational System: A Geographical Perspective", Compare, Vol.9, No.2, pp.119-131.

37.Marsden,W.E. (1977): (a) "Social Environment, School Attendance and Educational Achievement in a Merseyside Town 1870-1900", in McCann,W.P. (ed): Popular Education and Socialisation in the Nineteenth Century, Methuen, pp.193-230.

(1977): (b) "Historical Geography and the History of Education", History of Education, 6, pp.21-42.

(1978): (c) The Geographical Component in Educational History: An Annotated Bibliography, Education Library, University of Liverpool.

38.Bell,M. (1980): "Past Mobility and Spatial Preferences for Migration in East Africa", in White,P. and Woods,R.: The Geographical Impact of Migration, Longman, pp.84-107.

39.Hagerstrand,T. and Kulinski,A. (eds), (1971): Information Systems for Regional Development, Lund Studies in Geography, Series 8.

40.Hallack,J. (1977): Planning the Location of Schools: An Instrument of Educational Policy, I.I.E.P./O.E.C.D. In addition to this key volume a subsiduary series of ten case studies, mainly located in developing countries has been built up.

41.Goodenough,S. (1978): "Race, Status and Urban Ecology in Port of Spain, Trinidad", in Clarke,C.G. (ed): Caribbean Social Relations, Centre for Latin American Studies, University of Liverpool, Monograph Series No.8, pp.17-45.

42.Spolton,L. (1968): "Methodology in Comparative Education", Comparative Education, Vol.4, No.2, pp.109-115.

43.Fletcher,L. (1974): "Comparative Education: A Question of Identity", Comparative Education Review, Vol.18, No.3, pp.348-353.

44.Bereday,G.Z.F. (1964): Comparative Method in Education, Holt, Rinehart and Winston.

45.Hans,N. (1949): Comparative Education, Routledge and Kegan Paul.

46.Holmes,B. (1981): "Models in Comparative Education", Compare, Vol.II, No.2, pp.155-161.

47.Taylor,G. and Ayres,N. (1969): Born and Bred Unequal, Longman.

48.Coates,B.E., Johnson,R.J. and Knox,P.L. (1977): Geography and Inequality, Oxford University Press, pp.208-212.

49.Carron,G. and Ta Ngoc Chau (eds), (1980): (a) Regional Disparities in Educational Development: A Controversial Issue, UNESCO/IIEP.

(1980): (b) Regional Disparities in Educational Development: Diagnosis and Policies for Reduction, UNESCO/IIEP.

50.Brock,C. (1980): "Problems of Education and Human Ecology in Small Tropical Island Nations", in Brock,C. and Ryba,R. (eds): A Volume of Essays for Elizabeth Halsall: Aspects of Education, No.22, University of Hull Institute of Education, pp.71-83.

51.Grant,N. (1981): "The British Isles as an Area Study in Comparative Education", Compare, Vol.II, No.2, pp.135-146.

52.Ryba,R.: "Territorial Patterns of Diversity in Education", University of Manchester, mimeo, 1977 - paper presented at the 1977 World Congress of Comparative Education Societies, London.

53.Lechat, J-M. (1979): "University Influence on Regional Development: Example of a New Creation - the Louvain Catholic University at Louvain - La- Neuve", European Journal of Education, Vol.14, No.3, pp.239-250.

54.Brock,C., op.cit., (1980).

55.CERI, (1982): <u>The University and the Community: The Problems of Changing Relationships</u>, OECD.

56.Altbach,P. (1978): "The University as Centre and Periphery", <u>Journal of Higher Education</u>, Vol.4, No.2, pp.157-169.

57.Mallinson,V., op.cit., 4th Edition (1975), pp.29-37.

Chapter Eleven

THE IMPACT OF EXTERNAL CHANGES ON EDUCATIONAL DEVELOPMENTS IN THE 1980s *

Keith Watson

I. THE EDUCATIONAL CONTEXT OF THE 1980s

Those involved in education have become all too well aware in recent years of the widespread criticisms that have been levelled against schools and education systems, as well as against educationists and their theories generally. In fact, just as in the 1960s it was fashionable to boast about the socio-economic changes likely to result from investment in educational expansion, in the 1970s it became fashionable to criticise schools for their failures. Writers such as Bowles, Carnoy, Coleman, Illich, Gintis, Jencks and Reimer, largely writing for the American market, became universally household names. Fortunately, during the first few years of the 1980s, there have been several attempts at a more sober assessment of the situation from the Carnegie Commission in the context of the U.S.A.; from H.M. Inspectorate in the context of England; and from the World Bank and Simmons et al in the context of the problems facing the Third World.(1)
What are some of these criticisms?

- that schools are failing to prepare pupils adequately for society and for social change;
- that education is an increasingly expensive luxury;
- that the curriculum is unrelated to basic needs and skills;
- that academic standards have declined;
- that schools are instruments designed to maintain the political and social status quo;
- that educational investment has not resulted in improved access or increased efficiency or economic growth.

Let us cite one or two of the more damning indictments.
Torsten Husen, the eminent Swedish educator, has challenged the role accorded to and the assumption behind present day schools in industrial nations, arguing that they have become separate and distinctive institutions set apart from the

175

societies which they are supposed to serve. As a result,

> The essential drawback of the contemporary school,
> when it comes to socialising young people into adult
> roles and responsibilities is that it makes the
> student altogether a <u>dependent</u> .(2)

In other words school is failing to prepare pupils adequately
for the world in which they must live and, hopefully, work.

While commenting on progress made globally in educational
expansion, the first Brandt Commission Report observes that
education has frequently taken a disproportionate share of the
national budget and that "almost every country has begun to
worry about the problem of ´educated unemployment´, and has to
ask the question: are schools and universities teaching the
right subjects to the right people?"(3)

A similar comment has been made in one of the recent
Carnegie Commission Reports on high school education in the
U.S.A.(4) The Report cites the Stanford Research Institute´s
findings(5) into the decline in academic standards as partly
the fault of poor teaching of basic skills, partly the fault of
inadequate teacher preparation, but largely the fault of the
overcrowded curricula:

> the fact that the decline has occurred since the
> early 1960s must be explained in considerable part by
> the increasing tendency for all levels of government
> to require intermediate and secondary schools to
> adapt their curricula to concepts of career
> education, ethnic history, and culture,
> desegregation, sex and family education and the like.
> Thus, new subjects have crowded the curriculum and
> help to explain decreasing emphasis on more
> traditional subjects .(6)

I do not intend to answer these criticisms in detail.
Instead I wish to challenge the widely-held assumption that
schools are largely to blame and to show that they have had to
respond to new situations, unprecedented pressures and changing
relationships(7) to a quite extraordinary degree.

Since the time of Sadler, as Vernon Mallinson has so
clearly shown in his excellent paper, <u>"In the Wake of Sir
Michael Sadler"</u>,(8) all comparative educators have been
concerned to take into consideration the cultural, social,
political, economic and religious features of a society or
nation in analysing an education system. Kandel referred to
"the <u>forces</u> which determine the character of an education
system"(9); Hans concentrated on "<u>factors</u> often common to many
nations"(10) - natural, religious and secular; Mallinson
concentrated, in similar vein, on the <u>determinants</u>(11); and
King has talked about "the <u>contextualisation</u>" of an education

system.(12)

Sadler´s contention in his famous Guildford speech of 1900, that "what goes on outside school is far more important than what goes on inside because it influences and affects what goes on inside"(13); is well known to all comparativists, (though not necessarily to politicians and educational critics). Some of his equally perceptive remarks, however, are far less well known, as for example his comment that:

> great tidal movements of economic or spiritual change sweep over the world with irresistable force........ What the school can do is to bend all in its power to the task of understanding the inner significance of each new and perturbing movement. It should diagnose the symptoms, and seek to detect, and then bravely to remedy the evil against which the movement is a needful though more or less unconscious protest .(14)

Vernon Mallinson made an equally pertinent comment in the last edition of his Introduction to the Study of Comparative Education when he wrote:

> ... each country´s educational system is seen as having its present character, not entirely because it has developed in a certain manner, but also because it has had to make the effort (not always fully successful) to correspond with and adjust itself to the social realities of the times. (my emphasis). In this sense it can be claimed that the social history of a people allied to the national ideals (the cultural totality of the group) is much more significant in determining the nature of the schools than the acceptance of any particular creed or philosophy .(15)

He has also made the point, and in this he is very much in the Sadler and Kandel tradition, that comparative education, for all its use of statistical data and manpower forecasts, is concerned with human beings. Educational responses must essentially be humanistic ones. Because societies and the educational systems which reflect these societies are not static, but are living organisms, it is how they respond to changes that is often so important and so fascinating.

It is in this mould, as well as in the wide sweep of affairs and of history that has always characterised Vernon Mallinson´s writings, that this essay seeks to show how external influences and factors have brought about or are bringing about educational change. My thesis is quite simple: there are areas of change - population, socio-economic and political - which have had and are continuing to have a profound impact on the shape of school provision throughout different parts of the world. Schools and teachers have had to respond, often in very novel ways. Because their response has frequently run counter to the prevailing perceptions about the purpose of schooling, both schools and teachers have been subject to widespread and often violent criticism. How far such criticisms are valid if left to the reader's discretion.

II. POPULATION CHANGES

(a) During the past two to three decades there have been phenomenal increases in population growth on a global basis as can be seen from the following table:

Table I. Global Population Growth

		Number of years to reach the next 1000 million	Reached in the Years
1st	1000 million	2,000,000	1830
2nd	"	100	1930
3rd	"	30	1960
4th	"	15	1975
5th	"	11	1986
6th	"	9	1995
7th	"	6 ?	2001

(Source: Based on U.N. Population Statistics)

Although this growth rate has been slowing down, especially in the richer countries of the world, it is nevertheless increasing at the rate of one million new births every five days. Even allowing for mortality and a drop in the birth rate United Nations predictions are that there will be at least 6.5 billion people on this planet earth by the year 2000.(16) The impact of these increases on educational provision has been, and will continue to be, profound.

If it is considered that 50-60% of the population of Third World countries are under 15 years of age and that by the end of the century this figure will have risen to 65-70%, simply because 90% of births are taking place in the South, then demands for school places are likely to continue to increase for many years to come. This is largely because most Third World governments, influenced by the U.N. Declaration of Human Rights, Article 26 of which proclaimed education to be a basic human right, have recognised universal primary education (UPE) as a constitutional right as well. As a result many millions of parents have naturally demanded school places for their children, though there is now some evidence from countries like Ghana, that demand is actually declining as frustrated parents cease to recognise schooling as a form of upward social mobility.(17)

Demand has also been formed by the various UNESCO Regional Plans for educational expansion that took place in the early 1960s. The result of these plans was that many governments set 1980 as the target year for the achievement of UPE. Some countries have more than met their targets: many others have not, simply because of low economic growth, poverty or population growth.(18) In fact, in spite of the phenomenal increase in school provision in the Third World since 1960, there are over 250 million children and 600 million adults who have never had the opportunity of any formal schooling.(19)

Neverthless, in spite of failures and disappointments, some of the world's most populous nations - India, Bangladesh, Indonesia, Nigeria, Pakistan - are pledged to renew their efforts to provide UPE by 1985/86.(20) They are being encouraged in their efforts by UNESCO and the World Bank.

Perhaps one of the most striking and obvious reasons for the inability to provide enough school places is the inability to fund education along the lines expected by politicians and aid experts from the rich countries. The chart below highlights more dramatically than any amount of words the growing disparity in educational expenditure between the rich countries of the world and the poor countries, to such an extent that one must ask whether educational investment and provision - as understood in the North - is really only possible from a wealthy economic base.

Certainly many countries are beginning to question whether or not they can continue to provide education in schools and colleges for all their children along conventional lines.

What have been the responses to both the population pressures and the financial implications of meeting these pressures? Many countries, especially in the urban areas of Africa and Asia, have resorted to double, even treble, shifts, using the same plant and sometimes even the same staff for the different shifts. Many have sought to overcome teacher shortages and school place shortages by using volunteers or itinerant teachers or even radio and television. Volunteers and/or itinerant teachers have been used effectively as literacy workers in countries as far apart as Botswana, Cuba, Iran, India and China, while in Bangladesh and Ethiopia literate housewives are being used as community leaders and para-teachers. Educational television has been used with mixed results in Colombia, Mexico, Ivory Coast, Pakistan and Thailand, as well as in many of the more advanced nations such as Italy, Canada, the U.K. or the U.S.A. Far more effective however has been the use of radio and/or transistorised cassette players.

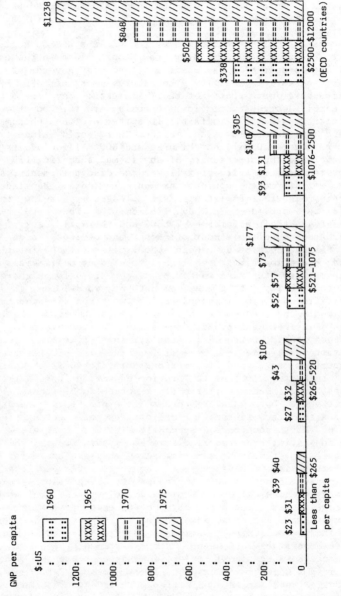

Chart 1:   Expenditure on Education (1960-78) per student

Source: World Bank Education Sector Paper, 1980

Many governments, following the examples of China and Tanzania, have sought to restructure schooling and the curriculum content so that courses at each level (primary, middle, secondary) are self sufficient and terminal. Pupils are not necessarily automatically prepared for the next stage of schooling. Indeed the intention is that very few will move on to the next stage.

Another feature is that in some countries (e.g. Cameroon, Colombia, Philippines, Tanzania, Thailand) schools are being seen as focal points for community development, with the result that local members of the community are expected to make financial contributions to the building and maintenance of plant and to the salary of the teacher(s).(21) In this way the financial burden on the central exchequer is considerably eased, but there is no guarantee that provision is equalised.

These responses to population pressures may be very different from those experienced in the more affluent parts of the world, but they reveal imagination and realism in the face of considerable difficulties brought about by population change. Inevitably, quality and traditional academic standards have suffered because of over-crowding and underfunding, and teaching standards and curriculum experimentation may have fallen because of the need to employ underqualified or unqualified staff, but the fact remains that many hundreds of millions have had the opportunity to enrol in school as was urged by those visionaries who drew up the United Nations' Charter over nearly forty years ago.

In the industrial nations of the world, however, the population problem is of a very different dimension. Here, with the exception of Japan, South Africa and Ireland, there has been a remarkable decline in the birth rate and in population growth. The implications for school provision are quite dramatic.

In England and Wales, for example, the decline in the number of children enrolled in school will drop from 9 million (1977) to 7.5 million (1987), a decline of 16% in the course of a decade.(22) Although the pattern is uneven throughout the counry, many inner cities and rural areas have been, or are being, badly affected, with the result that many primary schools have been closed or merged, while others have been put to different use (e.g. as community centres). Teachers can no longer be guaranteed long term contracts and school principals find that their autonomy over and flexible use of teaching staff and ancillary staff has been severely curtailed.

The decline in enrolments at secondary level, which will become most acute during the next few years, will call for even more severe readjustments. Schools will become smaller. For example, in many areas of Berkshire eight-form entry comprehensive schools (1979) will have dropped to five or even four form entry schools by 1989. In some LEAs, schools are already being closed. Fewer and smaller schools mean not only fewer teachers (and less promotion) but less flexibility in the deployment of staff resources and, inevitably, a reduction in the curricula offerings. If certain key members of staff leave, and are not replaced, some subjects may either be dropped from the curriculum or be taught by non-specialists. A basic core curriculum is as much a result of changed circumstances as it is of government decision. Inevitably, also, some of the pastoral care and extra-curricula activities which have made English schools so attractive and so "human" in recent years will have to be dropped. How to maintain standards and staff morale in times of contraction are major management headaches, yet the schools (and by implication the teachers) are blamed if standards are not maintained.

Although the above remarks relate to England and Wales they are equally applicable to Canada and the U.S.A., France, Germany and Sweden. In fact in some parts of the U.S.A. and Canada there are demands to cut out art and music and physical education as unnecessary "frills" on the curriculum. The Back to the Basics Movement is cashing in on the difficulties brought about by enrolment decline.

Moreover, as a result of contraction, many politicians and educationists are seizing the opportunity to question the whole structure of education during the late teenage period. Discussions about new forms of secondary and post-compulsory education which have been going on throughout Western Europe during the past decade are as much a result of changing circumstances and socio-economic and population change, as they are a result of pedagogical arguments.(23)

(b) There are two further problems of population change which must be mentioned which have had, or are having, a profound impact on educational provision. Chart II graphically illustrates them. Both are global phenomena but their effect on school provision has only recently begun to be studied,(24) partly because of population decline in the industrial nations, partly because of the concern for equalisation of access and facilities, though not necessarily of outcome, in most countries of the world, regardless of their political complexion. The first pattern is the gradual movement of people from rural areas to urban areas as they seek employment or a better life style.

In the earlier part of this century in the industrial nations, and since the beginning of the 1950s in Southern Europe and much of the Third World, the rural areas have become relatively depopulated and urban areas have grown first into cities and then into vast conurbations.(25) There have been attempts to reverse this trend, most notably in China, and in the world's most populous nations such as India, Indonesia and Pakistan, over 70% of the population still live in villages, but there is little doubt that even there the rural areas lose their attraction; there is a growing concentration of school

The Impact of External Changes on Educational Developments

Chart II.

The Impact of Population Change on Educational Provision

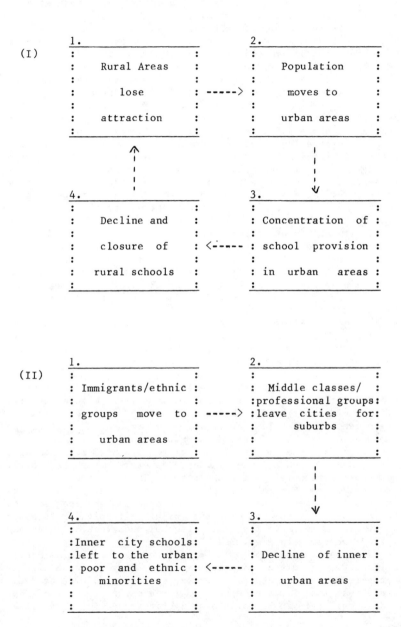

183

provision in urban areas and as educational expenditure fails
to keep up with increasing demand the rural schools decline or,
as in many parts of Scotland, Scandinavia and North America,
actually close, while, as already observed, some urban schools
begin to operate a shift system.

Inevitably school administrators and policy makers have to
adjust to these changes. In the U.S.A., for example, the number
of school boards dropped from over 40,000 in the 1930s to less
than 15,000 in the 1970s. There has been a similar decline in
France as the number of "mairies" and "départements" concerned
with primary school provision has dropped dramatically since
the 1950s, while in the United Kingdom local government
reorganisation in the early 1970s led to a reduction by almost
50% in the number of local education authorities. The effect of
such administrative "rationalisation" has been to increase
central or regional control over school provision at the
expense of local control, thus making a nonsense of the
argument that schools serve local communities: increasingly
they serve national or regional interests. Herein lies one of
the biggest conflicts in current educational provision.

(c) The most recent population shift with a direct bearing on
schooling is one long familiar in the U.S.A. and Canada but is
a much more recent phenomenon in Western Europe, the United
Kingdom and Australia. This is the influx of migrant workers
and immigrant groups from Southern Europe, West and East
Africa, the Caribbean, the Indian Sub-continent and South East
Asia. Countries traditionally mono-cultural or mono-lingual (or
at the most bi-lingual) in terms of educational provision have
in the past 20/25 years found themselves becoming consciously
multi-cultural or culturally plural societies. Table II gives
some indication of the size of the issue with regard to Western
Europe.

In the EEC countries for example the estimated numbers of
non EEC migrants range from 13 to 16 million with at least 6
million of these being children or young persons. Germany,
France and the Benelux countries have imposed a total ban on
immigration and have resorted to "expulsions" or termination of
work permits as a means of reducing the numbers. Denmark,
Norway and Sweden and the U.K. have severely restricted entry.
But these are only partial solutions. The most pressing needs
are for coherent educational policies. Government policies have
invariably lagged behind events and schools have been left to
decide how best to cope with the influx of foreign children in
their midst and have frequently been blamed if things have not
worked according to plan.(26)

The issue of educational provision for ethnic minority
children is so often politically contentious because it is
connected with race and also because it is linked with academic
standards. The Rampton Report on the underachievement of West
Indian children in Britain highlighted these two points.(27)

Table II

Migrant Workers by Origin (1975)

Host Country	Workers from the EEC		Workers from non-EEC Europe		Workers from outside Europe		Total	
	Number	%	Number	%	Number	%	Number	%
Germany	431.641	20.8	827.711	40.0	811.383	39.2	2.070.735	100.0
Belgium	130.000	56.5	47.000	20.4	53.000	23.1	230.000	100.0
Denmark	12.851	31.2	5.996	14.6	22.353	54.2	41.200	100.0
France	300.000	15.7	796.000	41.8	809.000	42.5	1.905.000	100.0
Luxembourg	29.300	64.7	14.300	31.6	1.700	3.7	43.300	100.0
Netherlands	49.800	43.1	20.217	17.5	45.483	39.4	115.500	100.0
United Kingdom	630.000	37.8	102.000	6.1	934.005	56.1	1.666.005	100.0
Total	1.583.592	26.1	1.813.244	29.4	2.676.924	44.0	6.073.740	100.0

Sources: EEC internal document: Social Affairs, April 1976 op.cit. See Table 1, Chapter 1.

The issue is compounded because of the heavy concentration of migrant groups in certain urban areas - Amsterdam, Birmingham, Bradford, Coventry, Hamburg, Lyons, London, Leeds, Manchester, Marsailles, Paris, Stockholm or Stuttgart - with the result that professional and middle class indigenous groups have left the inner city areas for the suburbs, which in turn has led to a decline in inner city schools. (see Chart II (II)). That such a decline might have happened in any case is immaterial. Ethnic minorities have been blamed and teachers have had to respond to situations for which they have been ill prepared.(28)

Both the Council of Europe and the EEC have argued in favour of bi-lingualism and culturally plural curricula, though these policies have not necessarily been pursued, except in Switzerland and Sweden. In the majority of cases, multi-cultural curriculum theory and classroom practice remain poles apart. France has chosen to ignore or not to differentiate ethnic groups for educational purposes, with the result that they are expected to be assimilated into French society through the medium of the French language. In West Germany, policies vary from Land to Land. In some Länder there are bilingual classes; in some, German is introduced only after fluency has been gained in the mother tongue; in others, children of migrants are absorbed into the mainstream of the school society as soon as possible. In the U.K., policies have varied from one local education authority to another and even from one school to another.

The growth of multi-raçial and culturally plural societies is not new. In the European - and Australian and Canadian - contexts, it is the speed at which change has taken place that has caught so many educators unawares. During the 1980s, the issues that must be resolved, if a whole generation of children is not to be alienated, are how much the school curricula should reflect the different ethnic groups in society, how much tuition should be in the mother tongue and how best teachers should be prepared for teaching in ethnically plural schools.

So much for the impact of population changes on educational provision. Schools and teachers have had to cope, adjust and respond to new and changing situations. That they have done so and continue to do so with great skill and ingenuity is no mean feat. That certain cherished traditions may have suffered is inevitable.

III. SOCIO-ECONOMIC CHANGES

Turning next to the socio-economic changes which have affected or are affecting educational provision, there are again three aspects that I wish to mention - family and social breakdown, unemployment and community involvement.

The Impact of External Changes on Educational Developments

(a) Family/social breakdown

In the U.S.A., a staggering one out of two marriages end in
divorce. Over 50% of the crime committed and the arrests made
are amongst the 16-25 year old age group. Many inner city
schools are policed by security guards as violence, drug
trafficking, murder and anti-authority demonstrations increase.
That classroom behaviour, motivation and learning should be
adversely affected is inevitable.
A not dissimilar picture is emerging from West Germany,
Italy, Japan and South Korea, all industrial nations where
schooling and society appear to be pulling in opposite
directions. In the International Evaluation of Achievement
survey conducted amongst 22 nations in the late 1960s/early
1970s, Sweden ranked bottom in matters pertaining to student
boredom and alienation from the system.
In the U.K., though figures for England are worse than
those for Scotland, three out of ten marriages end in divorce;
one out of five families are one parent families and in some
cities (e.g. Birmingham) 40-50% of children are "latchkey"
children - i.e. mother is out at work when the child returns
from school. In addition, there is a growing incidence of
disease, including mental disorders and depression, indirectly
related to unemployment in industrial areas, while television
viewing (25-30 hours per week) has taken over as the major
entertainment agency. It is similar elsewhere. In Japan, over
50% of 15 and 16 year olds are "latchkey" children.(29) In the
USSR, 52% of urban children and 35% of rural children come from
one parent families.(30) In the U.S.A., T.V. viewing figures
are as high as 40 hours per week in some areas.(31)
These social attitudes are having an impact on pupils'
attitudes and behaviour and on teachers' morale and how they
cope in class. In England and Scotland during the past few
years, for example, many teachers have felt threatened by the
mounting campaign of the minority group STOPP (Society of
Teachers Opposed to Physical Punishsment) to ensure the
abolition of any form of corporal punishment in school, while
Militant tendency, the National Front and numerous racist
groups have been actively distributing leaflets in schools.
What effect is this having in the classroom? Of a class of
30 children in an English classroom, for example, at least 12
will suffer from the traumas of marital breakdown, 9 will come
from families where there has been at least one divorce and
remarriage, between 12 and 15 will have mothers out at work,
2.5 will have one parent chronically sick, 3 (an underestimate)
will have the father unemployed.(32) Not all schools or
classrooms fit these statistics, by any means. In many cases,
some children will suffer from multiple deprivation; in others,
they may be scarcely affected. Inevitably, where there are
social problems academic standards suffer and social
relationships are affected. Are schools equipped to cope, so

that as well as teaching academic subjects teachers can play socially supportive and pastoral roles? Is it any wonder that there is classroom disruption and academic work suffers? Yet schools are blamed for what is basically a social, family or parental matter. Unfortunately, schools in the U.K., other parts of Western Europe and North America are being starved of funds for pastoral work and counselling and the growing pressures from teachers for "isolation units" ("sin-bins") for disruptive pupils are not being favourably received by hardpressed administrators.

These social pressures will inevitably continue to grow in the 1980s and measures must be taken to enable schools, and the teachers in them, to face up to and to adjust to them.

(b) <u>Unemployment</u>

Closely linked with many of the changing social attitudes commented on above is the vexed issue of unemployment, especially amongst young school leavers in industrial societies. By 1983 as many as 60% of school leavers in the U.K. were unlikely to find employment. This figure is roughly the same in West Germany, France, the Netherlands and the U.S.A., though in all these cases there is greater provision made for children to stay on at school or other educational institutions beyond the age of 16 than is the case in Britain, even allowing for the new 16+ extension year proposals. In Italy, Finland, Australia and Canada, however, the situation is even more depressing. By February 1983 there were 3.4 million unemployed in the U.K., over 2 million in Belgium, 1.9 million in France and 2.3 million in West Germany. In the EEC countries as a whole over 12 million are unemployed, 5 million of whom are 16/17 year olds who have given up hope of finding a permanent job.

As we have seen, schools are frequently blamed for not adequately preparing youngsters for the job market - though many liberal educators would heatedly argue that this is <u>not</u> the role of the school and many others would argue, with some justification, that it is almost impossible to prepare children for the rapidly changing world they are likely to find themselves growing up in - but unemployment is an <u>external</u> socio-economic factor which is having a direct bearing on what happens in schools, the least effect of which is that many children are staying on beyond the school leaving age in the hope of improving their examination grades.

The World Bank and UNESCO have long pointed out the problem of graduate unemployment from both school and university in Third World countries. India must top the league with four out of five graduates or diplomates unemployed, not only in the arts subjects but also in engineering, science and agriculture. The problems are also acute in Indonesia, Pakistan, Bangladesh, the Philippines, Nigeria, Zambia and large parts of Latin

America. Solutions range from restructuring the curriculum to insisting on some form of voluntary or community service after secondary level - (Botswana, Tanzania, Ghana, Zambia, Iran and China are just a few of the countries that have tried to introduce this concept); from the redirection of graduates to the rural areas as part of their service to the state, as happens with doctors and teachers in Malaysia and Thailand, to alternative forms of selection, other than the traditional examination for employment.

Now that the industrial nations of the West are faced with a similar problem, governments are unsure how best to tackle it.(33) Although the communist bloc countries, because of the so-called "polytechnic principle", have theoretically had an element of manual, practical or vocational training as part of the school curriculum and have no unemployment because of overmanning and because such a state of affairs would be contrary to state philosophy, there are growing concerns about graduate underemployment. This is particularly so in China. Several western countries, most notably West Germany, Austria and Switzerland, have also had strong apprenticeship and manual training schemes, with a remarkable degree of success, but in the U.K. there has been a dramatic decline in this area because of the recession and the high cost of young labour.

Recently, however, there have been pressures in the U.K., in France, and to some extent in the U.S.A., to ensure that some of what is taught in schools is directly linked to industry and other employment. In France, companies have the legal right, which they frequently exercise, to insist upon having some say over what is taught on the very wide range of technician courses. In Sweden, employers not only sit on curriculum advisory panels but at the same time they co-operate in link schemes between schools and industry. The latter have been a feature of many schools in England and Wales. In England and Wales, where additional courses in craft, design and technology are now being developed in many schools, the Schools Council Industry Project is designed to bring industrialists into the classroom, and children and teachers into industry. There is some scepticism about whether the whole scheme has come years too late, but it cannot be without significance that successful industrial countries like South Korea, Taiwan, Japan and Singapore have <u>all</u> their pupils at secondary level doing some technical and vocational courses.

There is also considerable discussion about what to do with school leavers who find themselves in the dole queues. Raise the school leaving age again? Compulsorily enrol them into further education classes? Send them on some form of community service or national (i.e. military) service, as is being tried in so many developing countries? There are moves afoot in the U.K. - and in France, Germany and Sweden, they are well developed - to enrol teenagers into special courses in further education colleges and/or in the English context, in Sixth Form

Colleges. This is seen by many as an indirect way of raising the school leaving age. It is interesting that very similar approaches have been recommended by the Carnegie Commission in the U.S.A., urging greater use of vocational community colleges, and suggesting that official State bodies should be established to oversee all 16-19 year olds, whether they are in school or not, and suggesting the introduction of community service for all not in full time schooling.

But are these suggestions the answer, or are they only part of the answer? If it is acknowledged that unemployment is here to stay because of automation, the silicone chip, robots, computers or even because of the pruning of the workforce, and if it is acknowledged that we are undergoing a social and industrial revolution, ought we not to be more seriously considering those technical and craft skills which could, or should, be usefully taught in school for those unlikely to get jobs easily, but which could be used in personal job development - e.g. metal/woodwork, bricklaying, plumbing, electrical training, etc?(34)

Whatever decisions are reached, education and work and unemployment are bound to be to the forefront of the educational issues facing planners and teachers throughout the 1980s. Their impact on the curriculum and syllabus and on attitudes to examinations and job selection could be profound. It is imperative, therefore, that politicians, educationists and employers join together to identify new approaches to the curriculum, rather than merely tinkering with subject content.

(c) Community education

In an attempt to recreate a sense of local community, partly because of the sense of individual alienation in the urban sprawl of many modern cities, partly because of the remoteness of so many educational decision makers and government organisations; in an attempt to cut costs; and in an attempt to provide useful outlets for unemployed people to develop hobbies or to cultivate new interests, another development of recent years has been that of community education.

In the U.S.A. and Canada, where schools are essentially neighbourhood schools and large community colleges offer vocational courses, this movement is not new. In many parts of Western Europe and Australia, however, where there has been a sense that schools have been divorced from the communities from which they draw their children, the movement is strong.(35) There is a belief that if only schools can be made smaller, relate to the local community more closely, be open to community involvement, embrace adults learning alongside children, even allowing some to teach their own skills and expertise to children, then many of the social issues already touched upon could be counteracted, or at least minimised.

At least that is the theory. Unfortunately, many of the

policies of the present government in the U.K. are destroying
the idea of community and/or small rural schools in the
interests of financial efficiency, but in many countries,
particularly in the Third World, where they act as focal points
for community development,(36) they are flourishing and at
least 40 countries have now developed some form of community
schools. On the grounds of economy, joint use of facilities,
making provision for vocational and general educational courses
for unemployed youths and adults, there is much to be said for
the community school concept. There are likely to be
considerable developments during the next decade and the impact
on school organisation and management, curriculum content and
the types of courses offered could be quite marked.

IV. POLITICAL CHANGES

The last area of change to be considered is that of political
change, not so much in terms of specific governments, but in
terms of disparities, regional and global. It is particularly
worth noting that in all cases where there has been a swing to
the right (in e.g. the U.S.A., the U.K., Australia, Iran, even
China) or to the left (in e.g. Nicaragua and France), an
increased concern for basic standards, together with
conservative views about the role of schools, has gone hand in
hand with a decline in financial commitment to education.

(a) Regional disparities

Whereas the concern of the 1960s and 1970s was for greater
equality of educational opportunity and a fairer distribution
of educational provision, there has been a growing awareness in
many countries of the world that educational expansion has in
fact highlighted disparities amongst minorities, the
economically weak, and the regionally backward areas within and
between countries.

The OECD and IIEP, both Paris-based organisations, have
become increasingly concerned about the need to recognise
diversity within national unity and with the need to point out
the dangers of potential revolution unless there is greater
equalisation of provision and funding. They have suggested that
the only way to prevent resentment in certain backward or
ethnic minority areas or regions from turning into opposition
to the central government, or even into revolution, is through
the allocation of funds to these regions. They have sought to
stimulate discussion about the best means of developing
backward regions and areas, economically and educationally.
This might involve varied school curricula, different languages
of instruction, preferential staff:student ratios, special
quota systems for futher and higher education, or additional
financial help with building programmes.

How to overcome regional disparities is a new and uncharted

field of inquiry. There is no clearly defined, let alone agreed, theory of disparity. Its causes can usually be identified, but solutions to disparity often defy logic because they create other, often unexpected, disparities. Nevertheless countries as diverse as Hungary, Spain, Switzerland, Cameroon, Nigeria, Kenya, Madagascar, and Thailand are actively involved in reconciling national unity and regional diversity with equality of opportunity and educational provision. The political survival of many regimes may depend upon how they tackle the problems of unequal schooling and many decisions will be made which have a direct bearing upon school provision, even curriculum content, but which have more to do with internal policies than with pedagogical justification. There is, of course, nothing new in this, but what is new is the inevitable concern with differentiated school provision on a regional basis.(37)

(b) Global disparities

Even more important, because it will be far more damaging in the long run if nothing is done about it, is the global disparity as highlighted in the annual World Bank Development Reports and most clearly in the two Brandt Reports. World alignments are changing, in the Middle East, South East Asia and Latin America. The communists will exploit the suffering and poverty of the Third World, and the United States and Europe will continue to be maligned, especially in Latin America, for their wrong diagnosis of the real development needs of the region, and confrontation between North and South will increase unless the size of the problem is recognised and action is taken. Table III highlights a few of these disparities.

The attitudes of the British and American governments to the message of the Brandt Reports, even after the near financial collapse of Mexico, Brazil, Bangladesh, Romania and Poland, and the subsequent IMF meeting in Ottawa, have been at the best lukewarm, at the least negative, insular and shortsighted. Neither government accepts the thesis of global interdependence or of the need for government intervention, believing instead in the "free working of market forces". While the public in the U.S.A. has largely ignored the Reports, in the U.K. the Brandt Reports have been best sellers and the government has been forced to modify its position under pressure.

It is, however, the implications both of the Reports and of global disparities for schools and education generally, especially in the North, that concern us here.(38) Brandt calls for schools and colleges to make known the relations between North and South (p.259) because its authors believe that we live in an interdependent world ecosystem which is increasingly in danger (hence the subtitle of the first Report, "A Programme

The Impact of External Changes on Educational Developments

Table III.   North-South: Some of the Disparities

1. Wealth

    60-70% of the world's population live in the South yet they
    have only:

        one fifth of the world's income;
        one sixth of the world's wealth;
        one seventh of the world's industrial output.

2. Between 70% and 90% of these people live in rural areas in
    villages or isolated hamlets.

3. Per Capita Income

    36 countries have an average income of less than $370 p.a.
    55 countries have an average income of between $380 and
    $4000.
    while the industrial countries have incomes ranging from
    $4000 to over $14000.

    (i.e. the richest countries on average are 40 times as
    wealthy as the poorest countries).

4. Health

    Life expectancy in the North is 70+ years;
    Life expectancy in the South is between 35 and 50 years.
    The average number of doctors per patient is:
        in the North: 1:650   in the South: 1:22,000.

----

for Survival"). They argue that there is a need to highlight
the wrong attitudes of governments, business and electorates in
the North; to highlight the gross international mis-spending on
armaments (p.14); and to make people aware of the unjust
economic structures between North and South. The Report also
argues,   perhaps   novelly,   that   because   of   global
interdependence, reduction of unemployment in the North is
closely linked with investment in the South.
    There has been, and continues to be, much heated discussion
about the Brandt Report proposals, but there is little doubt
that during the 1980s and for the rest of this century, the
issues of rich country/poor country relationships will increase

sharply and schools will be and should be involved in educating the young about these relationships as part of the curriculum. As Brandt observes, "it is essential that the educational aspects of improved North-South relations be given much more attention in the future".(39) The comparative educationist is in a unique position to teach about these relations.

CONCLUSIONS

This paper has touched upon a wide range of issues and topics. It has deliberately not been concerned with academic standards, educational performance, assessments, etc. with which so many educationists become bogged down. Instead, it has been concerned with showing that many of the educational issues of the 1980s are not the making of teachers and schools, but are a direct result of other changes in society. It is the unique role of the comparative educationist to seek to explain, as far as he can, these changes and to show how they affect different societies. It is the lot of those working within the education systems of the world, as Vernon Mallinson has commented, "to adjust to and to respond to the social realities of the times". The latter role is always a far more difficult one.

NOTES AND REFERENCES

* Some of the ideas for this paper originated in lectures given to teachers from Pennsylvania State University, and Bemidji State University, Minnesota, U.S.A. and first appeared in the Canadian Administrator, XX, 4, 1981 under the title "Coping with Changes - Pressures on Educational Administrators in England and Wales" and in Educational Administration, 8, 2, Summer 1980 under the title "Education for Uncertainty - Issues facing Educational Administrators in the 1980s".

1.Carnegie Commission (1979): Giving Youth a Better Chance, Options for Education, Work and Service, Jossey-Bass, San Francisco.
World Bank (1980): Education Sector Paper, Washington, D.C.
Simmons,J. (ed) (1980): The Education Dilemma; Policy Options facing the Developing Countries in the 1980s, Pergammon, Oxford.
D.E.S. (1981): Curriculum 11-16: A Review of Progress, HMSO, London.

2.Husén,T. (1979): The School in Question, Oxford University Press, London, p.130.

3.Brandt,W. (1980): North-South: A Programme for Survival, Pan Books, London, p.58.

4.Carnegie, op.cit.

5.Larson,M.A. et.al. (1977): Better Basic Skills for Youth: Four Proposals for Federal Policy, Stanford Research Institute, California.

6.Carnegie, op.cit., p.57.

7.Toffler,A. (1981): The Third Wave, Pan Books, London.
    King,E.J. (1976): Education for Uncertainty, Inaugural Lecture at King's College, University of London.

8.Mallinson,V. (1981): "In the Wake of Sir Michael Sadler", Compare, 11, 2, pp.175-184.

9.Kandel,I.L. (1933): Comparative Education, Houghton Miffein, Boston.

10.Hans,N. (1949): Comparative Education, Routledge and Kegan Paul, London.

11.Mallinson,V. (1975): An Introduction to the Study of Comparative Education, 4th Edition, Heinemann, London.

12.King,E.J. (1979): Other Schools and Ours, Holt, Rinehart and Winston, London, 5th Edition.

13.Sadler,M. (1900): How far can we learn anything of practical value from the study of foreign systems of education? Note of an address given at the Guildford Educational Conference, 20th October 1900. Discussed in Higginson,J.H. (1961): The Centenary of an English Pioneer (1861-1943): International Review of Education, 7, 3.

14.Higginson,J.H. (ed) (1979): Selections from Michael Sadler, Dejall and Meyorre, Liverpool, pp.31-32.

15.Mallinson,V. (1975): op.cit., p.265.

16.U.N. Demographic Trends 1980; Brandt, op.cit.

17.Blakemore,K. (1975): "Resistance to Formal Education in Ghana: its implications for the status of school leavers", Comparative Education Review, 19, 3, pp.237-251.

18.See International Journal of Educational Development (1981) I, for discussion papers of the UNESCO Regional Plans.

19.World Bank Education Sector Paper, op.cit. Brandt, op.cit.

20.Watson,J.K.P. (1981): "The Impact of the Karachi Plan on Educational Development in Asia". International Journal of Educational Development, 1, 1, pp.32-49.

21.Sinclair,M.E. and Lillis,K. (1980): School and Community in the Third World, Croom Helm, London;
Watson, Keith (1982): Teachers and Community Schools as Instruments of Rural Development: The Rhetoric and the Reality, International Community Education Association, Melbourne.

22.Briault,E. (1980): Falling Rolls in Secondary Schools, NFER Publishing Company, Slough.

23.King,E.J., Moor,J. and Mundy,J. (1974): Post-compulsory Education: A New Analysis in Western Europe, London, Sage.

24.Furter,P. (1980): The recent development of education: regional diversity or reduction of inequalities? in Carron,G. and Ta Ngoc Châu: Regional Disparities in educational development, UNESCO/IIEP, Paris.

25.Jacobs,J. (1972): The Economy of Cities, Penguin Books.
Lloyd,P. (1979): Slums of Hope, Shanty Towns of the Third World, Penguin Books.
Elkins,T.H. (1973): The Urban Explosion, Studies in Contemporary Europe, Macmillan, London.

26.Bullivant,B. (1981): The Pluralist Dilemma in Education. Six Case Studies, Allen and Unwin, London.
Bhatnegah,J. (1981): The Education of Immigrants, Croom Helm, London.
Megarry,J. et.al. (1981): The Education of Minorities, World Yearbook of Education 1981, Kegan Page, London.
Watson,J.K.P. (1979): "Educational Policies in Multi-Cultural Societies", Comparative Education, 15, 1, March, pp.17-31.

27.Rampton,A. (1981): West Indian Children in Our Schools, HMSO, London.

28.Watson, Keith (1982): "Comparative Education in British Teacher Education" in Goodings,R., Byram,M. and McParkland,M. (eds) (1982): Changing Priorities in Teacher Education, Croom Helm, London.

29.Cummings,W. (1979): Education and Equality in Japan, Princeton University Press.

30.Dunston,J. (1977): Paths to Excellence and the Soviet School, NFER, Slough.

The Impact of External Changes on Educational Developments

31.Large,M. (1980): <u>Who´s Bringing Them Up?</u> T.V. Action
Group, Gloucester.

32.Based on Clark,R.D. (1979): "Education Stragegy for the
1980s" in <u>Education in Science</u>, April, pp.17-22.

33.See Watson,K. (ed) (1983): <u>Youth, Education and
Employment: International Perspectives</u>, London, Croom Helm, for
a more detailed account of measures to resolve unemployment.

34.Watson,K. (1981): "Education for Life: Some of the
Educational Implications of the Brandt Report" in Garrett,R.M.
(ed): <u>Noth-South Debate: Educational Implications of the Brandt
Report</u>, NFER-Nelson, Slough, pp.101-112.

35.Sinclair and Lillis, op.cit.
    Watson,K. (1980): "Community Education - prospects for
the 1980s", <u>New Era</u>, 61, 1.
    Watson,K. (1980): "The Growth of Community Education in
England and Wales", <u>International Review of Education</u>, XXV, 3.
    Poster,C. (1982): <u>Community Education: its development
and management</u>, Heinemann, London.

36.Watson,K. (1982): Teachers and Community Schools, op.cit.

37.Carron,G. and Ta Ngoc Châu (1980): <u>Regional disparities
in educational development</u>, 3 vols. UNESCO/IIEP, Paris.

38.Garrett, op.cit.

39.Brandt, op.cit., p.259.

Chapter Twelve

"PRACTICAL BIAS" IN COMPARATIVE STUDIES WITH SPECIAL REFERENCE
TO CURRICULUM DEVELOPMENT AND INSET

Paul Mercier

The conference, held at Reading University in 1965, which
initiated moves to found the British Section of the Comparative
Education Society of Europe (parent of the British Comparative
Education Society), was appropriately entitled: The Place of
Comparative Education in the Training of Teachers.(1) Vernon
Mallinson was, of course, a leading spirit behind these
initiatives, and his own address to the conference not only
echoed its title but was, in a deeper conceptual sense, its
keynote. He insisted that "comparative education, properly
taught, must, by constructively challenging the myths and
objectively assessing a given culture pattern, lead to a more
effective international understanding and to a greater level of
communication".(2) Mallinson´s emphasis was chiefly on initial
training, especially within the then expanding colleges of
education with their proposals for new B.Ed. courses. His three
basic messages, however, were these: first, know your own
system well; secondly, in addition to your study of the
documentation, go observantly and analytically abroad; and
thirdly, do not omit attention to a society´s creative
literature as a primary source of understanding its educational
culture. This remains useful practical advice to any student of
comparative education. The present writer remains particularly
grateful to Mallinson for the third of these messages, which
was later extended into a full length article,(3) since it has
given additional dimensions to his reading in both literature
and education.
        During the year following this 1965 conference, the present
writer, acting as information officer for the infant British
Section, circularised all United Kingdom colleges of education
with a questionnaire that sought to establish the quantity and
range of existing courses in comparative and international
studies. Much of the evidence from this enquiry was at that
time encouraging to comparativists, as a revised review of the
findings by Keith Watson(4) has since shown. One hundred
colleges replied to the 1965 questionnaire, 49 of which
indicated that some comparative education was taught, 5 at PGCE

level, 44 at certificate or proposed B.Ed. level. All the
colleges except two arranged for some overseas visits or staff
exchange, while 25 of them had overseas visitors or students
attending courses at the college. Thus in a general educational
sense an even wider range of potential interest in education
overseas was evident.

Watson's own more recent and more ambitious 1981 survey of
the 106 teacher training institutions which responded to his
inquiry showed that 68 of them (including UDEs and Polytechnic
Schools of Education) taught aspects of education that have a
clearly definable comparative component. The two surveys are
not directly comparable in their statistical evidence, as the
1981 one includes reference to award bearing INSET courses for
teachers, as well as to initial teacher education and training
programmes. Despite evidence of increased provision of
comparative education courses since 1965, however, Watson's
survey contains much disturbing evidence about current and
future developments. Not only has there been an inevitable
decline in overall provision as the teacher education cuts and
the decline in academic appointments in higher education start
to bite, but there is also a general absence of concern and
interest in comparative and international educational studies.
This is particularly noticeable in the field of multi-cultural
education, where students are taught about developments in the
United Kingdom with little or no reference to the similarities
and differences in other pluralistic societies.(5) Watson
concludes:

> Unless there is greater concern to develop practical
> biases to comparative studies and there is less
> concern for debates about theoretical models and
> methodologies of approach......comparative education
> could be reduced to becoming an academically
> respectable subject undertaken by a few students at
> higher degree level only. The need for a comparative
> and international dimension to the study of
> educational issues is possibly greater in times of
> contraction than in times of expansion but the voices
> of those involved in the field need to be heard more
> clearly than they have been hitherto. ......The need
> is to continue to make contributions to national and
> local debates on educational issues wherever and
> whenever possible and to fire the enthusiasm of
> younger teachers as they train for their chosen
> profession.(6)

The implication that comparative education in training
institutions might become little more than an academic study
contrasts with the way that "practical biases", involving
information about the process and practice of education
overseas, have increasingly formed an important part of

official education reports in England and Wales, often backing recommendations for future national and local policies. The Robbins Report(7) of 1963, for example, contained a significant section of international information from the educational systems of other advanced industrial societies which was used to justify some of its recommendations for the expansion of higher education in this country. The most recent example of the consideration of international dimensions in an official educational document has been the Cockcroft Report, Mathematics Counts,(8) published early in 1982. The report points out, for instance, that the existence in Scotland of a single examination board and the use of centrally developed materials at both primary and secondary school levels seem to exercise a unifying effect on the mathematics curriculum compared with the diffuseness of the English experience. While these unifying factors may be as powerful in the Scottish system as elsewhere in Europe where there is national or regional government control over textbooks, the requirement for teachers of centralised curricula to exercise professional judgment in their mathematics teaching seems in no way diminished.

Cockcroft Committee members were impressed with the degree to which courses (and not least those in mathematics) for some 15 year olds in West Germany were much more vocationally orientated than in this country, and at least one U.K. industrialist made clear his regret that similar provision was not made in England and Wales. On the other hand, neither European nor U.K. industrialists confirmed the widely-held myth that they were profoundly dissatisfied with the mathematical capabilities of those whom they recruit from the schools. The report, indeed, uses international comparison to support one of its major recommendations: "that there should be an investigation into ways in which a requirement (i.e. teachers of mathematics at secondary level should hold a minimum mathematical qualification) might be introduced over a period of years, and that the first steps towards introducing such a requirement should be taken as soon as possible".(9)

In the same mode, the present Secretary of State for Education and Science, Sir Keith Joseph, is manifestly seeking convincing overseas evidence, from U.S.A. and from Scandinavia respectively, to support alternative economic policies for financing national provision at both school and higher education level - with regard, for instance, to an educational voucher system and to the concept of student loans (although what he finds "intellectually attractive" in the evidence from the Alum Rock experiment(10) in educational vouchers is difficult to comprehend!).

Curriculum Development in its own growth as a professional and academic discipline has not been slow to embrace a "practical bias" in international cross-reference, particularly in its use of case studies. It is perhaps significant that Raggatt in his contribution on "Comparative Education" in

Educational Research and Development in Britain 1970-80(11)
reminds us of the tradition of participant observation in
comparative pedagogy. Rejecting the search for general
principles, as he also did in his plea for a process rather
than an objectives model in Curriculum Development, Lawrence
Stenhouse whose thought and practice helped shape a generation
of educators, argued that comparative education should be used
"to illuminate the particular...... through a grounded
representation of day-to-day educational reality. Descriptive
case studies are the appropriate method".(13) A vivid example
of such descriptive case studies to illustrate possible
solutions to a national INSET problem concludes the present
paper.
    In its early heady days the English Schools Council
nourished the faith that international comparisons were of
practical value to an English teaching profession which, while
dispensing with the myth that it had autonomy in Curriculum
decision making, nevertheless rightly believed that it must be
the least dispensable of the partners in that exercise. The
English teaching profession, invited as the de facto curriculum
developers, persisted in this belief in the face of the massed
ranks of U.S. professors and Canadian administrators who
attended a Schools Council conference held in Oxford in
1968.(14) Gradually, however, they moved to a greater
sophistication as is evident from the report Styles of
Curriculum Development(15) of an OECD conference held at
Allerton Park, Illinois, in 1972. Both reports were edited by
Stuart Maclure, Editor of the Times Educational Supplement. It
was notable that the English "team" had been strengthened by
the presence of administrators and "curriculum developers"
(most, it must be acknowledged emerging from successful
teaching in schools to curriculum project leadership) compared
with the Oxford membership of four years earlier. The Allerton
Park conference membership was also more truly international
with representation from many European countries as well as
from the American continent and Japan.
    Styles of Curriculum Development analysed in an
international context have continued to pre-occupy Maclure
during the 1970s. In 1975, together with Tony Becher he
produced for OECD/CERI a Handbook on Curriculum
Development.(16) Later in 1978, again in association with
Becher, he produced Politics of Curriculum Change.(17) Both
volumes have a strong international dimension. The present
writer is very aware of the practical usefulness of the Becher-
Maclure analysis and tabulation of political, bureaucratic and
diffuse curriculum styles in European curriculum development.
Higher degree students, who are also practising teachers in
posts of responsibility engaged in actual curriculum decision
making in primary and secondary schools, respond to their
analysis with considerable interest and enthusiasm. Similarly,
Rudduck and Kelly in their Dissemination of Curriculum

<u>Development</u>(18) have analysed dissemination processes in several European countries in an attempt to throw light upon the process of curriculum dissemination in England and Wales.

The Organisation for Economic Co-operation and Development has not only fostered awareness of the international dimension of Curriculum Development but has encouraged "practical bias" in the critical analysis of systems as a whole, as exemplified by its <u>Reviews of National Policies for Education</u> - France 1969, Netherlands 1976, Italy 1979, etc. More recently OECD has turned (within the CERI programme) to a series of descriptive and analytical outlines of national policies and practice in "Innovation in INSET" programmes. The contribution by Ray Bolam on the United Kingdom(19) and Nathan Deen and E. Boeden Rijdes on the Netherlands(20) display two contrasting modes in disseminating comparative information. Bolam, although he includes case studies, concentrates on the validity of variant change agents, while the Dutch study offers very specific case studies only.

The close connection between curriculum development and INSET is widely acknowledged, and nowhere more forcefully than by Malcolm Skilbeck in his contribution to <u>In-Service Education and Teachers´ Centres</u> edited by Elizabeth Adams and entitled "School-based Curriculum Development and the Task of INSET".(21) Here he pleads for priority to be given to providing the support services essential to prepare serving teachers to become curriculum developers. High quality INSET would need to become more system-based rather than offered on a highly individualistic basis as at present. Skilbeck´s paper, written in 1975, starts with a comparison between American and British attitudes to life-adjustment schooling and the directions taken by consequent curriculum development. It is ironic seven years later, to realise how quickly his optimism about the greater buoyancy and endurance of British progressive movements compared with those in the U.S.A. has been less than justified as the Curriculum debate has brought critical H.M.I. reports on much progressive practice both in 5-11 primary and in middle schools.

William Taylor´s <u>Research and Reform in Teacher Education</u>,(22) one of the European Trend Reports on Educational Research commissioned by the Council of Europe, contains four chapters on "Trends in the Continuing Education of Teachers": "The Extension of In-Service Study Opportunities", "Development of the Induction Sequence", "In-Service Education and Curriculum Development" and "Problems and Trends in Continuing Education". The last two are, perhaps, most seminal to the present discussion. The first of these describes a 1973 report of a group of teachers, researchers and administrators in West Germany which recommended the establishment of a network of regional educational centres throughout the Federal Republic of Germany, thus bringing about an explicit interrelation of curriculum development, INSET and advisory and guidance services. Emphasising how this illustrates the conviction of many European educationists that a "downward" sequence of research development and dissemination has not been successful, Taylor relates it to the continuing criticism of the English Schools Council for Curriculum and Examinations. He shows that despite the strong teacher involvement and membership through the teachers' associations, it, too, embodies a "centre-periphery" model of curriculum change which is no longer viable.

"That curriculum development can ultimately occur only in one place - the classroom"(23) - gives credence to the changes in Schools Council policies since the re-organisation of its committee structures in 1979. These have concentrated resources on INSET contacts with and support for local curriculum development already fostered by L.E.A. advisory services, teachers' centres or the schools themselves through the Five Programmes: Purpose and Planning in Schools; Helping Individual Teachers to Become More Effective; Developing the Curriculum for a Changing World; Individual Pupils; and Improving the Examination System.

The last of Taylor's chapters pleads for a complete re-conceptualisation of what is entailed by the term "INSET" if full advantage is to be taken of the advanced study opportunities for teachers now being developed in most European countries. Communication (different people profit from different forms of this), participation, continuity and coherence are the desiderata for a professional model of INSET, and he concludes by describing a number of ways in which there are common European trends in its provision.

In his timely Evaluation of In-Service Teacher Training(24) - and there has been until recently no more neglected field in educational research as Taylor demonstrates - Euan Henderson also uses international perspectives. He compares the scale and format, and the obligations on teachers of in-service provision in England and Wales with those in the U.S.A., in Western Europe (with special reference to Sweden) and in Eastern Europe. In contrast, however, the 1980 World Year Book of Education(25) (once the most distinctive academic platform of comparative education scholarship) which took as its special theme The Professional Development of Teachers, shows a certain parochiality compared with most of its predecessors in that, out of 28 contributors, 16 are from the United Kingdom, dealing almost exclusively with the United Kingdom context.

The current INSET scene in England and Wales is chiefly concerned with making good the claims advanced for an emphasis on school-based or school-focussed INSET. Its second concern is with the continuing debate over the desirability of provision of specific central government grants for INSET. Sir Keith Joseph now seems prepared to negotiate a specific grant of several million pounds to local authorities, provided that priority is given to courses in senior management in schools;

mathematics in the curriculum, following the findings and recommendations of the Cockcroft Report; craft, design and technology; and helping children with special needs in ordinary schools.

It is, therefore, particularly apposite that a valuable comparative study with "practical bias" has recently become available to assist thinking and planning about the first of these priorities: training for senior management in schools. This has come about as a result of the initiatives of the Association of Education Committees rather than from academic departments in universities or colleges. The Association's trust has established an annual fellowship, the main intention of which is to allow educational administrators from England and Wales the opportunity to study some aspect of educational administration in Continental Europe. The holder of the first fellowship in 1980 was Derek Esp, deputy chief education officer (schools), Somerset, who took as his theme: <u>The Training and Selection of head teachers and senior staff in secondary schools in the Netherlands, France, Sweden, Norway and Denmark</u>.(26) Case studies on all these follow a general introduction that concludes with recommendations for both national and regional policies.

Esp argues that all school leaders need to be trained in skills of team leadership; experience and natural ability are no longer enough. In much of their content and emphasis, developments in Europe reflect trends across the Atlantic that have begun to influence training initiatives in Britain. So-called "administration" courses for heads have changed from being specifically academic into those which offer more general leadership skills, group work, and opportunities for tackling the complexity of understanding human relationships.

Compared with the U.K. provision, the scale and scope of training programmes in all the European countries that Esp visited were impressive. For instance, the French compulsory training programme which was introduced in 1974 has provided a 3 months' course (April - June) for teachers taking up their first appointment as head or deputy head in the following September. In Sweden the course for school leaders and principals is a programme of 25 days over a 2 year period. This includes 4 weeks of practice. In France, the Netherlands and Sweden a national training team is charged with the task of co-ordinating, developing and evaluating the training. The French national agency "Service de la Formation et Administration" has developed a bank of case studies and a catalogue of training methods.

In contrast to continental practice, even bearing in mind the inevitable fragmentation and devolution of English initiatives, the ˙image of the autonomous head, the sensible chap coping with everything coming his way, still dominates our attitudes to training at a time when the supposed freedom of action of the head is already being eroded by education and employment legislation, falling rolls, diminishing budgets and demands for participation and accountability.(27) The needs and problems of the English head, therefore, given the opportunity of such objective observation as Esp´s, look very like those of heads in the countries which have taken greater training initiatives than ourselves. On the other hand, continental colleagues seemed to envy English selection procedures which are essentially based on a promotion ladder which is recognised and accepted by the profession.

Esp´s general introductory report ends with comments on a possible structure for a national scheme of training for English and Welsh heads, influenced by some of the training methods he saw in Europe.

Because people "grow in the job", on the job training would enable a head to develop his own strengths in a particular context while using his junior colleagues´ abilities to the full. Part of a secondary head´s training programme, however, should be alongside that of other administrators, advisers, primary heads, community leaders, etc. Rather than a national staff college, it would be better, in the English cultural context, to co-ordinate existing resources on a regional basis: ideas, experiences and major research tasks, including the continued monitoring and study of school leader training in other countries, could be "farmed out", pooling both L.E.A. and higher education resources.

Esp´s report, thus inadequately summarised, serves as an admirable example of "practical bias" of the kind pleaded for by Watson (op.cit.). Teachers and administrators, whether on in-service courses or as part of their individual study to widen their professional knowledge, will continue to welcome the support that the additional dimension of comparative studies can give to assist sound decision-making on the job; and the initiative taken by the Association of Education Committees Trust is one to be applauded, and, if possible, emulated.

NOTES AND REFERENCES

1.Mercier,P.J. (ed) (1966): The Place of Comparative Education in the Training of Teachers, University of Reading Institute of Education.

2.Ibid., pp.35-36.

3.Mallinson,V. (1968): Literary studies in the service of comparative education. Comparative Education, 4, 2, pp.177-181.

4.Watson,J.K.P. (1982): "Comparative Education in British Teacher Education", Changing Priorities in Teacher Education, Croom Helm.

5.Ibid., pp.220-221.

6.Ibid., p.222.

7.Higher Education (1963): Report of the Committee appointed by the Prime Minister under the Chairmanship of Lord Robbins, H.M.S.O.

8.Mathematics Counts (1982): Report of the Committee of Inquiry into the Teaching of Mathematics in Schools, H.M.S.O.

9.Ibid., p.237.

10.Macklenburger,J. and Hostrop,R. (eds) (1972): Education Vouchers: From Theory to Alum Rock, ETC Publications.

11.Raggatt,P. (1982): "Comparative Education" in Cohen, Thomas and Manion, (eds): Educational Research and Development in Britain 1970-80, p.68, NFER-Nelson.

12.Skilbeck,M., quoted in Education, Vol.160, No.13 (September 1982), p.234.

13.Stenhouse,L. (1979): "Case Study in Comparative Education: particularity and generalisation", Comparative Education, 15, 1, pp.5-10.

14.Maclure,S. (ed) (1968): Curriculum Innovation in Practice, H.M.S.O.

15.Maclure,S. (ed) (1972): Styles of Curriculum Development, O.E.C.D.

16.Becher,T. and Maclure,S. (1975): Handbook on Curriculum Development, Chapter I, O.E.C.D. (C.E.R.I.).

17.Becher,T. and Maclure,S. (1978): The Politics of Curriculum Change, Hutchinson.

18.Rudduck,J. and Kelly,J. (1976): Dissemination of Curriculum Development, N.F.E.R.

19.Bolam,R. (1976): Innovation in INSET (United Kingdom), O.E.C.D. (C.E.R.I.).

20.Deen,N. and Rijdes,E.B. (1976): Innovation in INSET (Netherlands), O.E.C.D. (C.E.R.I.).

21.Skilbeck,M. (1975): "School-based Curiculum Development and the Task of In-Service Education", in Adams,E. (ed): In-Service Education and Teachers' Centres, Pergamon.

22.Taylor,W. (1978): Research and Reform in Teacher Education, N.F.E.R.

23.Ibid., p.196.

24.Henderson,E. (1978): The Evaluation of In-Service Teacher Training, Croom Helm.

25.Hoyle,E. and Megarry,J. (eds) (1980): The Professional Development of Teachers, (World Year Book of Education), Kogan Page/Nichols.

26.Esp,D. (1981): The Training and Selection of head-teachers and senior staff in secondary schools in the Netherlands, France, Sweden, Norway and Denmark, Society of Education Officers.

27.Ibid., p.9.

Chapter Thirteen

COMPARATIVE STUDES AND EDUCATIONAL REFORM

Edmund King

THE CHANGING EDUCATIONAL CONTEXT

There is, of course, no need for academic interests and other
enthusiasms to justify themselves with a useful purpose - at
least, in all cases. The study of pond life, of etymology, of
place-names, or indeed ethnology may arise from spontaneous
interest and continue with that emphasis. More systematic
information and insights, and perhaps utility for some
practical application, may result directly or indirectly; but
that outcome was not part of an original purpose.

Some criticism might be levelled against such pursuits if
they absorbed time and resources which ought to be spent on
other, more urgent, matters; or if those urgent matters were
grievously neglected in research centres - as the physical
sciences, the life sciences, and the modern human sciences were
long neglected in universities while theological and similar
abstractions occupied gifted minds. Such a "treason of the
clerks" still taints some Latin countries´ universities and a
few departments elsewhere; but as a rule dilettantism in the
modern world is offset by human concern and a strong sense of
professional obligation. What Americans have recognised as the
"public service" function of higher education for over a
century inheres in many learned investigations, and is
certainly marked in what we all now accept as the teaching
responsibility of higher education. In that respect comparative
studies of education have a particular commitment.

Today´s context - especially since the multiple crises of
the early 1970s - surrounds and pervades the perceptions of
every teacher, student, and researcher. For the comparative
educator this altered context not merely means that there is a
wider span of countries, systems and populations engaged in
formal education and indeed its evolution or reform to be
studied but it has also introduced a quite different horizon of
concerns and a reordering of priorities within any study. Our
own experience alone would insist on that; but we are not alone
in the relevance of our experience. The experience and insights

of far more people on far more occasions over a whole life-span are now recognised as the proper test-bed of theories and experiments once expounded with priestly assurance. Indeed, not only "feedback" to "experts" but effective "participation" by a much wider representation of humanity are now seen as essential for successful scholarship.

The later 1970s and the opening 1980s have established a new climate as well as a new context for scholarship of every kind. Comparative studies of education naturally share and are affected by the circumstances which constrain and condition us all materially - not just in resources or in the data before us but more in our appreciation of what can, and must be, done because comparative studies are studies of education, concerned with ameliorative activity.

Whereas (let us say) the study of philosophy or even of animal species and communities still keeps us "outside" the object of our research even when our study requires some empathy with the behaviour we investigate, an effective study of education does not allow us the luxury of distant detachment. Of course we try to obtain objective data, to categorise them "scientifically" and to process or compute them in a way that makes them universally relevant or at least intelligible; but there are two special pitfalls for the student of education which do not beset students in other areas of inquiry. The first is that involvement of the observer in the process of observation(1) has been preconditioned by his own idiomatic upbringing and educational expectations - quite apart from his academic preoccupations. The second is that everyone's expectations of education have undergone a marked change over the past two or three decades. That change has a special bearing on questions of reform, urgently demanded on so many fronts.

PRESSURES FOR REFORM

Let us look first at what we might call the outer, environmental conditioning of reform (quite apart from the world's financial and similar crises). The context of public opinion, the institutional nexus, and occupational prospects must all be right before any reform can "take on" - or, still more, - "take off". We have all seen this truism repeatedly in failed French educational reform. Mitterand revives and refurbishes Haby; before him (and Fontanet's essentially similar plans for secondary education) there were reforms stampeded through by de Gaulle after May 1968; and before that there were Langevin and Wallon in 1947 and the Compagnons de l'Université Nouvelle in 1918 - all with substantially the same master-plan and many similar details, but all waiting for a war, a civil crisis or an electoral turnabout to give, first the impetus for acceptance and, secondly, the socio-economic and technological matrix for a new educational life-style. The

Comparative Studies and Educational Reform

French example can be parallelled elsewhere.

No less important than the domestic ecology for education in one country is a wider type of conditioning influence. The years soon after 1945 were marked by opening doors and by wider recruitment. From the 1950s to the early 1960s the mood was one of confident expansion - expansion of provision, of staffing, of curricula. Alongside the necessary structural reorganisation and facilitation of access and transfer there developed a glorification of method - sometimes spuriously attaching to itself the suffix "-ology".

What was the point of this preoccupation? It was symptomatic not only of academic inflation, which over the years has deflated esteem for even genuine studies of education, but also of a concern for "process", which in North America produced "input-process-output" models and "cost-effectiveness" scrutiny and other supposed mechanisms for "efficiency". Why put the word "efficiency" in quotation marks? Because concern was not with effectiveness of education as perceived and profited by at the receiving end. The mechanics of the systems proposed depended on the concept of people doing things to other people, especially doing civilising things to less civilised people so that they could be assimilated, or encouraged to conform, or be "predicted" as manpower, and so forth. (Elsewhere I have called this phase the "second technological/educational idiom" characterising the logic of high industrialisation).(2)

True, most of us really need better management in our professional services; but until the end of the 1960s or even into the early 1970s it was not realised that management in education was special to education, or that management was not enough. It is no use "transmitting" culture or "delivering the goods" if they are left on the doorstep. At least as early as the Berkeley remonstrances of 1964, the "flower power" phenomenon and other symptoms of rejection made it clear in highly schooled countries like Sweden and Denmark, with their respective problems of truancy and free school(s), that educational endeavour fails unless the learner accepts and identifies himself with what is offered - and, indeed, takes it further in his own idiom. During the past decade that same message has come back to us repeatedly from Third World countries. We are just beginning, too, to recognise its full relevance to the case of our own "lower orders", to most young adults, and to the unemployed.

So the early post-1945 comparative studies of structural reforms with their "juxtapositions" and tabulations and confident predictions that this or that "model" would prevail in retrospect look like preliminary classifications before an effective study could take place of what really went on both within and without school systems. "Competency" training of teachers and "efficient" training of heads and administrators were both, no doubt, pre-requisites to something; but to what?

210

Obviously, to the <u>effective</u> self-education of the student, particularly in the later secondary stages and in life afterwards. During international researches and many discussions in the early 1970s it was difficult to secure appreciation of what "effective" education meant - at least among teachers and administrators. In several languages there is no separate word for "effective", to distinguish it from the notion of "efficiency"; and in international statistics the word "effective" was used simply to denote a body enrolled in a classroom - nothing to do with a mind engaged and a real-life commitment afterwards. But students themselves knew only too well what "effective" education meant for them; and the majority of the age-group <u>not</u> enrolled, or "failing" within or dropping out of the system, knew even more acutely what was "effective" in formal education and what was not. They also knew only too well how much education was left out of formal schooling.

Hence it was deeply important to investigate not what was supposed to go on, or what providers intended to lay before the populace, but what actually was perceived as going on at the receiving end. Several international investigations of "the view from inside" began in the early 1970s, including the 3-year, 5-nation, study of Post-Compulsory Education undertaken by the Comparative Research Unit at King's College in the University of London.(3) In most instances it was the very first time that teachers - let alone students - had ever been asked for their opinions and insights. Though the LEA investigation of <u>Achievement in Mathematics</u> (1967), directed and edited by Torsten Husén, in many ways blazed a trail for empirical research in comparative studies, it was marred in so far as it emphasised the aspects of manipulation and control by providers. So were many of the ideas then current in OECD and the International Institute for Educational Planning. Elsewhere, "computable models" of school systems (often called "educational systems") were proposed. The big turnabout followed consumer reaction, which was sometimes disastrous for education in the short term as parents and electors took issue with providers, although in the long run comparative studies of <u>students'</u> reactions may help us to a far truer understanding of education's needs and feasibilities today.

Let us look at the same shift of emphasis in relation to the notion of "partnership". In Sweden, France, and many other countries with centralised administrations, there was no nonsense about "partnership" in determining educational policy and content. (Sharing expenditure was another matter). In Britain the tradititon of "partnership" was exemplified in the sharing of provision, expense, and day-to-day responsibility for ultimate satisfactoriness. But until 1977 and the Taylor Report there was little official recognition that the "partnership" included parents, though of course some local authorities did so. The notion that school students might also

share in school government had an even tougher passage, despite
the fact that at 18 they can help to elect the country's
government, or, if employed, participate in works' councils'
affairs from the age of 16. The "partnership" envisaged was
therefore one of managing the provision, as though from on
high, or externally.

The related word "participation" is also worth examination.
In many publications from OECD, the Council of Europe, and
other international agencies, the word was used as a synonym
for "enrolment". The only sharing considered was that of taking
up whatever was set out by others, at least in education. That
seems odd, especially when participation in a game or similar
activity implies interlocking and relevant activities, perhaps
even teamwork.

That notion of really counting for something within the
entire system was certainly taken up by countless American
school boards during the 1970s. The United States system of
administration has long devolved responsibility for most
educational decisions, including costs, on to such local
boards, where parents may be the boards' direct electors. But
the "grass roots" rebellion against superintendents, management
and teachers' practices during the 1970s introduced demands for
"accountability" (i.e. for cash spent), cuts in school taxes,
and some growing preference for private high schools -
especially as a result of nationwide comparisons with other
districts or other states of the Union.(4) International
comparisons by Husén et.al. in the LEA surveys had prepared the
ground but had not directly occasioned such parental distress
or legislative onslaught on the entire state system - as in
California's Proposition 13. All of these and related phenomena
exemplify a public demand for real participation in the process
of education which is beginning to be world-wide.

THE ECOLOGICAL FRAMEWORK

At the present stage of international comparative study, it is
vital to recognise the experiential dimension in our
investigations and teaching. By that I mean the element of
profiting from experience - our own and others' - not only in
order to understand better, but also in order to teach
theorists and paper reformers what actually goes on when
educational reforms are embarked upon. It is not simply that
the world as a whole has moved on in its general experience,
though that is tellingly true, but it is even more important to
recognise that education in particular has moved on and to
acknowledge two things: (a) that education essentially is a
matter of organising experience into a personal system; (b)
that this occurs within an idiomatic but evolving "educational
system" - part of a wider cultural pattern, and within a larger
social/economic/technological system which "makes sense" (or
nonsense) according to the perceptions of that place,

population, or occasion. It is our business as comparative students of education to know the realities of characteristic systems and subsystems of education, to feel within the occasions and <u>crises of judgement as experienced by the protagonists</u>, and of course to adduce from one situation to another what may be helpful parallels or interpretations. In short, we must "teach" in the sense of offering aids to judgement, to more effective participation, and (when need arises) to reform.

Thus our function is distinct from, though complementary to, that of students of politics whose concern is to show and classify examples of the interplay of power, or of sociologists demonstrating that in all societies there are particular groups and pressures. True, pressure groups may <u>use</u> or frustrate education (in the narrow scholastic or the wider cultural sense) in order to exercise power or to re-order society; but the human beings involved in the process (especially at the receiving end where real education does or does not take place) can accept or reject these manipulations in ways which we should know from an <u>educational</u> angle. Educational systems formally set up, or the more diffuse folk-ways and local or topical "inside view", positively <u>teach</u> their populations to react in particular ways. These are part of our stock-in-trade, as foreign languages and comparative linguistic studies are the stock-in-trade of the comparative philologist. We know them with some precision; we teach about them; we know characteristic situations and present trends. Some generalisations are permissible - as hypotheses only, to be substantiated or refuted with reference to precise situations. Not for us the "ideal types" of the sociologist. People do not react that way, even in the mass - and least of all in the inevitably intimate encounter which education constitutes by its very nature.

It has been said with some truth that any given curriculum is 100 different curricula for 100 different people. So much for what we might call "lateral" comparisons within a tiny bit of a system. Still more, continually over time and in a series of evolving contexts, we all re-engage ourselves and whatever we have learned. To some extent that evolution is personal; in other respects it depends on our group contacts, each one of which obviously forms part of a great complex of connections and communications. The point of repeating this truism is that many standard studies of education (especially, perhaps, comparative studies) pay far too little attention to two dimensions: (a) the general ecological dynamics surrounding "the process" at any time or place; and (b) the long-term completion or frustration of the formal educational process. Perhaps more telling in the long run is the study of what that formal process omits, or fails to take account of in the formative context surrounding it. The feeding into our study of fresh perceptions, unanswered questions, perhaps even questions un-asked hitherto, presents a potent challenge to comparative specialists. In this matter as well as in more traditional ways we can make reform attempts more realistic.

Nor should it be supposed simplistically that the reactions and questions just referred to occur with spontaneous clarity to individuals and groups, or that because of our common humanity there are universal responses and needs in education at any one time. As I have pointed out elsewhere, thoughts and preferences in education (and many other social matters) clothe our minds idiomatically like language. Language is learned - and __taught__ - unconsciously and consciously by parents, peer groups, and day-to-day communications, long before formal instruction in a language takes place. In that sense, educational expectation and preference are taught too. It is very hard to un-think ourselves from our schooling, and still more to dissociate educational essentials from the apparatus, traditions, and intentions of the schooling industry. We think and talk its language because we have been taught it. Are there alternatives? Could there be alternatives because of changed technological/occupational necessity, or because of altered occupational/career expectations? These are potent questions for comparative study, especially now.

NATIONAL CHARACTER

Before coming to a closer analysis of these things, we may give a bow to Vernon Mallinson and "national character". A few critics on some occasions (more among the sociologists than among students of education) have taken a swipe at the notion of "national character". I have yet to find Vernon Mallinson saying that "national character" is, so to speak, acquired through the genes. We all know that, to go no further, Western Europeans living in rather flat lands open to the sea and on migration routes have been invaded time and again by sundry bands of youngish men who hardly ever brought many women with them. They found them on the spot. Where there have been larger migrations of both sexes, they have eventually merged with or been swamped in turn by others - often the indigenous population, itself mongrel. Genetically, in most countries, we are all mongrels in varying degree. Yet through language differentiation, cultural and trading contacts, religions, motherhood, and other __teaching__ institutions, we have in sundry ways learned to recognise and prize ourselves as members of tribes, nations, or whatever. We __teach__ our children all about it, build fences, and resist or even attack neighbours. Since nation-states developed, and especially since formal school systems, often backed up by religious or socio-economic apparatus, were nationally invested with colossal powers of at least hidden persuasion, we have certainly been imbued with the notion of corporate character; and in our less conscious smugness or prejudices we bloat ourselves with the myth. Myth perhaps it is, in any totally objective sense, except that it really exists as a form of self-recognition - just like "class", in fact, which the sociologists accept while rejecting the notion of "national character" as a system of self-ascription.

Myth it may be, like Hitler and Rosenberg's myth of the master-race; but as a justification for particular kinds of indoctrination (and self-identification) it is still an educational phenomenon to reckon with, if nothing else. Anyone who has been inside a situation where "national character" dominates consideration of educational aims and practices, as for example, in Afrikaner society, is left in no doubt of its potency in educational decisions, and in the fanatical adherence of many young members. Not dissimilarly, we witness a rising appeal to nationhood and "national character" in many revolutionary nations. Iran's overweening national pride is not simply in the Islamic (or even Shia) complement of its revolution; it does not forget the former glories of the Persian empire. Indeed, in England too, we still suffer from hidden or overt appeals to a supposed "national character" - not only in resisting dictatorial regimes far away but in being too "gentlemanly" to take educational account of the technological revolution in our midst.

PRESSURES FOR CHANGE AND NEW EDUCATIONAL FRONTIERS

That technological metamorphosis of our time is of urgent concern to comparative students of education, and above all to those endeavouring to assist reform. The interface between national systems and internationally comparative considerations is more contentious than it has ever been. Moreover, the shifts in technological and educational emphasis between the era of heavy industrialisation and its associated commerce on the one hand and the microprocessor world of communications on the other are full of profound challenges for comparative study, both of educational responses as it actually happens and of projections for the future. Projections and planning in considerable detail are now part of the data before us. Altered expectations of young adults - in school or college, in "the transition from school to work", in unemployment, and in returning to education and/or training - open up vistas of comparative investigation without previous example. Furthermore, associated changes have brought about huge migrations of underprivileged workers (often of alien culture) into hitherto well-settled systems, with resulting problems of multicultural education - even for previously self-satisfied monocultures - and numerous internal problems of urban decay, flight to the suburbs, and so forth. Hardly any of these problems were recognised as even contingent fields of comparative study a generation ago, when the foundation studies of our discipline were established. Our comparative commitment

must therefore be not simply lateral in some contemporary
sense, but developmental and prospective too.

Since, as teachers no less than as scholars, we care so
much for _effective_ education, we must now pay far more
attention to the receiving end - indeed, we must think of it
not as a "receiving end" but as a situation where education (or
reform) begins. That is particularly so when we examine in the
industrialised countries all those frontier situations where a
new educational style is demanded. These manifestly include:
the huge and varied increase in the enrolled over-16s in many
countries, latterly accentuated by unemployment; the
intermittent experience of paid employment and unemployment
which now characterises the entire 16-25 population in the OECD
countries of Western Europe generally, and in urban centres
around the world in particular; the need to "catch up" with
education and/or training at this _level_, though not at the
usual age; and the case of new demand from hitherto neglected
social categories such as migrants, girls, country people, and
the old. In the less industrialised countries and in the Third
World generally, educational needs are now expressed (and must
be answered) in terms alien to those familiar in the formal
education industry of the industrialised "West" and North. No
longer is it sufficient to think in terms of "feedback"
(presumably to providers) from these frontier regions of
education. Our study must now be based upon the "view from
inside", shared even for academic purposes with the local
participants, and shared still more if we are to help in
educational development and reform.

There are important ways in which all systems of schooling
(and of education beyond and around that) have become frontier
areas in industrialised countries too. Reform must be radical
and continuous, from our inner concepts outwards through our
institutions and practices - not just for reasons of social
amelioration and so forth, though these are integral to our
contnuing civilisation, but also for reasons of technological
necessity.(5) School systems as we know them are largely by-
products of industrialisation, as H.C. Barnard and others have
reminded us.(6) Following systematisation by Horace Mann and
others in the United States, with mass availability of high
schools and higher education in due course, the expansion of
most forms of education throughout the industrialised world has
been based on assumptions of assimilating people into the
cultural and occupational mainstream of the host society,
according to the ability and readiness of those being
assimulated as well as in processing people as described
earlier.(2) The big reorientation is necessitated by what I
have called the "third technological/educational phase".(7)
Others, like Daniel Bell, have spoken of a "post-industrial" or
a "communications" society. Whatever the name, today´s society
and industries call for a much wider range of aptitudes and
qualities, varied fields of interest and knowledge, differently

developed and constantly re-adapted skills. In place of much compliant convergence, adaptive divergence and judgement are continually needed. Furthermore, this continuum of re-learning and re-creating is spread over a lifetime. This idiom or phase of education recognises the <u>provisional or conditional status</u> of the present state of knowledge or understanding.

Obviously, too, microprocessors and computer-assisted diffusion and analysis of knowledge, almost incalculably accelerated in little more than a decade, both demand and facilitate the <u>participation and relevance</u> of many people and activities not so far considered as partners in the educational process. The crumbling of industrial/occupational structures since the early 1970s, combined with the redistribution of much of the world's industry to new locations, has brought unemployment and job-changes into near-normal expectation in all the heavily industrialised countries of the Western world. At the same time, the "communications society" has thrust new concepts of learning relationships and feasibilities right down into the primary school stage - with, of course, a perspective of electronically supported learning and relearning throughout life.(8) More than any change since formal education became a major state commitment, this challenge demands complete rethinking of educational aims and practice. For comparative studies of education this metamorphosis challenges our supply of data, our analysis of aims, and our skills in reassessing all learning relationships - not just once for all time, but in a commitment of unforeseeable duration and complexity. By the same token, it puts our studies at the very centre of any reform plans.

All effective education now must be a preparation for uncertainty,(9) for responsible participation rather than indifferentism. Educational development and planning too must take the same stance, in preparation for varied and flexible response to ever-changing "crises" (that is, literally, <u>judgements</u>). "Predictions", "laws" and expectations of convergent assimilation have no place in our study - if they ever had. We need careful study of what <u>is</u>, what is moving by way of response and experiment, what is planned for, and how the implementation proceeds in the world's national and cultural workshops. The microprocessor revolution and the advent of a "communications society" mean that the world shares technological apparatus and opportunities as never before; but by the same token a plurality of responses is as evident as the plurality of fashions on our streets, indeed more so because cultural individuality is not only prized but persistently taught and identified with. Who could expect one thousand million Chinese to be Russified, Americanised or even internationally neutered in culture - no matter what technologies are imported? Who could therefore expect education to have other than a national base, with national experimentation, and a latterday sense of being "central" no less than in the days of the "Central Kingdom". A Chinese is Chinese, in whatever period of time we are referring to. We have thus not altogether abandoned Vernon Mallinson's discussion of national character.

Nonetheless, within each of the national systems still responsible by law and with financial responsibility for so much of the world's schooling and the educative media, pluralism is growing not only as a self-evident feature of daily life but as a desideratum in education. We do not seek a "melting-pot" or a farrago any more; we recognise that a multiplicity of perceptions and probably values too is essential to true civilisation. In search of whatever human essence may be we maintain the great conversation of mankind with comparative scholarship, as well as civilised acceptance of others' complementariness to our own perceptions and practices.

Nor can we stop at the personal level, or in each nation's classrooms, or with any one of the increasingly comparative development plans put out by education ministries (often in English for international study - as in the Netherlands' Contour Plan, the Danish U90, and the Swedish U68). Debates about reform are internationally comparative even when striving to make the most of a country or a culture's special virtues and strengths.

Further afield from the industrialised world, comparative students have to ask if "Western" education can be afforded by any more human beings. Should it be? If so, how and where? How may education be re-engaged in the lives of learners, workers, and teachers? In any country whatsoever, how may education be phased and programmed and experienced in a life of rapidly shifting relationships at home, at work, in communications of every kind? Who will organise the whole cybernetic feedback from experience (whose experience?) which will keep educational development on course? Obviously the answers must be sought continuously in comparative studies, and in Comparative Education's unfailing committedness to educational reform and its sensitive implementation.

NOTES AND REFERENCES

1.The involvement of observers in whatever is observed was admirably discussed in A.N. Whitehead's Adventures of Ideas, (1933). See also my Comparative Studies and Educational Decision, (1968), especially Chapter 2: "Is our study of education objective?"

2.See Other Schools and Ours (5th edn., 1979), pp.36 and foll., especially p.40.

3.Reported in King,E.J., Moor,C.H. and Mundy,J.A.: Post-Compulsory Education I - A new analysis (1974), and Post-

Compulsory Education II - The way ahead (1975).

4.See, for example, F.E. Armbruster's report of studies by the Hudson Institute in his book: Our Children's Crippled Future, (1977).

5.Examined in some detail in my article on "Education's steps towards computer-assisted learning" in European Journal of Education, Vol.15, No.2, 1980.

6.See particularly Barnard,H.C.: A History of English Education, (2nd edition, 1961), p.54.

7.Other Schools and Ours, (5th edition, 1979), p.40; also Boyd,W. and King,E.J.: The History of Western Education, (11th edition, 1975), Chapter XV.

8.See the reference in Note 5 above.

9.See King,E.J. (ed): Education for Uncertainty, (1979); and King,E.J. (ed): Reorganizing Education - Management and participation for change, (1977), especially Chapter 1.

Chapter Fourteen

VERNON MALLINSON´S PUBLICATIONS

Graham Geoghegan

The following pages list the publications of Vernon
Mallinson in chronological order. A brief study of them will
reveal the enormous breadth of interest and scholarship that he
has brought to all his writings.

BOOKS

Lire et Ecrire (for School Certificate forms). Dent, 1938.

Ecrire: a "creative" French composition for middle forms. Dent,
1939.

Amusons-nous (A French Reader for middle forms). Dent, 1940.

Tendances nouvelles dans la littérature anglaise contemporaine:
le roman, la poésie, le théâtre. Bruxelles, Edition Lumière,
1947.

Extraits de Poil de Carotte. Edités par Vernon Mallinson.
Heinemann, 1947.

Creative French, 3 Vols. Heinemann, 1948-52.

The adolescent at school: experiments in education. Edited by
Vernon Mallinson. Heinemann, 1949.

Nous les Gosses. Heinemann, 1949.

Monsieur Maubenoit, philatéliste; raconté par Vernon Mallinson,
d´après le roman de Frédéric Lefèvre. Heinemann, 1953.

Teaching a modern language. Heinemann, 1953.

None can be called deformed: problems of the crippled
adolescent. Reissued; New York, Arno Press, 1980. Heinemann,
1956.

Introduction to the study of Comparative Education (1st edition). Heinemann, 1957.

Introduction to the study of Comparative Education (2nd edition). Heinemann, 1960.

Choix de poèmes. Edited by Vernon Mallinson. Heinemann, 1963.

Power and politics in Belgian education, 1815-1961. Heinemann, 1963.

Introduction to the study of Comparative Education (3rd edition). Heinemann, 1966.

Modern Belgian literature, 1830-1960. Heinemann, 1966.

Belgium (Nations of the modern world). Benn, 1969.

Introduction to the study of Comparative Education (4th edition). Heinemann, 1975.

The Western European idea in education. Pergamon, 1980.

WORK IN PROGRESS

Erasmus on education.

Sage of Ferney: the last years of Voltaire.

Tradition and change in French education (1815-1980).

PERIODICAL ARTICLES

A Plea for "freer" Free Composition. Modern Languages, XIX, I, pp.32-38, (October 1937).

French Poetry in School. Modern Languages, XIX, 4, pp.159-166, (June 1938).

Where the Rainbow Begins. Journal of Education, 71, pp.276-282, (May 1939).

Creative French - A Challenge. Modern Languages, XX, 4, pp.170-173, (June 1939).

The Old Order Changeth. Journal of Education, 72, pp.10-11, (January 1940).

The Social Factor. Journal of Education, 72, pp.120-121, (March 1940).

Choosing the Text Book. Journal of Education, 72, pp.215-216, (May 1940).

The Textbook and the LEA. Journal of Education, 72, pp.329-330, (July 1940).

Talk and Chalk. Journal of Education, 72, pp.406-407, (September 1940).

The Junior School. Journal of Education, 72, pp.516-517, (December 1940).

The Middle School. Journal of Education, 73, pp.82-83, (March 1941).

Note of Jean-Paul Sartre. New Statesman and Nation, 30, p.403, (1945).

Training the Modern Language Teacher. Modern Languages, XXVIII, 1, pp.17-19, (December 1946).

The Novels of Julien Green. Revue des Langues Vivantes, 5, pp.236-241, (1947).

Aftermath of occupation. Times Educational Supplement, No.1712, p.109, (February 1948).

Outlines for an analysis of prejudice. New Era, 29, pp.27-28, (February 1948).

Balzac and England. Revue des Langues Vivantes, 3, pp.235-242, (1950).

Educational reconstruction in Italy. Journal of Education, 84, p.432, (September 1952).

Comparative education studies in Great Britain. British Journal of Educational Studies, 1, pp.60-63, (November 1952).

Modern language studies in the sixth form. Journal of Education, 85, p.282, (June 1953).

Belgium. Year Book of Education, pp.358-368, (1953).

Education in France today. Journal of Education, 86, pp.161-163, (April 1954).

France and the "collège moderne". Journal of Education, 86, pp.265-268, (June 1954).

Education in Belgium today. Journal of Education, 86, pp.361-363, (August 1954).

Education in Holland today. Journal of Education, 86, pp.450-456, (October 1954).

Education in Western Germany today. Journal of Education, 86, pp.541-544, (December 1954).

British and German Education: comparison of aims and ideas. Journal of Education, 87, pp.45-47, (February 1955).

Education in Italy today. Journal of Education, 87, pp.212-216, (May 1955).

Some sources for the history of education in Belgium. British Journal of Educational Studies, 4, pp.62-70, (November 1955).

The Cultural Way of Life in France Today. Modern Languages, XXXVII, 2, pp.50-51, (March 1956).

The voluntary principle in French education: a dual system. Dublin Review, 473, pp.121-128, (1958).

The development of the idea of "école unique" in France. Forum 2, pp.112-114, (Summer 1960).

A vindication of Maeterlinck: a centenary appraisal. Modern Languages, 43, pp.46-52, 109-114, (1962).

L'Actualité de Maeterlinck. Revue Générale Belge, pp.13-29, (July 1962).

Editorial (with Brian Holmes). Comparative Education Review, 9, pp.129-131, (June 1965).

Church and State in French Education. World Year Book of Education, pp.67-77, (1966).

Morals without religion in continental Western Europe. World Year Book of Education, pp.228-237, (1966).

Education in Belgium. Comparative Education Review, 11, pp.275-287, (October 1967).

Literary studies in the service of comparative education. Comparative Education, 4, pp.177-181, (June 1968).

Scholar and humanist: salute to a nonagenarian (H.C. Barnard). Comparative Education, 10, pp.97-99, (June 1974).

Erasme d´Angleterre et sa Révolution Pédagogique. Revue Générale, 1, pp.41-57, (1975).

The hope of unity. Times Literary Supplement, No.3962, p.262, (3 March 1978).

Time of crisis in Western European education. Aspects of Education, 22, p.84-94, (1980).

In the wake of Sir Michael Sadler. Compare, 11, pp.175-183, (1981).

Emeritus Professor J.A. Lauwerys (1902-1981). Comparative Education, 17, pp.261-262, (1981).

MISCELLANEOUS WRITINGS

Modern languages in the secondary modern school: report of the Secondary Modern Schools Committee of the Modern Language Association. 1951. Professor Mallinson was a member of the Committee.

John Locke (1632-1740). In: Château, Jean. Les rands pédagogues. Paris Presses Universitaires de France, 1956.

Modern languages in the sixth form: report of a committee of the Modern Language Association. 1960. Professor Mallinson was a member of the committee.

The place of comparative education studies in teacher training. In: Mercier,P.J. (ed): The place of comparative education in the training of teachers. Report of a conference held in the University of Reading, September 1965.

General education in a changing world: a discussion. In: Comparative Education Society in Europe: General education in a changing world. Second general meeting, Berlin, 1965.

Factors prompting curriculum reform and their implications for British education. In: Comparative Education Society (British Section): The changing school curriculum. Report of the Third annual conference held at Bolton College of Education (Technical), September 1968.

Common problems and opportunities in teacher education. In: Comparative Education Society of Europe (British Section): Trends in teacher education. Report of the fourth annual conference held at the University of Reading, September 1969.

Pre-school education. In: Lauwerys,J.A. and Tayar,G. (eds): Education at home and abroad. Routledge and Kegan Paul, 1973.

Vernon Mallinson's Publications

Based on a series of BBC programmes.

Educating the Gifted Child: A Comparative View. <u>In</u>: Povey, Robert, M.: <u>Educating the Gifted Child</u>. London, Harper and Row, 1980.

L'Education en Grande Bretagne. <u>In</u>: Mialaret,G. et Vial,J.: <u>Histoire Mondiale de l'Education</u> (1515-1815). Paris, Presses Universitaires de France, 1981.

L'Education en Grande Bretagne et Ses Colonies. <u>In</u>: Mialaret,G. et Vial,J.: <u>Histoire Mondiale de l'Education</u> (1815-1945). Paris, Presses Universitaires de France, 1981.

COLIN BROCK — is a Lecturer in Education and the Director of the Overseas Education Unit at the University of Hull.

GRAHAM GEOGHEGAN — is the Librarian of the Reading University Education Library.

NIGEL GRANT — is Professor of Education at the University of Glasgow, Scotland.

W.D. HALLS — is the Senior Tutor at the University of Oxford and the Senior Lecturer at the University's Department of Educational Studies.

HARRY HIGGINSON — is a former Warden of Sadler Hall, University of Leeds and a former Principal Lecturer in Education at Christ Church College of Higher Education, Canterbury.

BRIAN HOLMES — is Professor of Comparative Education at the University of London Institute of Education.

WILLIAM KAY — is a research assistant at the University of Southampton School of Education.

EDMUND KING — is Emeritus Professor of Comparative Education at King's College, University of London.

SIXTEN MARKLAND — is Director of the Institute for International Education, University of Stockholm, Sweden.

PAUL MERCIER was a Senior Lecturer and Director of In-Service Teacher Education at Reading University.

JOHN OWEN was formerly Director of Professional Studies at Newland Park College of Education, Buckinghamshire.

KENNETH SMART was a Lecturer in Education at the University of Reading.

MARGARET SUTHERLAND is Professor of Education at the University of Leeds.

KEITH WATSON is a Lecturer in Education at the University of Reading.

RAYMOND WILSON is Professor of Education and Chairman of the School of Education at the University of Reading.